Where Are You?

Dear Frank and Wendy,
      Ruth and I have gained a great
deal of blessing by reading together
each day selected portions of Scripture
with a brief commentary. We hope
that this book will prove to be a source
of enrichment for your Christian lives.
      Love,
      Bob and Ruth

1/3/92

Henry De Moor

Where Are You?

Daily Readings With The Bible

PAIDEIA PRESS
Jordan Station, Ontario, Canada

ISBN 0-88815-078-4
Printed in Canada.

But the Lord God called to the man, and said to him, "Where are you?" (Genesis 3:9).

Where am I?

His voice speaks, and heaven and earth come forth. Again the Word speaks and God's world unfolds like a flower opening to the sunlight. And it is good, very good—a home made ready for God's children. Then He speaks once more, this time telling me of the profound simplicity of our relationship and of the importance of my work in this world. And so this is where I am: living as God's co-worker in His beautiful creation.

But another voice whispers that there is no love in my Father's heart, only tyranny and arrogance. Like the hiss of a serpent, it escapes—the frustrated anger of one who has lost the battle of the rebellion. Yet strangely enough, I listen to that voice—a thousand and a million times. And when I obey it, the catastrophe starts to happen; the beautiful world turns into a vale of tears. Now I dare not look into God's face, and I want to escape His voice. This is where I am: hiding in a world that I ruined.

Then begins the greatest mystery of all time. Heavy with disappointment, His voice nevertheless sounds as calm as if all the problems I have created have already been solved in His great heart. He simply calls, "Where are you?" Of course He knows. Yet He is stretching out His hands to me, calling me out of my hiding place. Why should I hide? His Son has offered Himself for my sins; He will crush the serpent. My Father's voice is not revengeful; it forgives and invites me to come back. When I start to tell Him of my sins, He kisses me and tells me of the celebration of His love in which I may share. Where am I? In His embrace, in spite of all I did!

And now He tells me of thorns and thistles, labor and sweat, tears and yes, even death. But He is ready to lead me through this maze and He points one to a new paradise, far away but sure and beautiful and pure.

Where am I? I stand looking up a long narrow road. I must move on; in my Savior, there is much to be done.

Genesis 1-3

Then the Lord said to Cain, "Where is Abel your brother?"
(Genesis 4:9).

Beneath the smile of God's redemption, lie flocks of sheep and
the fruits of the earth. It is good to live and to work and to be
merry: the earth has given its wealth.

Who owns it all? Obviously this is my world, and these are the
fruits of my labor. Of course, I will give some of it back to the One
who gave it to me—a token offering, a generous symbol of my love
and gratitude. It looks good to go to church and pay my pledges.

But One knows exactly what I am doing and thinking. He rejects my naive efforts to fool Him. He strips away my false
pretenses and lays bare my selfishness. When I see that the Lord accepts only the heart that gives *itself* to Him, I am deeply jealous.

There is only one thing to do: I must silence the voice that
unknowingly keeps accusing me. One well-aimed blow will finish it.
And when the blood of my brother trickles upon the ground, I am
satisfied. Now at last I can expect peace.

Then I find that there is no peace. A Voice that I could not kill
keeps asking, "Where is your brother?" Am I my brother's
keeper? I am busy living my life, enjoying the good things in this
my world. But the Voice insists, "Where is your brother?" At last
my eyes are opened to this cruel fact: I would not have hated my
brother if I had not first hated my brother's God. When I don't
love my Father, how can I love my brother?

Easy enough to avenge the blood that is crying from the earth:
let my blood mingle with it upon the ground. Instead, I hear a call
to repentance. His arms are still wide open, for the sprinkled blood
of Jesus covers the blood of Abel. God wants to wipe out violence
by love. And I cannot frustrate that Love, for it is stronger than
death.

In this world rife with hatred and jealousy and bloodshed, the
question, "Where is your brother?" rings in my ears. It calls me
back to my Father.

Now I have a question: What can I do for my brother?

Genesis 4-6

And the Lord shut him in (Genesis 7:16).

I sometimes wonder: Is God's path through this world a dead-end street? He doesn't seem to get anywhere. People who don't love Him take this world of His and seem to make it theirs. Agriculture is developing well (Jabal), music and art are emerging (Jubal), and industry is beginning to dominate the world (Tubalcain). But the church grows smaller and seems more insignificant. Finally only one family is left.

Where is the coming of God's kingdom? No one in his right mind would give the Lord a chance anymore. I try to close my eyes and ears so that I don't realize how weak God's case is. But deep down, I fear that I believe in a lost cause.

However, God gauges His work in the light of His promises in Christ, the Messiah. He does not depend upon the people and their willingness to serve Him. Through Noah, Christ is coming. God holds His hands around the little flame that is still alive; in the ark, He safeguards His promises.

This beautiful world is nothing in itself—a little water will wash it away. But that same water will carry the ark safely to a new world where God's praise will ring out again and where altars will be built once more.

When His people enter the ark, they don't have to close the doors; their Father shuts the doors behind them, separating them in Christ from a perishing world. Amid the uproar of the animals in the ark, we hear a new world emerging.

God saves not only my life, but also my work, my future, and all that I have received in Him. He puts His hands on all of creation, still claiming it for Himself.

Knowing that, I no longer have to close my eyes and ears. Who cares how many other people want to serve Him? I must do all I can. Then I may give myself and all that I love into His care. I can say with profound faith, Amen! I don't have to worry anymore. For the Lord shuts me in.

Genesis 7-9

I will bless you, and make your name great, so that you will be a blessing (Genesis 12:2).

The Lord is preparing for the celebration of Christmas. The man from whom Christ will be born is being called to claim Canaan, the land in which the Savior will die. Why does God call Abram? Abram is not the most likely father of the Messiah. First of all, he is childless. What *does* he have that makes him so useful in the coming of the kingdom? Nothing besides God's calling. God doesn't need impressive abilities from Abram; all He asks is that Abram trust Him and obey. And without understanding the meaning of this calling, Abram obediently goes where the Lord wants him.

Why does God call me? What is there in me that the Lord loves? Do I really know much about my place in His kingdom and His work of salvation? No, but as long as I believe that it all makes sense, I don't have to see it clearly. I can trust Him for that.

Abram leaves his country and his kindred and his father's house and sets out for a very uncertain future. But he can be certain that God will keep his promise to bless him. Since I too may serve and share in that unmovable kingdom, my life has meaning. The Lord is with me and I may be with Him. All of His gifts await my asking.

Abram receives the promise that his name will be great. And I may take the name Christian, one who belongs to Christ. Once this name was used to mock Christians, but now I cherish it. It describes all that really matters about me. Likewise, only in the coming of Christ is the name of Abram meaningful and great.

Finally, God does not command Abram to be a blessing —when he lives as a child of God, he will be. Someone who is that rich cannot help but spread his wealth. Therefore I too will be a blessing. When I am not a blessing, something is definitely wrong with me. I am not listening to His calling. I am not trusting and obeying.

Thanks, Lord, for still calling me.

Genesis 10-12

Behold, a smoking fire pot and a flaming torch passed between these pieces (Genesis 15:17).

In Abram's time, a covenant was sworn to insure a relationship between two parties: master and slave, conqueror and conquered, family and family, man and his God. The ritual described in this passage was common. Sacrificial animals were cut in two and laid down facing each other. The contracting parties then passed between the parts of the slain animals, calling upon themselves the fate of those animals should they violate the agreement.

Now, for the sake of Christ's coming, God chooses to make a covenant with Abram. It will symbolize that God and he belong together, that they are partners. In a vision, a deep dream, Abram is told to slaughter the animals and to put the halves on either side of a path.

The penalty for setting aside this covenant is clear—death. I will die if I don't want to live in covenant with God. But God Himself says that *He* would rather die than break His Word of love. He proved that true at Calvary. Amazing!

Then, in the darkness of the night, Abram prepares to walk with God between the killed animals. But instead, the Lord walks all by Himself to show that His promises are the only ground of salvation. Certainly the Lord wants me to keep His covenant. But it is good to know that God's kingdom does not rest on my feeble promises.

How does Abram see God? In a smoking fire pot and a flaming torch. Around Him hover darkness and clouds. The world and satan still oppress me. What can I expect as a sinful person living in a sinful world? God's holiness will have to burn out all that is dirty. There will be lots of smoke. But within all that smoke burns a fire—just like Moses saw in the burning bush and the Israelites saw over the tabernacle of the Lord, Yahweh.

I can find comfort in the fire of His Holy Spirit, and in the smile of Him who said, I am the Light of the world. I see the smoke, but I may walk in that Light.

Genesis 13-15

So Sarah laughed to herself (Genesis 18:12).

It is simply ridiculous. Sarah knows that she is not going to have children anymore. God should know it too. And yet the Lord has promised that the Messiah will be a descendant of her son. That promise does not depend on the biological condition of this woman; it depends on His Word. He is saying that He will do what He promised, even though the situation seems to be impossible. Of course, Sarah laughs. For crying out loud!

That is the problem with the whole gospel: it is all so ridiculous. I am a sinner and God calls me righteous. I have no hope and God speaks about my future. I have no talents and the Lord tells me to use them. I see a church that is being defeated on all fronts, and God tells me that hell will never conquer it. Impossibility seems to be the theme of the whole Bible.

We laugh, but He who laughs last laughs best. God laughs at the limitations we put on His power and faithfulness. That is the reason why Sarah's son will be called Isaac. *God* has made laughter —a reminder that salvation is His work in spite of all the odds against it. When I remember to look to Him, suddenly everything is possible. All my sins are forgiven; I am a new creature. There is hope for this world, and a new Jerusalem is ready to receive me. As long as I listen to His Word, I may have a good laugh.

Sarah seems to have another problem: "But when Isaac is born, everyone who hears will laugh at me!" I know what she means. People will say, Do you really think you can be righteous before God? There will be smiles all around. I can even hear satan laughing. But the good fight of faith is to overcome this reluctance to believe God's Word.

Who says that miracles don't happen anymore? I live in the great miracle of God's love in Jesus Christ. For laughing out loud! I don't care anymore about the laughter around me. There is a joyful laughter in my heart.

Genesis 16-18

Take your son and offer him (Genesis 22:2).

What kind of a God is this? First He gives a son, the answer to prayer. Then He decides to have him killed. He forbids us to bring human sacrifices; yet He commands us to do it. The hope of a Savior is concentrated in Isaac, and now He tells Abraham to extinguish that flame of hope.

It is hard to trust this God. I know. He tells me that I am His child, and then hides His face behind the pain and sorrow of life. He promises a happy life, and then lets joy and idealism be crushed. Is this a God of love? Or is God a despot who toys with the life of His children, seeming to enjoy their frustrations?

He does provide a ram that can be killed in Isaac's place. But that does not take the hurt out of the first command.

God promises to give hope and life in the coming Savior. But His promises do not depend upon the possible and reasonable. He asks, Will you believe in My promises even when there is no reasonable chance that they will be fulfilled? When I have lost all human hope and see no possible fulfillment of God's Word, the only thing I have left is unshakable trust in a God who can do the impossible. That is the deepest ground of my faith. As long as He is sure, I am sure.

He who had received the promises was ready to offer up his only son, of whom it was said, "Through Isaac shall your descendants be named." Abraham, according to Hebrews 11:17, 18 "reckoned that God was able to raise men even from the dead." God has ways where I can't see them. Even death is no obstacle for His work of salvation; Jesus Christ rose from the dead. When the ram is found in the thicket, a substitute for Isaac, a mysterious, prophetic hand points to a cross and an open tomb.

I must learn Abraham's absolute trust. No matter how things appear to me or what satan tells me, God is my Father. And He asks me, Do you put your trust in Me alone?

Genesis 19-22

Then Isaac brought her into the tent, and took Rebekah, and she became his wife; and he loved her (Genesis 24:67).

Just imagine! Your father's servant brings you a girl whom you have never seen or even heard about, and right away you marry her. And, even stranger, you love her. That is ridiculous. How can that be real love? You may accept the customs of your time, but are they the basis for a good marriage? Only your own heart—and of course hers too—can tell you whom to marry. And even so, many problems may have to be worked out; it could end in failure.

But Isaac knows that this woman is not the servant's, or even his father's choice. Wanting to build God's covenant, the two men searched for a life partner for Isaac from whom the Savior one day could be born. Isaac's personal taste and preference were not the only factors to be considered.

When I live in God's kingdom of love, the most important consideration is never my own happiness. However, when I want to serve my Lord, even in my own marriage, there will be joy. Jesus told me that love is not just something I find somewhere, but something I do, a command that I obey. Loving God makes it possible to give myself to Him, and therefore to the other one in my life.

God had chosen Isaac's helpmeet. The servant tells Isaac how the Lord had led him to find the right girl. He had brought them together with His own hand.

That is still the way in which true love can be found. Certainly customs have changed. But God still leads His people. Who can tell me what to do in this delicate area of marriage and love? God can. But then, I must be willing to accept His will. It could be that the Lord leads me to no partner at all, or that He wants me to crush a budding attraction to someone who is clearly not given to me by my Savior. He can also take away the one I love because He has another task for me.

No longer do I first ask, How can I be happy? Rather, I ask, How can I serve Him better? How can I love my partner with love that begins with God? What matters most is to love Him. He who is Love Himself can teach me to love.

Genesis 23-25

Then Isaac trembled violently (Genesis 27:33).

Isaac and Rebekah asked the Lord to give them children. But an answered prayer does not always mean happiness. Esau marries heathen women, sells his birthright for some food, and cares nothing for God's promises and covenant. He makes life bitter for his parents. Jacob, named Cheater from birth, deceives his father in order to receive his blessing. The peace of Isaac's old age is greatly disturbed.

The worst part is that those things don't just happen. Isaac favors Esau in spite of God's prophecy that Jacob will be the forefather of Christ. Rebekah stirs up her younger son to deceive his father. When Isaac finds out that he has been double-crossed, no wonder he trembles violently. With rage, indignation, frustration? Maybe. But there is more.

All of a sudden, Isaac knows that more than human maneuverings are at work here. At the birth of the twins God told them His plan; in Jacob He would bring the salvation of the world. God does not want the strong and straightforward Esau; He wants the sly and deceitful Jacob.

God chooses what is rejected and despised in my eyes to be the carrier of His covenant. He has put His hand upon me, not because I am worthy of it, but because He has chosen me.

What's more mysterious, God can use the sins of men to do what He wants. There is no excuse for the sinful actions of the parents and the sons. But I am assured that somehow God can use even my despicable sins for His purposes.

God is able to use everything to the coming of His kingdom. Yes, this is the very basis of my salvation; He uses even me. When I stumble upon this amazing grace, it is no wonder that I tremble violently. Curse is turned into a blessing!

I love the Lord with fear and trembling.

Genesis 26-28

"This time I will praise the Lord"; therefore she called his name Judah (Genesis 29:35).

Judah is the son of Jacob who, in the line of generations, will be the forefather of Christ. Why did the Lord choose him? I want to know because I want to know how the Lord prepares me for His service. Judah must have been a very special child.

But when I start looking for his qualifications, I'm stymied. He is neither the oldest nor the youngest child; he's number four. His mother is not Rachel, the woman Jacob loves; he is born of Leah. And he is conceived because Leah wants to humiliate and spite Rachel. She is maliciously proud of all the sons she is giving to Jacob.

When still a young man, Judah marries a Canaanite girl, though he knows that this hurts his parents. His marriage hardly shows interest in keeping God's covenant and the coming Messiah. Later he gets involved in adultery and his daughter-in-law bears him a child. His life seems dirty and cheap.

But God takes this man, puts His hand upon him, and calls him to His service. Judah is the one. Why? Simply because God can use anybody. There are no special conditions to be met.

I do not serve God because I am qualified. I serve because He wants me. I may even think that I am not the right one for His service. What talents do I have? What is so special about me? Nothing. But He puts His hand upon my shoulder and says, You are the one.

Leah must have felt something of the importance of Judah's birth. When the first three children were born, she gave them names that expressed her frustrated love and her pathetic effort to win back the love of her husband. But when Judah is born, she simply says, "This time I will praise the Lord."

The Lord will later equip Judah to be the lion who protects his brother Benjamin. And when the Lion of Judah's tribe is victorious, He will make me what I should be. It is the mystery of His work.

There is only one thing for me to do: I will praise the Lord.

Genesis 29-31

I will not let you go, unless you bless me (Genesis 32:26).

Jacob has it cased. If you want to be successful in life, you have to be smart and dodge problems. Help yourself; nobody else will. God? Sure He has given promises, but you're safer trusting your own wits.

But now his brother Esau is coming to meet him. All Jacob's sins rise up against him, and he faces the prospect of being the loser. He attempts to bribe his brother into a peaceful attitude, and he tries to protect his family and possessions by dividing them into groups. It is clever, but will it work?

But then God comes to wrestle with Jacob. Now there is no escape; he has to fight for his life. There will be no cheating, no clever tricks, no dodging problems, for he has to face God. Other problems can be solved only if I make peace with God; my relationship with Him comes first.

Jacob must come to know the power of God's covenant by which he can stand and conquer. The Lord wrestles him in order to teach him how strong he is when he stands in the promises of the coming Christ. And Jacob learns quickly, he has the courage to tell God: I will not let You go, unless You bless me. Is this the sinner, the crook, the frightened man? Yes, this is a child of God responding to His love and calling.

God asks, "What is your name?" God knows, but Jacob has to confess it. "I am Jacob, cheater." Then, lovingly, God gives him a new name: Israel, man of God.

This leads Jacob to an even bolder request. Lord, tell me Your name! Now God has to calm him down. God will reveal Himself in Jesus Christ, but not now. Jacob receives the blessing, that is enough.

In the morning, Jacob may meet his brother as a king who has wrestled with God and conquered. But he will meet him also as a man with a limp. When he approaches Esau, limping Jacob demonstrates that his power is not in himself. He is weak, but his God is mighty.

As a child of God, I don't have much to boast about. When I am weak, then I am strong. From there, God takes over and solves the problems.

Genesis 32-33

You have brought trouble on me by making me odious to the in-
habitants of the land (Genesis 34:30).

Success is not always the same as blessing. Dinah, the daughter
of Jacob, has been raped by Shechem, the son of the prince of the
land. Shechem is very willing to marry her, and he offers a royal
marriage present: free use of the land, and free trade. It seems to be
a good deal.

But the sons of Jacob smell a better deal. True, they are indignant about the way Dinah has been treated, but they are more interested in money and possessions.

I too can be very upset about what happens to me, and yet care
little about justice and righteousness. When sin affects me and my
position, I erupt in phony indignation.

Jacob's sons propose that all the Hivites be circumcised before
there is any reconciliation. They use the sacrament of God's covenant to hide their evil desires. The Hivites agree to their demand,
and while they are still weak, Simeon and Levi kill all the males and
take all their possessions. Their scheme is a tremendous success! A
dismaying event turned out to be a windfall.

How can children of God justify such actions? When Jacob
asks them why they did it, they reply, "Should our sister be treated
as a harlot?" Revenge and greed, murder and robbery take on the
guise of justice.

(What are *my* real motives? Is the honor of God and my fellow
Christians my real concern?)

Jacob is very upset. When God was with him, the tribes
around him feared and respected him. But his claim to be
something special with God has lost its credibility. Will they still
respect Jacob?

When I become worldly, the world will treat me on its terms. I
must give up my special position and become just one of them.
Revenge and hatred will swirl around me.

But God protects Jacob for Christ's sake, and He will protect
me too.

Genesis 34-36

What is this dream that you have dreamed? (Genesis 37:10).

Joseph is a conceited brat who asks for the troubles he gets into. His father is partly to blame. Jacob treats this son of Rachel irresponsibly; he spoils Joseph. And his favoritism is all too obvious.

No wonder Joseph tries to take advantage of his position. He spies on his brothers and tells his father all the bad things they do. After a dream, he tells his brothers that they all will have to bow down to him. After the second dream, he even claims that his parents will bow down to him. As a result his brothers hate him and his father rebukes him.

The moral of the story seems clear: don't play favorites with your children and/or don't brag.

But there is much more to this story. Joseph is indeed the man whom God will use to protect His people. Years before a catastrophic famine will plague the small family of Israel, the Lord is preparing to protect the coming of His Son into the world.

The Lord has revealed to me that He will use me in His mysterious way for the protection of this world. The world will be saved through His church. I have a tremendous task, a calling and a position that makes me the firstborn of His creatures. He has revealed this, and it is true.

But when I start bragging about *my* being a Christian, and the importance of *my* church and *my* doctrine and *my* activities, people will start to hate me and the God who has chosen me to be His instrument. I need a humble spirit. I cannot approach the lost around me with claims that I can save them. When I tell them how poor they are without Christ, I may not sound boastful about my riches.

I cannot and may not give up my dream. But without love and concern, I don't reveal my God of love. I am God's child, but I should not act like a spoiled child.

Genesis 37-39

Can we find such a man as this, in whom is the Spirit of God? (Genesis 41:38).

Why is Joseph chosen to be the ruler over all the land of Egypt? One reason is that he says yes to God and no to sin in the moment of temptation. He rejects the easy route out of slavery—to become influential in his master's house. Sin never brings real happiness. Obeying God brings him prison, but it is better to be there with God than to be a slave of men and sin.

Even in prison, Joseph serves his God in his fellow men. Saying no to sin is not enough. Through this service and obedience to God, Joseph comes in contact with the people that later will lead him to a position of honor.

There is far greater reason, however, why Joseph is chosen to rule Egypt. The Spirit of God is in him and tells him what human minds would never have known.

At every step of my road, no matter how dark, I have the comforting knowledge that the Lord is still with me. I have His Word and Spirit. I may not understand His ways, but I know what He has given me, and through Him I am more than the conqueror. When people get frustrated and puzzled by all the complexities of life, I can help them by telling them what He revealed to me. Even when God speaks to other people, they may still be confused. But by His Spirit, I may know how to help. The more I study the Bible, the clearer its guidance becomes. I have a word for the world.

It is not so strange that Joseph has such patience. Though his childhood dreams seem to be utter lies, Joseph knows that God is still with him. Then it is not so hard to obey Him, to give up sin and to serve the people around him. I know that in Jesus Christ, God is living in me. His Spirit dwells in my heart.

Genesis 40-42

So it was not you who sent me here, but God (Genesis 45:8).

Since God wants to keep His people alive for the coming of His Son upon earth, He provides food for them in the years of famine. And Joseph is an instrument in His plan to do so.

It is a hard and long road to this goal. For Joseph, it means slavery in Potiphar's house, followed by imprisonment. For father Jacob, it means the "loss" of his favorite son of Rachel. The brothers must endure their guilt and later the agony of their visits to Pharaoh's palace. Wasn't there a shorter and easier way? Couldn't God Almighty just *give* bread to His starving people? Can't there be healing without an agonizing wait?

The Lord does not want to give bread only. First of all, He gives Himself, a God who answers when I can't find answers. What good would all gifts be to me if I didn't see the Giver? Therefore, He waits and leads me through frustrations until I see Him well.

God also takes no shortcuts to save this world. There must be grief and pain, a cry in the darkness, and a tomb, and a stone rolled away.

And now it takes a long time for Jesus to come back, and the church will keep suffering while she waits for Him. But God's promise is sure in Christ. And I may know that He is at work in the world around me. "It was not you who sent this all to me but God."

There is still another message in this passage. Jacob's favoritism, Joseph's conceit, the murderous envy of his brothers, the wickedness of Potiphar's wife, the ungrateful forgetfulness of the chief butler—it all found a place in God's plans. He is victorious over all the powers of sin and satan. Nobody, not even I, can sin God's victory in Christ away.

Genesis 43-45

God will visit you, and you shall carry up my bones from here (Genesis 50:25).

Joseph has enjoyed a rich, long life before he dies at the age of 110. After his days of trouble, God has comforted Joseph. His life in high office has been a blessing for his adopted land and his own people. He has seen his great-grandchildren. His life has been full of the goodness of God, and so he dies in peace and satisfaction. Thank You, God!

But Joseph looks not only backward, but also forward. God will lead His people to the promised land. And when they go, they are to take Joseph's remains and bury them in the little cemetery with his fathers. Is that nostalgia? No, it is hope. Joseph knows that the time Israel spends in Egypt is not an end in itself, but is a preparation for the glorious fulfillment of God's promises.

I know that my life here is extremely important. But it is not everything. If I belong to God, I remain restless until all His promises are fulfilled. What is the promised land for me? One day I will be at home with God forever, knowing that He has done what He has promised.

That does not take the joy out of my life here and now. With my Father, I can live a meaningful life and work and love and laugh. Because the future is secure, I need not fear.

Joseph knows that Egypt will become the house of bondage. Many tears will be shed. The good life in Egypt is very uncertain. God has visited His people by giving them happiness and prosperity in Egypt. But He is going to visit them even more fully when He leads them out of Egypt toward their real destination.

Without the moment when God visits His people in the coming of Christ, life is meaningless. But life is good, not meaningless, because in God the future is secure.

Genesis 48-50

The child grew and she brought him to Pharaoh's daughter, and he became her son (Exodus 2:10).

The Bible is full of humor.

The new Pharaoh of Egypt, frightened by the tremendous growth of the people of Israel, starts to oppress them by hard labor. When this doesn't work, he tells the Hebrew midwives to kill Hebrew baby boys right after birth.

Satan is laughing. Pharaoh is a splendid instrument to serve his evil designs. Perhaps the Messiah will not come and destroy him; perhaps God's promises will not come true.

When I am a child of God, I have to face the hostility and brutal attacks of the evil one. He attacks on many fronts, in many disguises. Satan will use nations and their rulers, society and its alluring false ideals.

The anti-Christian forces in the world are getting stronger and the church is suffering. I belong to an embattled church. In a way, that makes me proud—a burglar does not break into an empty house.

The prospect of battle does not scare me because it is God's cause. Now I hear Him laughing at the futile efforts of the enemy.

The Lord not only saved the life of Moses, the deliverer, but He takes him to the palace of the very man who ordered Israel destroyed. Pharaoh's daughter is going to give Moses an upbringing that will equip him to be the great leader of Israel. For eighty years no one will know this secret weapon of God; it will seem He is doing nothing to help His people. Pharaoh is sure that he will win the battle, but all the time Moses is growing up in his own palace.

Moses' parents, who obey God rather than Pharaoh, have a share in this salvation. I too may be an instrument in God's hand by my simple trust and obedience. But towering over my faith is God's faithfulness in Jesus Christ.

Exodus 1-3

Surely you are a bridegroom of blood to me! (Exodus 4:25).

God has called Moses to go and deliver His people. Although Moses has searched for excuses, in the end he must submit to God's calling. He returns to Egypt in obedience, knowing that the Lord is with him. Everything seems promising now.

But that night, the Lord turns to him in anger, for Moses had circumcised his first son but not his second one. Why not? Because his wife did not like it. Being a Midianite, she found it a bloody, repulsive affair. Her influence upon Moses had prevailed.

But surely, I have to compromise sometimes in order to stay out of trouble. Life is give and take. No, the Lord does not approve of compromise. He owns me as He owns Moses and his family. The token of His covenant declares symbolically that I can only be strong when I totally belong to Him. How can I preach the covenant when I am not living it myself? God's kingdom is an all-out affair; He demands complete obedience.

Zipporah, Moses' wife, knows what is wrong. In anger she circumcises her son to save her husband's life. She bloodies her husband's feet and cries, "Surely you are a bridegroom of blood to me." The price of her husband's life disgusts her. She cannot love Moses' God: He is cruel.

Many people have called the Biblical message a theology of blood. A God who wants blood to pay for sins seems to be a cold, loveless God. However, God has given the blood of His only Son to restore peace between us. When the blood of Christ is sprinkled on my head and on the heads of my children, I feel reluctance. Was that really necessary? But then I underestimate what I have done, how I have angered the Lord by my sins. Because of sin, God shed the blood of His own Son.

Now I have to accept that covenant in His blood without compromises. I have to be faithful to it.

Exodus 4-6

But Aaron's rod swallowed up their rods (Exodus 7:12).

God tells Pharaoh, "Let my people go." His people must live in freedom so that they can serve Him. God illustrates His meaning by turning Aaron's rod into a serpent. The rod is the symbol of God's leadership and protection; this rod and staff comfort me. But when I don't accept it because I don't accept God's rule, it turns into a serpent, a dangerous animal that can kill me.

However, the magicians can also turn rods into serpents. The world seems to have much the same power as God. So I begin to wonder: Can the world make me just as happy as the Lord can? Is it really necessary to follow His way to find meaningful life? Are the promises and threats of God, the staffs and the serpents, for real? Anti-Christian forces try to convince me that God has no monopoly on wonders. Satan is trying to make me doubt the reality of God's leadership. This moment of near-doubt is agonizing for Moses and Aaron.

But then comes a strange and wonderful message. Aaron's serpent swallows up the rods of the magicians. Suddenly everything has changed. The magicians' rods can lead no one; their serpents can bite no one. There is a roaring laughter from heaven. The promises and the threats of the world are swallowed up. The staffs of anti-Christ cannot compare to the staff of the Good Shepherd!

There will still be oppression in Egypt: blood, sweat and tears. But the moment will come when Aaron's staff will lead Israel into freedom. God's staff will cleave the sea and will lead His people to the promised land.

I will fear no evil for Thy rod and Thy staff, they comfort me.

Exodus 7-9

Your loins girded, your sandals on your feet, and your staff in your hand; and you shall eat it in haste (Exodus 12:11).

This is the great night of the Exodus. Tonight the dark shadows of death will fall over Egypt, and tomorrow morning the light will rise over God's people. Is it possible? Nine times now the plagues have scourged their oppressors and the Israelites' hopes have risen—each time in vain. After nine disappointments, why should the tenth time be different?

This time it *is* different. To put the blood of a lamb on the doorposts is to claim the promise that the Lord will spare them when all the firstborn in Egypt are killed. They are preparing the meal of joy in the shadow of death. A lamb will die in the place of their firstborn sons. They cannot know that God will sacrifice His own Son so that He can free His people from the bondage of sin. But they know that this is the night. When the cry of horror sweeps through the houses not marked by the blood of the lamb, they are eating and drinking to celebrate God's grace.

But there is more. They are told to be ready to journey. Loins girded, sandals on their feet, staffs in their hands, they must eat with haste. When I know that the Lord has given His Lamb for my sins, I cannot simply talk about it or reflect on it. Salvation has no meaning in itself; instead, it opens the door to new life. Salvation sends me into the service of Him who bought me with the blood of Christ. My life in the bondage of sin has ended. Vigorous activity in His kingdom must begin.

There will be moments in the desert when Israel will long for the relatively easy days in Egypt. It is not always simple to follow God. But the Christ who has given me salvation will give me His Spirit before sending me into a strange and hostile world to conquer it for Him.

Exodus 10-12

*But God led the people round by the way of the wilderness toward
the Red Sea (Exodus 13:18).*

The road from Egypt to Canaan isn't long. It leads straight
through Philistine territory. But the Lord directs Israel away from
the straight road to the promised land. Did He lose His sense of
direction? Didn't He realize that His people were eager to settle
down in freedom?

Often I think I have a better sense of direction than the Lord
does. He closes off the ways I want to go and leads me through a
wilderness. I know that finally I will get to the land of promise, but
hardship and frustration make me question the Lord's leadership.
However, here at the Red Sea, He makes it clear that He is never
mistaken.

Pharaoh chuckles about those stupid slaves who take the
wrong turn to Canaan. But Israel could hardly afford to meet the
Philistines; they would face a battle for which they are not yet
ready. So they head towards the Red Sea. Beside them are the
mountains, in front of them the sea, behind them the host of
Pharaoh. They seem to be trapped.

But when the Lord opens the sea for them, they walk through
it, and the army of Pharaoh is drowned behind them. Now they
have seen the unbelievable power and wisdom of the Lord. They
need that lesson for the future. Furthermore, all the enemies that
might endanger their existence have seen how God protects this
people and they tremble and lose the courage to attack them.

In the wilderness, Israel will meet its God at Sinai and receive
His covenant. In all their hardships, they will learn that they must
depend on the help of their faithful God. *Then* they will be ready to
go and take the promised land. In hindsight, the ways of the Lord
seem wise and good.

Why can't I trust my Father a little bit more? He does not
make any mistakes. *Everything* in my life is for good.

Exodus 13-15

Some left part of it till the morning, and it bred worms and became foul; and Moses became angry with them (Exodus 16:20).

Man shall not live by bread alone, but by every word that proceeds from the mouth of God. God speaks, and manna falls for God's hungry children. He provides plentifully and constantly. There are no limits to the care of my Father, and He can help me in any way He pleases. I must admit that I am not able to estimate His potential. The God of creation is my God and Father. Later, He will send His Son, the Bread of Life, into the world.

However, God adds a stipulation. His people should only gather enough for every day, one day at a time. Their security is not in what they own. Every morning they have to go out to witness the care of God again. Every day I have to pray, "Give me today my daily bread." I must know that I am constantly dependent on Him. I cannot live on what I received yesterday; I cannot save for tomorrow.

Some of the Israelites break this rule and they try to keep some of the food for the next day. I can understand that. One has to be wise. One shouldn't take any chances, just in case . . .

But their anxiety backfires. The manna becomes foul and breeds worms. Moses becomes very angry and in him the anger of God is apparent. Doesn't God understand my wish to have some security? No, God is disgusted when His children don't trust Him completely. This manna is one link in the great chain of events leading to the fullness of His kingdom. But His chosen people seem more concerned about their own security than about His promises.

I must learn from this anger that unbelief and doubt are *not* excusable. I may not grieve the Holy Spirit; I must love and trust God with all my heart.

Exodus 16-18

I am the Lord your God, who brought you out of the land of Egypt, out of the house of bondage (Exodus 20:2).

It seems that Israel is going to lose its hard-won freedom. A Ruler is demanding that they obey His commandments. How is He different than Pharaoh?

God starts by reminding Israel of His love and salvation. His children are to serve Him out of gratitude. When I am thankful for deliverance, I will gladly do my share in communion with my God.

Secondly, a covenant stands between God and Israel. Theirs is not a relationship of Master and slave. God rescues miserable slaves from the house of bondage that they may be partners in His work. When I obey the law of God, I become a co-worker with God in Christ, through the strength of His Spirit. We are joined together in the great struggle to redeem the world.

God talks to me in His law as a father talks to his child. When I don't obey His law, I am turning my back on Him. Sinning is not transgressing an impersonal law; it is saying "No" to His communion. Then the Holy Spirit is grieved, for He cannot work the joy of salvation in my heart.

If God had given me only ten commandments, I may have been confused about His demands. But those ten commandments describe just the start of a complete life of dedication to Him. Jesus puts distorted commandments back in proper perspective in His sermon on the mount. The Holy Spirit through the apostles tells me how to behave in changing times. And every day when I ask, "Lord, what do You want me to do?" He answers.

God gives me His law to heal my life. Sin destroys the joy and purpose of life, but serving God and my neighbor makes my life meaningful.

Exodus 19-21

You shall not exact interest from him (Exodus 22:25).

The laws of the world are meant to protect me and my property. But God's law is designed to protect my neighbors. It is the law of love. Since I have been saved by the love of my Savior, I must show His love to others.

"Love" sounds strange in a dog-eat-dog society. In this world, I must look after my own interests, I think. But I am mistaken. My Father will look after me; I am a rich child of a King.

In Israel a man could borrow money for which he did not have to pay interest. I am used to paying high interest rates on mortgages and loans. While I pay interest, the debt is reduced at a very slow rate, and I begin to feel that the interest is a block tied to my feet. I have no hope of getting anywhere. That is exactly what the Lord does not want. Present problems should not last any longer than necessary; they must not kill hope.

I can easily love my neighbor, but it is much harder to share my money with him. However, difficult love, a giving of self to another, is real love.

The basic question here is: Can I give without knowing that I will get richer by doing so? Am I willing to give one of God's people a chance?

I may already believe that all Christians should have a chance. But in this chapter, God tells me not to oppress a stranger. You were strangers yourself, God says; you should know how hard it is. My wrath will burn against you if you mistreat foreigners. The church exists to show outsiders that the love of Christ lives in their hearts, and that the Christian community is not exclusive but inclusive.

In a complicated society the problem of whether or not to charge interest is hard to solve. But the call to live in the richness of God and to show love is very actual and real.

Exodus 22-24

From above the mercy seat, from between the two cherubim that are upon the ark of the testimony, I will speak with you (Exodus 25:22).

God wants His people to make a beautiful dwelling place for Him. The tabernacle is a symbol of His constant presence. His children have to use the most costly material, and they have to expend much time and labor. But when the holy God resides among His people, nothing is too good and beautiful for Him.

The center of the tabernacle is the ark, the place where the Lord will particularly dwell. To express His holiness, two cherubim will keep watch over it. The cover, called the mercy seat, will be a golden plate on which the priest will sprinkle the blood of the covenant each year. From there, the Lord will speak with His people.

God cannot speak with me unless there is blood between us. The whole tabernacle with its jewels, gold, tapestries, works of art, and especially the golden mercy seat speaks of Him who actually should not deal with a sinner like me. Communication between us exists only because of the blood Jesus shed for me. He talks to me and I pray to Him in the name of Jesus.

God's presence and His communication with me is not a haphazard affair. It is constant and meaningful. If I do not listen all the time, that is my fault. If communication was worth the price of Jesus' blood for Him, it should be so precious a gift to me that I cannot neglect it.

The tabernacle does not exist anymore. But through His Spirit, God lives in me as His holy temple. Communication exists because of the blood of Golgotha. Now my whole life is temple-building, and that is even more exciting than participating in the old tabernacle.

Exodus 25-27

Thus Aaron shall bear the judgment of the people of Israel upon his heart before the Lord continually (Exodus 28:30).

A high priest represented God to the people and the people to God.

God comes to me in a human being who understands me and knows how to deal with me. Jesus Christ is a high priest who is able to sympathize with my weaknesses, one who in every respect has been tempted as I am, yet without sinning.

And a high priest pleads my case before God. When I think I can go my way alone and do not bother coming before God, God has a high priest for me who is in the sanctuary continually. In Jesus Christ I am always in the presence of God, for He is there for me. How determined God is to stay in contact with me!

The breastplate which the high priest wore symbolized his two-way function.

God cares deeply for the tribes of Israel. Twelve precious stones are embedded in the breastplate, each with the name of one of the tribes on it. When the priest goes into the sanctuary all the tribes are represented. The stones are well attached with golden chains and rings so that they never can be lost. Likewise, nothing can separate me from the love of God.

The Urim and Thummin of the breastplate represent God's communication to the people. When wearing them, the priest can make judgments and decisions on behalf of God for the people. God will speak to Israel and make His will known to them in very practical matters.

God's revelation is concrete. The Lord is concerned about a viable, vibrant contact with me. I know what the Lord wants me to do generally. But often workaday decisions have to be made for which I also need God's guidance. Apparently God does not want to speak to me only in generalities. Through the Holy Spirit, Jesus Christ leads me through the maze of my life.

Exodus 28-30

Aaron made a golden calf; and they said: These are your gods (Exodus 32:4).

Moses has been on the mountain so long, talking with the Lord. It seems to Israel that God and their leader are very far away. They want a more concrete religion. It is not easy to believe in a Savior who has ascended into heaven. My heart should go out to the living God, but it is much easier to be involved in things that I can see and grasp.

So Israel substitutes a golden calf for God. Then the people have a tangible symbol before which they can bow down and worship. I too may replace my Father by a church, a ritual, the Bible—holy cows which I adore. I may love the routine of service to God more than I love the living God Himself.

That makes the Lord very angry. I have a living Savior in heaven who does not want to be replaced by an image. He knows my misdirected worship deserts Him, even though I claim that it helps me serve Him better.

Furthermore, the golden calf is a symbol of God that does not fit Him. Perhaps it expresses the power of the Lord who broke out of the fences of Egypt like a young bull calf. Certainly strength is one of God's virtues. But that is only a small part of His being. The golden calf says nothing about His tender love, His holiness, His wisdom, His redemption. Brute power can be attributed to any god. But all these elements describe the true God.

When I make my own image of God, I don't see and respect Him for what He is. A distorted picture of God dishonors Him.

Who is God really? In Jesus I find the real God. I may know Him through His Word and Spirit. Then I need not make an image of Him.

Lord, teach me to love You as You are.

Exodus 31-33

Moses did not know that the skin of his face shone because he had been talking with God (Exodus 34:29).

How does Moses receive the glory of God? He enters the awesome mystery of the holy God, covered by lightning and thunder, darkness and clouds. But even more important, Moses experiences the commandments of Almighty God and the authority of His Word. It takes courage to do that. When God speaks of peace and pardon, I draw near, but when He tells me of His holiness and His claim upon my life, or how He hates and punishes sin, I fear to come to Him.

But if I don't come, I will miss the glory of His communion with me. When on the Mount of Transfiguration Jesus meets with Moses, the law-giver, and Elijah, the preacher of a God who keeps His law, the glory of God surrounds them. The brilliance of God is with the risen Christ who has accepted the punishment for sin. When I meet my God who speaks of sin—forgiven—then I also discover His friendly face turned to me in mercy.

Moses asks to see the Lord face to face! Listening from a distance cannot satisfy him. His personal relationship to God is so real that he wants to meet Him eyeball to eyeball.

But Moses does not receive what he asks for. Nobody can see God's face in this sinful world. But when I am lifted out of my sinful life, then in perfect nearness I will see Him face to face. For now, Moses is allowed to see only the glory that remains when God has passed by. Yet even that slight remnant is enough to make Moses' face shine! What powerful glory must be His!

When I meet God in Jesus Christ, when I go to Him in His Word, when I believe in Him as He is and draw near to Him, the power of His glory surrounds me. The power and joy of the gospel must shine through for other people to see.

Exodus 34-36

Then the cloud covered the tent of meeting, and the glory of the
Lord filled the tabernacle (Exodus 40:34).

The tabernacle is ready. All the instructions of the Lord have
been observed in painstaking detail. Vast amounts of gold, silver
and bronze and thousands of hours of work have been spent. Now
Moses can proudly look upon the finished product: a house for the
Lord.

Still, it is only an empty shell unless the Lord moves in. Moses
can do nothing about that. He cannot draw God in; God has to
come as He pleases. So when the cloud at last descends upon the
finished tabernacle, Moses' heart fills with joy. God has accepted
the work of their hands, making it all worthwhile.

The tabernacle was built around the promise of His coming.
He was present while Israel built it, but now His presence is clear.
Now everybody can see that the living God is among His people. By
day the black pillar of smoke and by night the fiery glow of His
presence can be seen for miles around. In a hostile and greedy
world, the Lord protects His own. As long as Jesus lives in my
heart, there is nobody who can snatch me away from Him.

But protection is not enough. Israel is still far from the glory
of Bethlehem and the golden city. So God uses His cloud to guide
His children through the desert. When it is time to move on, His
cloud moves. I cannot simply sit and contemplate the beauty of
God's dwelling among us. No, the traveling days are not yet over.
So much has to be done! God is eager to get me to the promised
land where I will know Him and do His will perfectly.

At the same time God knows that I cannot always be on the
move. Knowing His children are weak, He stays sometimes and lets
His cloud rest upon the tabernacle. But His goal still waits ahead of
me.

Exodus 37-40

He shall lay his hand upon the head of the burnt offering, and it shall be accepted for him to make atonement for him (Leviticus 1:4).

The Israelites bring sacrifices to God for various reasons: atonement for their sins, gratitude for received blessings, or simply declaration of their love for Him.

But sacrifice is no simple matter. Many strict rules dictate the proper way to bring a sacrifice to God. They must bring an animal from their herd, one they have raised themselves and are attached to, not one they have just hunted down or bought for a low price. What I give to the Lord must be a part of myself.

The animal must be valuable too, one without blemish. God does not want something I don't value. He wants me and what I cherish. I have to give my love to Him, and that means sacrifice.

When a person puts his hand on the head of the animal, he is saying, "Lord, it is not only an animal. It is me. I am actually giving myself."

Sacrifice forces the people of Israel to recognize that they are sinful and should die, but that God accepts something in their place.

Jesus died for my sin, but in faith I must claim Him to be my sacrifice, my Lamb of God. He is mine, and He died in my stead!

When Israel brings sacrifices of thankfulness, they do much the same thing. I, too, can serve God only in person. God does not need my money and my church-going and my prayers; He wants me. When I look upon the sacrifice Jesus made, I understand how much I owe Him.

The amount I can give does not matter. In Israel the poor can bring lesser offerings. There are no unreasonable demands. But whatever I give, I must remember to put my hand on it. I must give over myself to God.

Leviticus 1-3

If anyone . . . sins unwittingly . . . the priest shall make atonement for him, and he shall be forgiven (Leviticus 4:27, 31).

I can sin without realizing it. In fact, it is quite understandable that I break a few commandments. Who can know exactly what is wrong and what is right? Even Paul says that he did not know that it was a sin to covet. Also, I may sin when I mean to do good. Meaning to do good must be a good enough excuse even when an action seems to break the law of God. As long as I don't break the law intentionally, God won't be very angry.

However, this passage tells me that the Lord is indeed very angry about such sins. He demands sacrifice; the priest must see to it that my sin is forgiven and my peace with God is restored.

Why? I was not aware of the sin. Or I had such a good reason for doing it.

God does not judge according to my good intentions or my ignorance. What is not according to His will is sin and deserves punishment. My ideas about justice are not the ones that count.

I am even guilty of being unaware of my guilt. I have not been able or willing to measure the depth of sinfulness in me. I should be overwhelmed by my need for a Savior to forgive me. If I deny that the Lord may be angry about my unintentional sins, I am obviously not willing to accept my guilt and bring it to the high priest for pardon.

I may sin with good intentions; it may be hard for me to know what the Lord wants me to do. But I must not sidestep the commandments of God. Trusting the Lord, I must do exactly what He has told me to do rather than rely on my own judgment. I need the guidance of the Holy Spirit to lead me in the law of God, and I need the gift of humility to accept the fact that Father knows best.

Leviticus 4-6

*And Moses killed it, and took some of its blood and put it on the
tip of Aaron's right ear and on the thumb of his right hand and on
the great toe of his right foot (Leviticus 8:23).*

There are so many details in the description of the rituals in the
temple service that I start asking, "Is this all God's Word? Does it
mean anything to me?" But even today, those symbols, so crucial
to Israel's knowledge of God, have meaning for me.

It is time to ordain Aaron as mediator between God and His
chosen people. After cleansing him, Moses puts on Aaron each
carefully made and highly symbolic part of the high priestly rai-
ment. Certainly Aaron looks impressive.

But God smiles. Aaron is still not good enough to serve Him.
He is just as prone to misunderstand God's words as I am; human
hearts are very unreliable. Blood is put on his ear so that he will
hear and understand. His hand, which will touch the mysteries of
God, also must be purified by the blood of atonement. His foot
must go the way of the Lord, and so the blood of forgiveness and
cleansing is put on his foot as well. Aaron may seem like an exalted
person, but, like any human being, he needs the perfect High
Priest who will eventually be the perfect Mediator between God
and man.

When I see the blood on Jesus' head and hands and feet, I
know that no matter how high I may be in my own estimation, I
need Him. The splendor of the highest of all priests among us,
Aaron, is not good enough for God. That is a very humbling
thought. I cannot reach God unless He comes to me in forgiving
goodness.

This passage reminds me, as I enter His service, of my
unreliable heart. Lord, do I hear Your Word correctly? Am I still
serving and following You?

If I do work at serving God, the way will not be easy. But,
thank God, the High Priest is leading me.

Leviticus 7-9

If a woman conceives, and bears a male child, then she shall be unclean seven days (Leviticus 12:2).

On the one hand, the Bible teaches that the birth of a child is surrounded by joy. God does not frown upon sex and childbirth; rather, they are beautiful gifts entrusted to us. Because sex and marriage are so precious to God, He becomes angry when I abuse them. I should not make common or unclean what God has given as a joyful and holy present to men.

But now in this passage, God seems to say that childbirth makes a mother unclean. Why? Isn't that a contradiction?

No. In the first place, this is a ritual uncleanness, meant to point to a deeper truth. That truth cannot be denied: when a child is born, joy is mixed with sadness. People may call a baby a "little angel," but he is not. He is a child conceived and born in sin, and so the chain of a sinful generation continues. Awareness of this fact is certainly not romantic, but it is realistic. When I am willing to face the reality of being conceived and born in sin, I may also receive the comfort of hope.

When a boy is born to her, a woman cannot enter the temple for forty days. Her time of purification is twice as long when a girl is born. The birth of a boy hints at the hope of the coming Messiah. As a further reminder of God's promised salvation, all male children receive the token of His covenant after seven days. And when the time of purification expires, the woman is cleansed and may go again to the house of God.

Someday, the birth of Jesus Christ will break the chain of sin. He is the One who is not conceived and born in sin. He took away the gloom that used to hover over the birth of a child. I don't have to wait forty or eighty days; I may go into His house with praise.

Leviticus 10-12

The priest shall make atonement before the Lord for him who is being cleansed (Leviticus 14:31).

Leprosy is a contagious disease that is caused by bacteria; medical research has found cures for it. But God wants leprous people to go to the priest with a guilt offering. What is their guilt?

Sickness is a symbol, as well as a result, of sin. Leprosy shows clearly what sin has done to this world. The leper cannot communicate with other people. He cannot work in society. Because he may not live in a protected city, his life is in constant danger. Worst of all, he cannot go to God's house and worship Him there. That is the final symbol of the total meaninglessness of his life.

The leper, one of the "living dead," portrays what has come to all of us through sin. Even though he may not be personally guilty, he bears the sins of the world. And he warns me that life without God is frightening.

The healed leper has to show himself to the priest, and then he must bring sacrifices to God to atone for the sin that has shown itself so clearly in him. In so doing, he points to the only One who can heal more than diseases, the One who takes away the guilt and the sin of the world.

People may still shun the cured leper, afraid he is still contagious. Often people don't easily accept the fact that the Lord is able to make life new. God will erase the marks of my sin, but people may hold sin against me for a long time.

After the offering, the leper may indeed go to the Lord's house to praise His name. His life may become worship. He can work again, communicate and take care of other people.

Medical science may explain leprosy and cure it, but the Bible shows me how I can be fully alive. Christ has borne our diseases and carried our pains. In Him I can go to God's house and worship Him in my whole life.

Leviticus 13-15

Do not defile yourselves by any of these things, for by all these the nations I am casting out before you defiled themselves (Leviticus 18:24).

Many of the Levitical rules govern Israel's ethical behavior. Some touch the matter of sexuality, forbidding abnormal behavior. But there are also commandments against such things as child sacrifices, fortune telling, and eating meat which still contains blood. Even the sowing of the fields and the breeding of the cattle are regulated. Some of these rules may apply to my actions today, but most of them don't pertain to me at all. So what can Leviticus mean to me?

Leviticus 18 makes clear God's reason for all the rules. God knows that soon His people are going to be living among the heathen nations. So far, the Israelites have been protected by their isolation in Egypt, but soon they will see other cultures and habits. And yet they will have to live as God's peculiar people; a lifestyle of their own will glorify the covenant that God has made with them.

God knows that it takes courage to stand out from the crowd. As I follow His commands for clean, upright living, I begin to understand that He is interested most of all in my pride to be His child. The nations around me have no life and future. God will cast them out. But I may belong to Him and build up His kingdom.

To do that, I have to listen well to His will for my life. His will cannot be reduced to a whole list of do's and don'ts. But there are two basic rules: love God and love my neighbor. I need the guiding hand of the Holy Spirit to turn that golden truth into daily coin.

Leviticus 16-18

None of them shall defile himself for the dead . . . except for his nearest of kin (Leviticus 21:1, 2).

Two themes run through the Bible. The first is that God is very strict: "Be holy because I am holy." Strict holiness dictates that a priest not attend a funeral, even when his own good friends are buried. The priest is the symbol of the life which God gives to His people. Death speaks of sin and punishment, and God hates sin and death so much that He tells His priests to stay away from it. Jesus says, "Let the dead bury the dead, but you follow Me."

That means hardship for the office bearer. When a loved one dies, he may not go to say farewell. I too must give up things for God's service. Sometimes even showing sentiment can be contrary to my task of preaching the new life in Christ. I will have to crucify my emotions when they do not honor Him who brought me out of death into life.

But there is also a second theme in scripture: God is merciful and understanding. He makes exceptions to the rule. When father or mother, son or daughter, brother or sister dies, God does not command the priest to stay away from the funeral. And in the case of a sister who never married and has no one else to take care of the funeral, the priest-brother must show special concern and love.

The rules of God are not made to rob life of warmth. His people must never think that He is like the cruel and demanding heathen gods. He shows His loving heart. In holiness, He condemns sin, while at the same time in love He gives His only begotten Son to die for me.

May the Spirit help me to remember the balance between these two Biblical themes. I know a just God who loves me.

Leviticus 19-21

You shall rejoice before the Lord your God seven days (Leviticus 23:40).

Religion is a serious business. The book of Leviticus speaks of God's holiness and my sinfulness, of God's claim on my life, and the struggle of His people to live a life of dedication unto Him. But in this chapter, the Lord tells Israel to celebrate a seven-day feast, the feast of booths or tabernacles, at the end of the harvest when everything is in abundance. God tells them: "Eat and drink and have fun!" They are to take tree branches and make temporary dwellings for their celebration. Living as God's rich children, they will act as if hardship is gone forever.

Such celebration is certainly not easy. Ecclesiastes says that it is easier to attend a funeral than to have a good celebration. Christians sometimes think it somewhat frivolous to laugh and shout and live it up. It is hard for me to become a child again after I have learned to act the role of a wise and serious adult.

But God commands celebration. Since I have a heavenly Father who takes care of me, I can be carefree and joyful. For fifty-one weeks of the year I have to make ends meet. But for one week, I must show how rich I really am.

This is a test of my trust and gratitude to the Lord. Do I believe I have to do everything myself or do I know God has freed me from distress so that I can laugh and sing?

Later, after the exile, when Israel is freed from the bondage of Babylon, this feast is re-instituted. Again it is an expression of thankfulness for the Lord who led them out of Egypt and gave them freedom.

If I cannot be joyful, then I have not understood what God has done in the past and what He has promised for the future.

Leviticus 22-24

In this year of jubilee each of you shall return to his property (Leviticus 25:13).

There are two peculiar institutions in Israel: the sabbath year and the year of jubilee. In the seventh year, no crop is planted in the fields. The poor can go and harvest what the fallow land produces. After seven sabbath years, the fiftieth year, all the property that has been sold by bankrupt Israelites is returned to them. Slaves regain their freedom. Families that have lost their lands and their freedom get it back. Strange rules indeed!

God also provides for His people during this time off. He promises such a good harvest in the sixth year that Israel can easily live on it for three years.

What a blow to capitalism! One is not allowed to get all one can out of one's lands and good fortunes, for the Lord takes it back. He says, "It is Mine. You are only stewards who take care of My property."

God teaches me a good lesson. What I have may be the result of hard work, wise management and good fortune, but I may not claim it as my own. I live out of the Lord's hand. He has the right to give or to take back.

This is also a blow to communism. Not violent class struggle, but the mercy of God restores society and gives the poor a new chance in life. No one will become richer at the cost of another, for God provides for all, the rich and the poor.

This is a new concept in social justice. In God's world, people are called to help each other and to cooperate in the quest for happiness.

The sabbath year and the year of jubilee proclaim God's forgiving grace. Everybody gets a new chance. Some people will not live to see that fiftieth year, but their children will receive a new start in life.

That is the way the Lord wants to deal with me. The many problems of life will not last forever. God makes everything new in His time.

Leviticus 25-27

They shall encamp facing the tent of meeting on every side (Numbers 2:2).

The Lord counts His children like a proud Father. Despite the hardship of Egypt and the attacks of satan, a mighty army of God stands ready to travel to the promised land. People correctly say that numbers don't count in God's kingdom. The depth and the strength of faith in the Lord are most important to Him. David sins against God when, in pride, he counts the people of Israel, for he should know that the Lord can do His work even with a small group of three hundred soldiers. However, the Lord Himself may count and may rejoice in His victory, in His protection.

All of God's children will live in the camp with their tents facing the sanctuary where the Lord dwells. He wishes to live among His people, and He wants them to look toward Him. When they step outside in the morning, the first thing they will see is the tabernacle, a constant reminder that God is in their midst. The cloud above the tent of meeting by day and the fiery glow by night assure them that they are not left in the desert as prey to their enemies.

This arrangement is also a witness to all the nations around them. When they see Israel's camp, they notice that their tents do not open outwards. Apparently they do not need to fear outside dangers. Israel gazes at God's dwelling, trusting Him for protection.

The center of my existence is in my Savior. My safety does not depend upon the fences I erect around me and my children and my church. I know that there are terrible dangers in the world, but I need not tremble. My eyes are upon the Lord who is my salvation.

Numbers 1-3

He shall set the woman before the Lord (Numbers 5:30).

There are many strange laws in Israel, but this one beats them all. A man suspects that his wife has had relations with another man. He brings her to the priest who makes her swear an oath that it is not true. Then the priest takes holy water, puts dust from the tabernacle floor in it, and lets the woman drink the potion. If she is innocent, nothing will happen. But if she committed the sin, she will have bitter pain and a violent reaction which will destroy her ability to bear children.

What could possibly justify this seemingly superstitious ordeal?

The Lord knows how terrible jealousy can be, how suspicions can ruin a relationship. And because He cares for happiness and unity, the Lord provides a way out of a dilemma; He resolves uncertainty.

But the problem runs deeper. The man is upset, not only because his wife may have sinned, but also because it is extremely important that he know that he is the father of any son which is born. The Israelites know little specific about the future in Christ; nevertheless, they share in that future through their sons.

The woman's part in that future also lies in the children she could bear. Once she cannot have any more children, she cannot have a part in the coming of Christ.

So husband and wife have to work together. Uncertainty kills their joy and cooperation in the Lord.

We have to be sure about each other to work together. We must know that we are all involved in God's church with our whole hearts. Otherwise there is no real growth in Him.

Jesus said, "Let your yes be yes, and your no be no." No suspicions may separate us. Too much is at stake. We must find each other before the Lord.

Numbers 4-6

He who offered his offering the first day was Nahshon the son of Amminadab, of the tribe of Judah (Numbers 7:12).

With due respect for the Word of God, this chapter might well be the most boring in the whole Bible. Now that the tabernacle is ready, the leaders of Israel, one from each of the twelve tribes, bring their gifts to consecrate the tabernacle. The offerings are mentioned in detail, even though all the offerings are exactly the same. The names of those who presented the gifts and even their fathers' names are recorded. Wouldn't there be a less tedious way to describe this event? Why all the repetition?

This Scripture tells me first of all that God remembers what is given to Him. He recognizes the love of His children in their gifts. He knows what I have done for Him in gratitude, in simple faith and dedication, even though my efforts often seem insignificant to me.

Second, it is striking that every tribe brings the same offering. They are not trying to outdo each other or to compete in what they give unto God. When I wish to express my gratitude to the Lord, the thought of doing or giving more than others should not cross my mind. We have all received equal salvation from the Lord. So what we give to Him is the same too—ourselves.

Although the tribes come forward and give the same offering twelve days in a row, still the Lord continues to mention each and every one.

Judah is the first tribe to go to the tabernacle, though Judah was not the firstborn of Jacob's sons. God has chosen Judah to be the one from whom the Messiah will come, and obediently Israel lets him go first to present his offering.

My dedication to God is possible only because Jesus gave Himself first. Now, in and through Him, I may also come to the Father and present myself unto Him as a living sacrifice.

Numbers 7-9

Would that all the Lord's people were prophets! (Numbers 11:29).

Although Moses reflects the image of the great Mediator, Jesus Christ, he is only human. When the people begin to grumble and wail again, the Lord gives him seventy co-workers to lighten his task. In order to make their special appointment as elders of Israel clear, the Lord gives them some of the spirit that was on Moses, and they start to prophesy. The event is similar to Pentecost when the apostles speak in tongues.

Now two of the seventy elders, Eldad and Medad, do not take part in the official installation, but they receive the spirit anyway and prophesy in the camp. A young man, probably Joshua, is upset about that. He feels that since they did not gather around Moses at the tabernacle they should not prophesy either. Certain rules must be kept, after all.

Moses sees the problem, but he also sees beyond it. Their prophesying is the work of God; therefore it cannot possibly be wrong.

God will extend His Spirit far beyond the limits I have set. When the Spirit is poured out over all flesh on Pentecost, all God's people are prophets! Our rules and traditions are not wrong. God does work through office-bearers and official church activity. But nobody can put limits on what the Spirit will do. He is perfectly in command.

God smiles at Joshua who indignantly reports the irregularity to Moses. He means well, but he will see greater things than he expects to see. The work of the Lord will be proclaimed not only in the church, but also in the camp of the world. The Spirit shows His power not only through official channels but also in unexpected ways.

I will pray for the pouring out of His Spirit in wonderful ways. He can make even me a prophet!

Numbers 10-12

But your little ones, who you said would become a prey, I will bring in (Numbers 14:31).

Ten spies return from the promised land to tell the people of Israel that it will be impossible to conquer it. Only Joshua and Caleb point out that it is a good land, worth fighting for.

The Lord knows that it is not impossible to conquer Canaan. Without Him, they could not do it, but with Him nothing is impossible. Such unbelief and fear makes God very angry; in His wrath, He threatens to destroy His people. Only Moses' plea turns Him back from His anger.

God will not accept my choice to live without Him. He tells His people that it may be rough going with Him, but without Him, they will be dead in the desert. I cannot escape my responsibility to meet the enemy and go in God's power into the tribulations of life. The Lord is with me, and I may not fear.

One of Israel's arguments against going to the promised land is that their young children will suffer. Perhaps the Lord does not care so much for the young generation as they do. But the Lord laughs at those words. He tells them that He does care. In fact, the older generation will die in the wilderness, but the Lord will bring the young children into the promised land. He remembers His covenant.

When I am unwilling to cooperate with God, He can eliminate me and still fulfill His purposes. The Child in Bethlehem will be born, and there will be a new Jerusalem. He takes care of His work.

I may not see the coming kingdom. When a lack of vision is a lack of faith, I will be left out of the glorious victory. No one can stop the Lord of hosts.

Numbers 13-15

You have killed the people of the Lord (Numbers 16:41).

Korah is tired of carrying the tabernacle furniture through the desert. Why can't he be the priest? Dathan and Abiram are descendants of Reuben, the firstborn son of Jacob, so why can't they be leaders of Israel? The idea of new leadership appeals to 250 people, and a rebellion arises against Moses and Aaron, but actually, against the leadership of God. If this mutiny succeeds, Israel may very well perish. So the Lord, on Moses' prayer, punishes the rebels by death. The people are deeply impressed.

But the next day, they return to Moses and Aaron, this time to accuse them of killing God's people. Again, they are really accusing the Lord of being too strict, even cruel. They have not seen that the Lord was trying to protect them all. The sacrifice of human life was necessary to save His people.

Now the Lord becomes very angry and a plague starts to kill the murmuring complainers. Moses quickly sends Aaron out to stand between the wrath of God and His rebellious people. As intercessor, Aaron stops the plague, but not before 14,700 died.

Why was God so angry?

I constantly wonder and complain about the ways of God. If the Lord does not do what I see as just and wise, I accuse Him of being harsh and cruel. But how can I in my limited and sinful vision judge the Lord in His infinite wisdom and mercy? Admittedly I cannot always understand God's actions. But do I have to? If I trust Him, I will have to see things His way. The Lord, while protecting and guiding me, may have to use harsh and bewildering measures to accomplish His purposes. His love is so strong that He can do that.

I don't have answers to many questions. But I have one answer and that is enough. God is love, no matter what I think. His Word of peace must quiet the disturbing questions in my own heart.

Numbers 16-18

If a serpent bit any man, he would look at the bronze serpent and live (Numbers 21:9).

Edom will not allow God's people to go through their territory. Because the descendants of Jacob may not attack these descendants of his brother Esau, Israel has to make a long and bothersome detour. On this trip, the Israelites become fed up with all the hardships of the desert. They accuse the Lord of leading them in ways of hunger and thirst. How can they! The rock has supplied water when they have needed it. God sends them meat, and manna is on the ground every morning. Now they call it all worthless food.

When fiery serpents suddenly begin to kill many people, the children of Israel realize how beautiful life has been and how ungrateful they have been. Feeling profoundly guilty, they ask for forgiveness and relief from the plague.

The Lord orders Moses to make a bronze serpent and to set it on a pole in the middle of the camp. Now both punishment and redemption are clearly visible. The people hate the serpents and the wrath of God they represent, but they have to look at the serpents to experience healing.

The punishment for my sins is nailed to the cross with Christ. I have to look at Him and see what I have done. In the Lord's Supper, I must see the broken body and the shed blood and know that the justice of God cannot let my sin go unpunished. That is not easy. I would rather look the other way.

Why do I always have to be reminded of my sins? Because God wants to straighten out matters between us. Unflinching confrontation with Him will cure my sinsick life.

Whenever Israelites looked upon the serpent, they not only survived, they were healed. Healing is the end of animosity between a holy God and a sinful human being.

The bronze serpent itself did not heal. But Jesus can. When I look at Him who died for me on the cross, I find new health and life.

Numbers 19-21

A star shall come forth out of Jacob (Numbers 24:17).

Balaam has been called by Balak, the king of Moab, to curse Israel so that it can be defeated. Balaam is quite willing to do so, even though he pretends that he is unwilling, for he desires the money and honor that Balak promises. But when he tries to curse Israel, he cannot. Blessings for God's people come out of his mouth instead of evil curses. Balak asks Balaam to try again, but the second try is a worse failure. Balaam eloquently speaks of Israel's greatness. Embarrassed, he can only apologize, "God has blessed, and I cannot revoke it."

When Balaam makes a third attempt to frustrate Israel's power, he starts to speak of the Messiah who will come to rule and deliver His people. Suddenly a heathen is compelled by the Spirit of God to say more about the Savior than most of God's own children. Balaam sees Jacob's star rising in the future. As certainly as the rising of a star cannot be stopped, so certainly will Christ come to deliver His people and rule the world.

Now Balaam faces the anger of King Balak. Certainly he will lose the honor and money promised him. But what can he do against the Spirit of God Almighty? With opened eyes, he sees the vision of the kingly scepter rising out of Israel to crush all enemy forces.

The Roman officer on Calvary has to admit that the One who died was the Son of God. The evil spirits cry out that Jesus is the Messiah who has power over them. The Sanhedrin has to admit that Jesus rose from the grave and so bribe the soldiers to lie.

All these witnesses make me ashamed. Why do I hesitate when even His enemies accept His Word? It is because the archenemy of God tries to separate me from my Father by cutting my bonds to His reliable Word.

But most assuredly, the star is rising . . . has risen!

Numbers 22-24

Why should the name of our father be taken away? (Numbers 27:4).

Five girls go to the tent of meeting to talk to Moses. They want to get married, but they know that when they do, they will receive the names of their husbands. Then, since their late father had no sons, his name will no longer exist in Israel. There will not be a piece of land given to his name in the promised land.

They admit that their father was one of the people who died in the desert because of his unbelief, but he was not one of Korah's rebels. God's punishment for murmuring and unbelief (chapter 14) left the rights of succeeding generations intact, whereas the sinful revolt of Korah and his companions (chapter 16-17) affected their descendants. These girls know that even though their father did not believe God's promises, he still was a child of God. Sin can never break God's love.

So the daughters fight for their father's honor and name. They firmly believe that they will come to Canaan, and they want their father to have a share in the new land. The covenant and the promises of God are vital to them. They ask Moses to change the rules in cases like theirs. Could they not have a part of their uncles' possessions? Could their father's share be given to them? Moses is touched, but he has to ask the Lord about it. And of course the God of mercy permits them to do so. The law is changed, not only for them, but for all similar cases. When I seek happiness only in Christ, I too can count on the Lord's love and mercy.

Now the girls may be married, knowing that their father's legacy is safe. However, they may only marry within their own tribe so that the property of their late father will not fall into the hands of another tribe. And that restriction they accept gladly.

Now I can examine myself. Do God's promises and His covenant mean that much to me too?

Numbers 25-27

When a man vows a vow to the Lord, he shall not break his word (Numbers 30:2).

There are more than enough laws to obey and sacrifices to be brought. However, many Israelites want to do still more than the Lord has commanded. They pledge a vow; that is, they promise to do something special or to abstain from something that is not bad in itself. Sometimes they may be trying to make a deal with God. But usually, they simply want to show an abundance of love. To do more than absolutely necessary shows a loving heart.

The Lord accepts such vows with joy. He is honored by such dedication. If the Spirit of Him who gave Himself freely to me lives in my heart, I can pledge my vows easily to Him.

But the Lord insists that those vows be kept. He does not smile when people break a promise they have made to Him. God is not satisfied with emotionally charged spiritual highs; He demands continuing faithfulness.

However, God is not harsh. If a girl has made a vow rashly without realizing what she is doing, her father may nullify that vow. A wife who makes pledges that cannot possibly be kept can be released of them by her husband.

The Lord does not insist that an unreasonable vow be kept. Since He does not rejoice in people suffering under burdens too heavy to bear, He makes provisions for His people. Even a Nazarite can be released of his vow. A man may put a time limit on a vow he makes. And nobody is under any obligation to make a vow in the first place. God accepts true respect and reverence for Him with love and mercy.

In keeping my vows, I may reflect the image of Him who vowed His Son to me, even though it meant death.

Am I faithful to Him?

Numbers 28-30

We will pass over armed before the Lord into the land of Canaan (Numbers 32:32).

The long journey through the desert is coming to an end; the fields on the east side of the Jordan are already in Israel's grasp. Now the sons of Reuben, Gad, and Manasseh ask Moses to give them that eastern territory. They have big herds of cattle and the country is excellent pastureland. Their people could settle in fortified cities.

Their request is reasonable. Now that the days of hardship and exhausting travel are over, they look forward to building their lives in quiet and peace.

Moses is not unwilling to grant them their request. But he challenges them: Do Reuben and Gad simply want to dodge their responsibility to help conquer the promised land? Do they perhaps fear the up-coming battle? Is their motivation the same unbelief that forced Israel to stay in the desert for forty years?

They have to prove that this is not so. When Israel fords the Jordan to enter the promised land, they will have to be there too with their armed men. In the final battle, they have to stand side by side with the people of God. If they will not do that, their sin will find them out.

This makes sense. I thank God when I have achieved something and may experience rest. But I cannot then forget that I am still a member of the church militant and that there are still foes to be faced. As long as the Lord wars against sin and the devil, I will have to stay with Him.

Reuben and Gad have to join the other tribes so that all Israel may experience the communion of the saints. Some may not live in safe cities while others still have to fight to possess the promised land. As long as one of my Father's children is still struggling, I must stand with him and support him. The church of God is a family, knit together in the one Savior.

Numbers 31-33

He shall live in it until the death of the high priest (Numbers 35:25).

In the time of Israel, when a person is killed, another death will surely follow. A relative or friend will avenge the death by killing the killer.

But the Lord regulates this universal lust for revenge. An official "avenger of blood" is appointed and only that person may take action. In the case of premeditated murder, he needs more than one witness before the killer is sentenced to death. Human emotions and reactions are put under the justice of God who owns all life. He is very upset when a person, created in His image, is killed. But He is just as upset when I act as if I own life.

In the time of Israel, unintentional killing is also avenged—but not in Israel. God shows His mercy by designating certain cities to be havens for the unintentional killer. These cities belong to the Levites, the servants in the temple. God's servants would protect the innocent one from the avenger who in blind rage might try to wipe him out.

I can find comfort in this image. God knows what I have done and what is in my heart, but He is my refuge. He provides me a city of refuge where I can live in peace with Him.

The exile in the city of refuge will not last a lifetime. As soon as the high priest dies, all the people who have taken refuge in the cities are free to go where they used to live without danger. The death of a high priest means the jubilant homecoming of the exiled. Here I see intimations of the great High Priest who will die for sinners. He will give His life to make possible another, greater homecoming.

Numbers 34-36

You have seen how the Lord your God bore you, as a man bears his son (Deuteronomy 1:31).

Moses is looking back on the years in the wilderness. Just before his death and Israel's entering the promised land, he wants to recall all that has happened.

When I reflect, I often recall good things and conveniently obscure the bad. But a holy God cannot do that. And so Moses must remind Israel of all their sins and shortcomings: their unbelief, their worldliness, their lack of gratitude, their failures as a people of God. And that hurts.

Even though God forgives me my sins and does not hold them against me, hard lessons from the past should not be forgotten. When I know where I went wrong, I can learn why I did so and can prevent it from happening again. When the same problems face me time and again, I will learn to find a better approach to them.

Deep down I know that I am always inclined to hate God and my neighbor. I realize that satan is determined to lead me astray. Only in the Spirit of Jesus Christ can I find the strength to be more obedient. Coming to terms with the past, I can face the challenges of the future.

This reminiscing has another benefit. The people of Israel are learning more than a better attitude in which to approach the promised land. They are learning to look upon the Lord and marvel. Wherever and whenever the Israelites went wrong, the strong arms of God took up His erring children and bore them as a father bears his son. What loving patience! God knows how and where His children must serve, and He keeps putting them back on the road. He does so with compassion, but also with eagerness to go on. He is determined to keep me involved.

Looking at the work of God in my past opens a bright future for me.

Deuteronomy 1-3

Has any God ever attempted to go and take a nation for himself?
(Deuteronomy 4:34).

What is so unique about Christianity? Can I claim that all the other world religions are wrong and that we Christians are the only ones who know the truth? It seems extremely arrogant to do so. When I see how fervently other people hold religious convictions, I feel ashamed of my often half-hearted commitment. Perhaps the Lord thinks more of their strong dedication to their own faith than of my casual, lazy dealings with Him.

But listen to God's opinions about it. Jesus said, "Nobody can come to the Father but by Me." He declares that there is only one way of serving Him: the Christian way.

The religions of the world attempt to reach God through sacrifice and good works. Such an approach is plausible only with eyes closed to the stark reality of human sin and corruption. It is only possible if people draw God down to their level or imagine that they are very close to God's level. The proud heart never wants to give up the hope that it can accomplish peace with God.

God alone makes peace with me. Whereas other gods are high and mighty, waiting for people to get close to them, He stoops to me in my sin and misery. My Father is also the only one who ever attempted to take a nation for Himself. The word "attempted" describes fully how hard it was—and is. He takes a divine risk. He does not choose the "good ones" who will probably make it. God has not chosen me because I deserve His love. He knew that He would have to send His Son to die for me. But He chose to do it.

Now God looks around in justifiable pride. Is there any God who even attempted to do what He did?

I need not look down on the faithful of other religions. Admiring them, I can also feel ashamed that my dedication is not greater than theirs. But I must look up to God who succeeds in His attempts to save His people.

Deuteronomy 4-6

The graven images of their gods you shall burn with fire; you shall not covet the silver or the gold that is on them, or take it for yourselves, lest you be ensnared by it (Deuteronomy 7:25).

When Israel found idols among conquered nations, they had to burn them. The uneasy fear they felt when they burned the images had to be overcome by the glorious knowledge that the Lord is victorious over all idols.

Surrounded by the idols of the modern world, I must take my stand as a Christian, knowing that all power is given to Jesus Christ and that nothing will separate me from God's love. The idols of technology and science cannot take God's Word away from me. The idols of sports and entertainment cannot stop me from giving my time and heart to the service of my Savior.

But God goes one step further. While burning the idols, the Israelites would like to keep their gold and silver plating. Those precious metals might help them through the hardship and poverty of the first years in the promised land. But God wants Israel to destroy the metals so that they can never be used again.

Isn't that over-reacting a bit? As long as I stand strong in my faith, does it hurt to benefit from the idols of the world? This world belongs to Christ, the Lord of all; surely I may enjoy it.

God knows better than I do how easily I stray away from Him. So in His great protecting love, God says, "Be careful." All those good things may trap and entangle me.

Christ was radical in His rejection of the old. He knew that a new world and kingdom of God cannot be built on the foundations of the old one. He sacrificed His life to make a completely new start. Now He tells me to hate even the garment spotted by the flesh (Jude 23).

Obedience requires some hard decisions. It is not easy to know when I have to forego the niceties of the world. I must pray for the guidance of the Holy Spirit.

Deuteronomy 7-9

For the Lord your God is God of gods . . . , who is not partial and takes no bribe (Deuteronomy 10:17).

Moses describes the greatness of the Lord: He is the God of gods and the Lord of lords, the great, the mighty, and the terrible God.

So what? All the gods of the other nations claimed to be the same. One can stand in awe of power and strength.

But God is also kind to the helpless; He cares for all those who are forgotten and forsaken.

That is something different! In a world that admires brute force above all, I have a God who is so great that He can give Himself to the lowly and the outcasts. He goes to those for whom the world has no respect, no justice, and no love. He cares for those who have no helper. God tells me that I attain greatness when I too show love to the poor and afflicted.

The Pharisees were very upset to see that Jesus cared more for publicans and sinners than for people who had done their utmost to go the straight way. And here is where the idea of bribing God comes in. By fulfilling my religious duties, I may try to escape the command to love my neighbor. "Look God, I have offered so much for Your kingdom, I am so active in the activities of Your church, I have studied Your Word, I have shown that I really love You. What more do You want?"

God is not moved. I may try, with my obedience to the first table of the law, to bribe the Lord to ignore my failure to really love my neighbor. But He tells me that He takes no bribes. I cannot buy myself out of my task to reflect the image of my Savior in my whole being. God points me to the helpless, and the forgotten people in the world. The true test of my service to God is the compassion and love which I show to those who do not particularly appeal to me. If Christ lives in me by His Holy Spirit, I have to go with Him all the way.

Deuteronomy 10-12

You shall not listen to the words of that prophet (Deuteronomy 13:3).

In this passage, Moses describes an utterly confusing situation. A prophet or dreamer performs a miracle to prove that he is speaking the truth. Isn't it clear that the Lord stands squarely behind him? Or this prophet correctly foretells the future. Who but the Lord could have given him such insight? The people of Israel listen to him, for his credentials seem impeccable.

Moses agrees that it is the Lord who allows a prophet to perform a miracle or predict the future. But then, words to lead people away from the service of the God of Israel come from this same prophet. The people are told to refuse to listen to him then and even to put him to death, for he has tried to cut the relationship between God's children and their heavenly Father.

Apparently the Lord permits a false prophet to do a miracle or to predict the future so that He can test His children. Will they stick to His Word? Do they know His revelation of Himself well enough to be able to discern falsehood from truth?

Obviously, I must have an intimate knowledge of God's Word, for then I will be able to know whether the voices I hear are coming from God or not. Fortunately, the Holy Spirit will help me to know what is the truth and what is a lie.

It won't be easy. I hear many claims of miracles and of prophecies that come true. I must test these messages and doctrines against the Bible.

There is only one Chief Prophet who is the Truth. If I follow Him, I will see miracles happen and prophecies come true.

Deuteronomy 13-15

*You may not offer the passover sacrifice within any of your towns
which the Lord your God gives you (Deuteronomy 16:5).*

Passover is for the Israelites what Christmas is for me—one of
the greatest celebrations of the year. They would like to celebrate it
in their homes, or at least in their own towns. But God says they
have to take the long journey to Jerusalem, leaving the familiar
behind and mingling with the huge crowd of all those going to the
same city at the same time.

Why? The most obvious reason is that celebrating Passover
separately might lead to splitting up the whole of Israel into small
groups. The people might feel somewhat lost in the crowded streets
of Jerusalem, but that is better than forgetting about the unity of
all of God's children.

Sometimes I feel I can serve my God very well at home, in my
personal life. Who needs a church? My personal relationship to the
Lord is what counts. But God has put me in a communion of
saints, in the body of Christ. I am a small piece of the whole jigsaw
puzzle, and the picture cannot be complete if I am missing. I must
learn from other Christians and I can mean something to them in
return.

However, God has another reason for requiring this trip. The
one altar in Jerusalem symbolizes the one sacrifice made for my
sins. The priest there points to my great high priest Jesus Christ.
The tremendous variety among Christians is healthy. But we share
one God and Father and one Savior and are led by the one Holy
Spirit. There is only one way in which we can be saved.

Every time I am called to celebrate the Lord's Supper, I am
reminded that I am just a sinner finding his life in the only Savior. I
must sacrifice to go to Jerusalem, but the trip reminds me of the
great sacrifice of Christ. There I find other Christians, and I
discover that basically we are all the same: lost sheep flocking
around the good Shepherd, accepting each other as Christ has accepted us.

Deuteronomy 16-18

Your eye shall not pity; it shall be life for life, eye for eye, tooth for tooth, hand for hand, foot for foot (Deuteronomy 19:21).

People throughout the ages have heaped scorn and contempt upon the Old Testament Scripture because of this text. Even Jesus seems to disclaim it in the Sermon on the Mount (Matthew 5:38). Is this the spirit of love? May I take revenge? Where is compassion and mercy?

People do not realize that this text only applies to a government's official course of justice. In my personal relations, I should forgive and show love. The courts, which represent the justice of God, have to apply this rule.

This text speaks of a situation in which an accuser and two witnesses accuse someone of a crime. When the case is examined, it appears that the accuser and the witnesses have lied. No crime has been committed. The liars intended to destroy a neighbor's life. Not only did they act with malice and hatred, they meant to use the government appointed by God to perpetrate a personal murderous plot. Therefore, God rules that the false accuser and witnesses shall receive the punishment that would have been meted out to the accused if he had been guilty.

What a profound warning! The tongue that was created to praise God can be used as a sword that kills: what evidence of the work of satan, who kills with lies! The Lord is furious when His people are willing to serve as satan's co-workers. He will protect the innocent who should be safe in His justice.

I can kill those I hate with slander, gossip, and false accusations. But when I distort the truth in order to destroy someone else, I should know that destruction will return upon my own head.

I should be loathe to let myself be an instrument of satan. God has given me the potential of being a blessing for those around me; He does not want me to be a curse.

Deuteronomy 19-20

His father and mother shall take hold of him and bring him out to the elders. Then all the men of the city shall stone him to death (Deuteronomy 21:19, 21).

Would any parents in Israel ever obey this commandment? No matter how hard it may be to handle a rebellious son, can any father or mother bring him to court to be executed?

As with all laws, this law is prophetic; it reveals how God thinks about matters. It shows clearly God's attitude toward sin.

The son is a glutton and a drunkard. He squanders God's gifts and destroys the image of God in himself. In him I recognize my own selfish, wasteful way of life.

But this is not the worst of it. The son is also rebellious. He does not listen to his parents, nor to his heavenly Father who speaks through them. He rejects God's law and guidance.

I also want to be free. Nobody is going to tell me how to live; that's my business. However, when I mind the things of the flesh and don't want to be led by the Holy Spirit, I trifle with death (Romans 8:6).

It is possible that no earthly parents were ever so grieved by a son's sins that they surrendered him to court and a death sentence. But God takes sin that seriously. When He in His mercy leads me toward life in Him, but I prefer to go my own way, God is deeply grieved and angered.

Perhaps no parents followed this rule, but God Himself did. He saw His Son bearing my sins of waste and greed and rebellion. So God took His Son to the courts of the land and saw Him condemned to death. When Jesus cried to His Father, God hid the light of His face; in the darkness of judgment He let His Son die. Golgotha shows exactly what God thinks of sin.

God purged the evil from our midst, and He asks me to hate evil too. It is a part of my struggle to bear the image of God truly.

Deuteronomy 21-23

*You shall not muzzle an ox when it treads out the grain
(Deuteronomy 25:4).*

Here, among all the laws concerning relationships between
people, is this commandment dealing with an ox on the threshing
floor. In I Corinthians 9:9, Paul asks, "Is it for oxen that God is
concerned?"

Yes, He is. This is His world; Jesus said that He cares for the
sparrows. The owner of an ox is afraid that the animal will eat too
much grain while it works, so he applies a muzzle to save his full
crop. The Lord does not like that. Treading grain is hard work, and
it is cruel to deny the ox the tantalizing food that is in his reach.

God is concerned about the way I manage His world. The
earth is being contaminated and polluted for the sake of profit.
Animals are killed for entertainment and sport. Although I may
consider myself part-owner of this world, actually I am just a
steward for my Creator. The Christian church should be the first to
fight for the lives of plants and animals, for purer air, for the con-
servation of the beauty of God's world. I may use the creation, but
never abuse it.

But this law implies more than the proper care of animals. Un-
willingness to let the ox share in the riches of the harvest shows
greed, greed which will prevent sharing the harvest with poorer
neighbors.

I must have love and compassion for the poor of the world.
When I reap the harvest, I must leave something for the poor.
When I employ laborers, I must give them good wages and pay
them right away. If even an ox may share in the riches God gives,
how much more should those people in need be fed. Christians
should be leading in the struggle for social justice.

When Jesus saw the crowds go hungry, He told the disciples to
give them bread. We must all live and share together.

Deuteronomy 24-26

The secret things belong to the Lord our God; but the things that are revealed belong to us and to our children (Deuteronomy 29:29).

My God is a mysterious God. His actions raise many questions. I cannot always understand His purposes. Sometimes I can say in faith that I leave it all up to Him. But other times, I feel rebellious. If I had an explanation, it would be easier to bear my burdens. Job would agree with that!

However, in such rebellions, I am assuming that God has hidden something from me that I ought to know. Satan told this lie in paradise. But my Father is not so cruel that He would withhold vital information from me. I can only conclude that the things I want to know are not of any importance to me or perhaps would even harm me. God keeps secrets because He loves me. He does not tell me about the future; He does not explain the past; He may be silent about matters that bother me now. As a child of God I must simply respect and trust the Father.

There is also a second danger in this rebellious attitude. While constantly prying into God's secrets, I may totally overlook the revelation that He has given to me. I can be so caught up in what I do *not* know that I fail to see how much I *do* know. Satan wants me to desire the forbidden fruit so that I will not eat of the abundance of the fruit that *is* available to me. When my eyes are fixed on what is not given to me, I cannot see the fruit of the tree of life.

What has the Lord told me about Himself? What is His will for my life?

Israel has been sidestepping the clear Word of God by saying that God is too hard to understand. But God makes His will plain; His Word is very near to me. It is in my mouth and in my heart, so that I can do it.

All that I need to know is given to me. But do I know it?

Deuteronomy 27-30

So Moses the servant of the Lord died there in the land of Moab (Deuteronomy 34:5).

This was one of the greatest tragedies of all times! Moses' life work was to bring God's people to the promised land, but he may not enter it himself. Once when he was to show the power of God's Word to bring forth water from rock, he hit the rock in anger. Was that such a sin that his life has to end in this tragedy?

Yes. God becomes very angry when I hamper His work with His people.

Still, this is not the only reason why Moses may not enter Canaan. Although his work is a picture of the work of Christ, only the real Savior can lead His disciples into the new Jerusalem.

But the Lord takes His servant unto Himself in kindness. God shows Moses the promised land so that he can see that his work was not in vain. God repeats His promise that Israel will enter Canaan very soon.

My sins cannot stop the progress of the kingdom of God. When I believe in the perfect work of my Savior, I can already see and taste the victory. Life does not end in shambles, for I can behold the beginning of the fulfillment of God's promises.

Still more touching is the closeness between God and Moses. God is not angry anymore; His goodness surrounds His child. He leads Moses by the hand to the mountain top, shows him the glory of Canaan, talks with him about the future, and then carefully buries him with His own hand.

Israel can never honor Moses better than the Lord does, for the greatest honor is to be this close to Him. Nobody attends Moses' death but God Himself.

Who more do I need? My greatest desire is to depart and be with Christ. After a life of struggle in the desert, a cool wind blows over the mountain top. There is a vision of coming glory, a loving voice, and intimate closeness to God.

Is that a tragedy?

Deuteronomy 31-34

And Joshua the son of Nun sent two men secretly from Shittim as spies (Joshua 2:1).

Once again Israel is at the gates of the promised land. Forty years ago they could not enter it because of their unbelief. But this time the Lord has promised Joshua that everything will be all right. The land is given into their hands.

Still Joshua sends out spies. Doesn't this indicate distrust in God's Word? When the Lord leads me, shouldn't I simply follow?

Yes and no. The Lord and I work together. He will do His share and He expects me to do my share. That is the meaning of the covenant. God gives me the privilege of being in His service.

So, as Joshua prepares for the warfare at hand, the attitude and approach are different than they were forty years before. Then twelve spies had been sent out. Now only two are sent. Then they had to go through the whole promised land, now only to Jericho. Instead of staying away for weeks, they will be gone for only a few days. Since the people of Israel have already promised to obey Joshua's instructions, no tension tightens the faces of Israel's leaders. They can smile because the spies are confirming the promises of God.

The spies do barely escape with their lives. But the knowledge that the land is given to them keeps them on their feet.

The Lord calls me to serve Him; defending His kingdom and church will not be easy. But the Lord has told me that in Jesus Christ I have the victory; all things have to work together for good. I may smile peacefully. I should not underestimate my task, but at the same time I know that I can do all things through Christ who strengthens me.

Joshua 1-3

When the circumcising of all the nation was done . . . they kept the passover (Joshua 5:8, 10).

After forty years, Israel is ready and eager to enter the promised land. But the Lord delays them; they must take one more introspective look back.

During the journey through the wilderness, Israel's sons have not received the sign of God's covenant. A whole generation of Israelites is uncircumcised. They are no longer marked as God's people, distinct from the nations around them.

Why? For many reasons, no doubt, but basically because they have not clung to God. In fact, they are disappointed in the Lord's doings. Life has been hard in the desert; as the days and the years go by, the glory of God's covenant has worn off.

Now the Lord shows them His forgiving grace. Even when the sign of the covenant is neglected, the Lord does not forget His Word. "Look back," the Lord says. "You will see that your life has been kept by My faithfulness."

Now Israel has to endure a time-consuming ceremony. Hundreds of thousands of circumcisions must take place and then the healing process will take quite a while. Is that a delay? Actually not. Rededication to the Lord will make it easier for them to proceed in their work.

The rededication which typifies this first ceremony leads Joshua and Israel to a second ceremony. They celebrate the passover. Again they are looking back. Once the Lord led them *out* of Egypt; now they will be led *into* Canaan. Past delivery leads to future delivery.

When I see the body and blood of the Lord at the Lord's Supper, I realize how great a price has been paid for my salvation. Then my doubts about the future vanish. The Lord does not abandon what His hands have begun. When I am fearful of the future, I may need simply to look back.

Joshua 4-6

Then Joshua said to Achan, "My son, give glory to the Lord God of Israel" (Joshua 7:19).

Achan broke the commandment of the Lord by taking silver and gold from Jericho instead of devoting it to God. But must he be executed for that? Where would I be if the Lord would punish me for my sins? Is there no mercy?

As a rule, after a victory, soldiers may take the spoils of the enemy as a bonus or reward for their courage and hardships. But when Jericho falls, the Lord tells Israel that this time no spoils will be taken. The reason is obvious. No soldier fought; nothing was accomplished by men; God gave the city into their hands. At the entrance of the promised land, the walls of the first big fortified city disintegrated when God's children followed His battle plan.

The soldiers return all the beautiful things they find in the city to God, thereby expressing their faith in His redeeming love. Because Achan fails to do this, he loses his life. When I fail to confess God's love in Jesus Christ as the only power in life, I betray God's care for me. When I say no to His mercy, He has to say no to me.

Achan cringes in fear when the finger of God points at him as the culprit. But Joshua calls him "my son." Joshua knows the Lord very well; his name ("the Lord saves"), expresses the mercy that is always in God. God does not want to punish; He would rather kill His own Son than harm me. God is not out to get me.

While executing justice, God calls me back to Him. So Joshua says, "Give glory to the Lord God of Israel." The truth of God makes life meaningful in all circumstances, even in the moment when Achan has to surrender life. There is no harsh and uncaring justice done.

God does not want my death. In Jesus Christ, mercy and justice are one. He calls me to praise Him!

Joshua 7-9

So Joshua went up from Gilgal (Joshua 10:7).

The tremendous power of Israel frightened the people of Gibeon. So they tricked Joshua into making a covenant with them, claiming that they had come from a very far country, when in fact they were next-door neighbors. Since Joshua did not ask the Lord for directions, he fell for it and promised to save their lives.

Now the kings of the neighboring nations plan to attack Gibeon to show them that they did the wrong thing by surrendering to Israel's God.

When the Gibeonites see the armies approaching, they cry to Joshua for help. I might expect Joshua to shrug and say, You tricked us; now it's your problem. The Lord will punish you for deceiving His people.

But Joshua does the opposite. Immediately he mobilizes his army and goes to help Gibeon. This time the Lord is with him. God defeats the five mighty kings by throwing great hailstones on them, and He lets daylight linger so that Joshua can completely destroy them.

Why does God help these deceivers? Because they have at least acknowledged His power. Though there may be no faith or love in their acknowledgment, the Lord accepts their proclamation of His victory. And when they are in danger, God shows that they have not counted on His Word in vain. He protects them.

I sometimes hate people who have harmed me; I want to take revenge. I might even grin to see them in hot water themselves. It serves them right!

But I must remember that God moves in mysterious ways. Through Gibeon's deceit, which resulted in the five kings' attack on them and Gibeon's cry for help, Israel's army is brought to battle. With God's help, they deal death blows to all the resistance in Canaan. God gives the land to His people. He prepares for Bethlehem and Golgotha and the new Jerusalem.

Joshua 10-12

So now give me this hill country (Joshua 14:12).

Joshua and Caleb are the only survivors of the whole forty year journey through the desert. Of the twelve spies whom Moses sent, they were the only ones who believed that God was able to give them the promised land. Now Caleb is ready to claim his parcel of promised land.

Surprisingly, Caleb does not ask for the best area. He claims the hill country inhabited by the Anakim, the giants who scared the spies so badly in Moses' days. Caleb wants to face those mighty warriors and take God's promised land out of their power. Believing that those giants are no threat to God's children, Caleb wants to prove it. At eighty-five, he requests this opportunity to put his faith to work.

Remarkable! The other Israelites are clinging together in their camps. They don't want to move out to their allotted areas because a tremendous task awaits them there.

I can attend conferences about our outreach to the world, and have prayer sessions for it, and hear beautiful speeches about it. But to go and do it—that is hard. But that is what God demands of me.

Eighty-five-year-old Caleb stretches his hands to a task that must have been staggering. Unable to fell one of the cities, he promises his daughter to anyone who will conquer it, and he honors that promise when a man accepts the challenge. Caleb puts even his family life under the rule of the coming kingdom.

On Pentecost, twelve men enthusiastically set out to attack a mighty world. Faith cannot sit still and do nothing. I must show that I really believe that the victory is the Lord's.

Do I indeed desire to reach out to claim what Jesus has promised me?

Joshua 13-15

Go up to the forest and there clear ground for yourselves (Joshua 17:15).

The descendants of Joseph are complainers. Here we read that the house of Joseph has received a small area of usable land. Too small, say the leaders of the tribe, for the Lord has granted them many children.

They go directly to Joshua (not even to the special board that is set up to deal with these problems); however, their complaint is actually directed against the Lord. Since property was given to the tribes by casting lots, God Himself was parceling out the land. The tribesmen hint that the Lord does not keep His business in order: on the one hand He gives them all these big families, and on the other hand He grants them only a small portion of land.

Joshua is fed up with their complaining. He answers, If you are so numerous, go and clear the land. Cut down the forests; enlarge your portion by homesteading. There is enough room if you are willing to work for it. In the kingdom of God you cannot sit still.

The tribe of Joseph is not amused. Woodcutting is hard work; wild animals prowl in the forests. Worse, the Canaanites who live there are strong and have chariots of iron!

But Joshua repeats the same advice. If you clear the land and subdue the enemies, you will find that it is a beautiful country. You will have a double portion, but only after you have tested yourselves against the powers of nature and the strength of your enemies.

Complaining is a useless way to deal with problems. Rather than feeling sorry for myself and accusing the Lord and His people of injustice, I must stand up and tackle the problems. Victory is promised, but it will not come without struggle.

God does not present the world to me on a platter. He calls me to be His follower, to use the power He gives me in Christ. He does not treat me as a beggar. I am His co-worker in His kingdom.

Joshua 16-18

Ziklag, Bethmarcaboth, Hazarsusah, Bethlebaoth, and Sharuhen (Joshua 19:5, 6).

"All scripture is inspired by God and profitable for teaching . . . that the man of God may be complete, equipped for every good work." How does that apply to the long list of cities and towns with their tongue-twisting names? Of course, in the days when the tribes received their territory, this passage was important. But can any child of God receive comfort and strength from it now?

Yes. When I see how carefully the Lord divides the promised land among His children, I realize that my life and work are important to Him. When He sends His people into Canaan, He stays with them to work out every detail.

Simeon receives cities, but not a territory of his own. Just before his death, Jacob had declared that Simeon would not be given a place of his own. Because of his impetuous, fanatic actions (Genesis 34:30), Simeon is not trusted anymore. The tribe of Simeon is given cities inside the area given to the tribe of Judah, so that brother Judah can watch and control Simeon. Here we read that since Judah's territory is too large for them, Simeon will share it. But behind this fact is the voice of God who keeps His Word, spoken by Jacob.

This frightens me a bit. The Lord's judgment will come true. I cannot wipe out what I have done in my life. My sins are forgiven in the blood of Jesus Christ, but what I do and say still influences my role in God's Kingdom.

However, this should not frighten me. God is safeguarding all of His people by supervising one tribe. Supervision is not punishment; it is protection.

The tribe of Simeon soon loses its importance; eventually its cities become part of Judah. But God never forgets His children. In the new Jerusalem, the tribe of Simeon is also sealed in God's grace.

Joshua 19-20

But as for me and my house, we will serve the Lord (Joshua 24:15).

Just as Moses did at the end of his life, so Joshua tries to bring God's children to a vow of commitment to God. But his methods are different. Moses tells them, "Serve God, or else!" Mount Sinai thunders in his words. But the Lord does not shout at me because He hates me. Rather, in love, He prods me into the green pastures of His communion.

Joshua realizes that it is Israel's own decision that counts; nobody can make the commitment for them. Now Joshua displays exceptional wisdom; he uses reverse psychology. He tells Israel that they are too stubborn to serve God. This makes them indignant. Of course they can follow the Lord, they claim. And they will! But again Joshua tells them it is too difficult to obey God's commandments. Then Israel proclaims even more emphatically their determination to live in the covenant, loving and serving their God.

One day, Jesus tells the disciples to leave Him alone because it will be too hard to follow Him. Then Peter bursts out, "To whom can we go? You have the words of eternal life!" Because Jesus leaves them free to make their own decisions, their commitment is even stronger. Similarly, the father in the parable let the prodigal son go so that he would come back of his own will.

I may stress obligation too hard when I tell others that they have to obey and serve God. Do I myself feel that there is some slavery in God's service?

God does not push and force. His love draws me to Him, but I have to decide to come to Him myself.

Joshua adds that he has made up his mind. He and his house will serve the Lord. That kind of personal example is essential for bringing others to Christ. My personal commitment and the joy I experience because of it will make it clear that Jesus lives in me.

Joshua 22-24

It was only that the generations of the people of Israel might know war (Judges 3:2).

Why must I always cope with problems? Why does God allow trouble? His Word helps me to answer that question.

When Israel settles in the promised land, they don't wipe out the original residents completely. Now these heathen nations oppress Israel, lead them away from their God, and cause a lot of trouble. Why?

Partly because of Israel's sin. Israel allows the enemies to dwell among them. Sick of fighting wars, they hope that the problems will disappear if they don't face them. Sometimes I also want to take it easy. That is when the real troubles start, for satan waits for that. The Book of Judges shows how dangerous it is to assume that perfect peace will reign on earth here and now. I am still a member of the church militant.

But there is another reason for the trouble. God turns my sinful and lazy attitude into something good. Surrounded by enemies, Israel will know war. Temptations and oppression will keep them on their toes. They will learn that they are children of God involved in His great war.

I too am called to be a Christian soldier. Satan is still around, and I must be prepared for him and his tricks. With every action of the enemy, the Lord prods me into activity.

The Bible describes the tremendous fight the Antichrist is going to wage against the church of God. The Lord will win that war, but it will be a hard-fought struggle for which I need much strength. The Lord sends problems now so that I may be more than a conqueror in Christ Jesus.

Judges 1-3

The Lord will sell Sisera into the hand of a woman (Judges 4:9).

The Lord speaks to His people through a woman, Deborah. As a prophetess, she has to bring the Word of God. As Israel's judge, she also has to rule, deciding on matters of the law.

Because Israel again slipped into their evil ways after the death of Ehud, the Lord, true to His promise, has permitted Jabin, king of Canaan, to oppress them cruelly for twenty years. But the Lord hears His people's cry for deliverance; Deborah orders Barak to fight the king of Canaan and to defeat Jabin's general Sisera. When he is afraid to fight, Deborah leads the army into battle. When the battle is almost won, the cruel general Sisera is killed by Jael, who drives a tent peg into his temple and therefore gets the credit for his death.

Today I may accept women filling all these typically male roles: prophesying, ruling, commanding an army, executing the leader of the opposition. But what did it mean to Israel in those days?

Why are women ruling? Because the male population of Israel is not accepting the task that is theirs. They are afraid to act. Now the Lord is going to humiliate them. To get His work done, God will use unlikely kingdom-leaders. He bypasses the cowardly strong males, and calls the weaker ones who are obedient.

The point of this story is not how strong women can be or how their talents should be used. Rather, it declares that when I fall short in my work in God's kingdom, He will use other people.

Many who were supposed to be first will be last and the last will be first. Jesus takes a child and teaches me that I, with all my self-importance, should look up to that child.

On the other hand, what a comfort! I may fail but the Lord's kingdom comes anyway. His is the victory!

Judges 4-6

With the three hundred men that lapped I will deliver you (Judges 7:7).

The Lord wants to convince me that I am not delivered by my own efforts. When I feel depressed because I think that my failures must mean the end of God's glory, God just smiles.

An army of 32,000 Israelites has to battle against 135,000 enemies. First God tells Gideon to send home all the people who are afraid. 22,000 go; 10,000 remain. It is alarming that two-thirds of the Israelite soldiers are that frightened. Where is the power of faith and dedication? But the Lord makes a further cut in numbers. Only three hundred men are chosen to do battle—one percent of the original army. And even these three hundred have no arms—just some jars, torches and trumpets. Israel will never be able to say proudly to God, "Our own hands have delivered us."

These three hundred men are not chosen because they are strong or courageous. Their task: blow trumpets, wave torches, and break jars. They shout the cry of victory before the battle has started. Then God confuses the enemy. The future of Israel is secure again; God protects His people.

The message is clear. I must not build my hopes on visible strength. I must believe that God's almighty power to fulfill His promises is the only ground of my salvation.

The world is more confused and uncertain than it seems. God wants to show that confusion to me. In Christ I too can be more than a conqueror as long as I live in faith and hope.

When Gideon's men made all the noise that night, attracting the attention of an innumerable enemy, they put themselves in jeopardy. At least, that is the human view: Let's be quiet and hope to survive. But God says, Shout! He knows that the world has been conquered. As long as I know that too, I can be victorious.

Judges 7-9

Then say Shibboleth, and he said Sibboleth (Judges 12:6).

Jephthah is a great warrior who brilliantly defeats the Ammonite enemies of Isreal. He claims that he did so for the Lord, and indeed the Spirit of God was with him. Still, a closer look at the story reveals that his brothers had thrust him out of the family because he was the son of a harlot. When he is urged to become the leader of Gilead's army, he accepts on the condition that he will be their head after the victory.

After the victory, more trouble develops. The tribe of Ephraim cannot tolerate Jephthah and Gilead getting all the honor for defeating the Ammonites, so they accuse Gilead of purposely leaving them out of the war.

What does it matter? Isn't the defeat of God's enemies all that counts? No, not to those who seek their own glory. Because of hurt pride, the tribes of Ephraim and Gilead, brothers in the Lord, start killing each other.

Gilead wins this ugly battle and then starts killing the fugitives of Ephraim who try to return home after their defeat. Now the nastiness of this whole matter surfaces. At the fords of the Jordan, it is impossible to tell an Ephraimite from a Gileadite. They all look so much alike; they have the same language; they are all sons of the same father. Then Gilead discovers that the people of Ephraim cannot pronounce the *h* in *Shibboleth*. If a person cannot say *Shibboleth*, he is an enemy; he is to be killed. Forty-two thousand are slaughtered!

As children of God, we have our differences. Differences would be beautiful if we all loved the God who gives many varied talents and gifts. But as soon as egos are more important than love for God, those differences turn into divisions and even lead us to hate and despise each other.

Is the love of Jesus Christ in me so that I love God more than myself? Is my pride more important than the glory of God? Christ can heal!

Judges 10-12

And the Spirit of God came mightily upon him (Judges 14:19).

Samson's life portrays Israel's position in God's covenant. Samson is hardly a nice person. He marries a heathen girl against the wishes of his parents. He poses a riddle to the men at the wedding, knowing that no one will be able to solve it, thereby intending to rob them of thirty men's suits. When they get help from his own wife, Samson angrily kills thirty innocent men in Ashkelon to pay off the wedding guests. In a huff, he leaves his wife. Then when he wants her back and cannot get her, he burns an entire harvest. Such behavior is inexcusable.

At the same time, God is using him. God has told Samson's parents that he will be a special man in God's kingdom. God marks Samson's life by forbidding him to drink wine or cut his hair. In similar ways, Israel was set aside for the service of God. But when Samson gives up the secret of his life, surrendering his special position, he is blinded and becomes prisoner of the enemies.

God has also put His hand upon me to say that I belong to Him, not because I am nice, but because He wants to use me. In Christ, He has baptized me, marking me as His servant. If my distinctiveness disappears, I am powerless.

The Lord uses Samson despite his sin. Even when Samson is acting irresponsibly, the Spirit of God comes mightily upon him and gives him power. Because of Samson's actions, hostility between Israel and the Philistines flares up, and this leads eventually to the destruction of many Philistines through Samson's death.

God uses even my sins to the coming of His glory. Though He never condones sin, He takes it in His mighty hands and bends it in the right direction.

Judges 13-15

What have I left? (Judges 18:24).

Micah stole from his mother. But when he returns her money, he receives her blessings rather than her curse. With the money, she employs a metal worker to make an ephod and a graven image, and Micah puts these articles in a shrine so that he can worship God in his own temple. A wandering Levite is willing to serve as his priest. Everything seems right; Micah says, "Now I know that the Lord will prosper me because I have a Levite as priest."

But then people of the tribe of Dan, on the way to war, find his little temple. They take the images, the ephod, and the priest and leave Micah with an empty shrine. Micah falls into despair: Now the Lord will not be with him anymore.

The Danites did wrong to rob Micah. But his wrong is also deep. Micah is not willing to go to Shiloh to worship God. But in Shiloh is the altar on which the blood of Jesus is symbolized. There is the ark through which God says, "I am with you." Wanting his own worship, Micah doesn't care to commune with God's people. He refuses to make the long trip as a sacrifice to his God. His ephod will tell him all he needs to know, though it may not be what God wants to say.

If my faith rests not in God's promises but in my own convictions, I may think that everything is fine and that God is with me. But my confidence is based in only my opinion. I must go to the altar of Christ; I must listen to God's Word and obey it.

It is a merciful God who sends the Danites to take away everything that is separating Micah from his God.

Have I really given myself to Him; is my trust based upon His Word? God doesn't mind my confusion. When He starts building His temple in my life, He must first tear down my own little shrines.

Judges 16-18

Shall we go out to battle against our brethren? And the Lord said, Go up (Judges 20:28).

A terrible crime has been committed in Gibeah in the tribe of Benjamin. The men of the city demanded a guest in the city to be delivered to them for a homosexual orgy. When they were denied, they took the man's concubine and killed her with their gruesome lust. To make Israel aware of this unbelievable crime, the husband sends part of the body to each tribe.

All the people of Israel now instruct Benjamin to punish the men of Gibeah severely. But the Benjaminites, loving their own sons more than the Lord and His justice, ignore the instructions. Therefore the army of Israel must go out; they cannot stay home when human rights, protected by God's law, are being trampled upon.

I *am* my brother's keeper. Though I may wish not to get involved, God has given His law, which is my business. I may not stay neutral. When people are suffering injustice in this world, Christians are called upon to act.

When Israel asks, Who shall go up first? The answer is, Judah. The tribe of the coming Messiah goes first, because Jesus shows us the way.

However, when Israel attacks the Benjaminites, twice they have to retreat with loss of lives. Still the Lord tells them to go on. The third time, finally, they are able to restore order and justice.

Why, if the Lord is with them, must Israel suffer so much loss?

Trying to do the will of God does not protect one from pain. Correction and restoration are always painful processes. When God restored peace with mankind, Christ Himself cried out in darkness.

Judges 19-21

He shall be to you a restorer of life (Ruth 4:15).

While in Moab, Naomi's husband dies. After marrying heathen women, her sons both die. Now the name of this family will be wiped out from Israel. Naomi may have food and shelter in Moab, but what good is it to have the whole world but no inheritance in the kingdom of God?

Now Naomi looks again to the promised land. Without any hope in the world, she wants at least to live in God's presence. After she makes her decision, things start to change. The "stranger" Ruth becomes a daughter to her and a child of Israel's God. Because the man Boaz is mysteriously drawn to this woman, Ruth finds rich gleanings in the field, plenty of food for Naomi and herself. Finally Ruth and Boaz marry, and the son is born who will carry the name of Naomi and her husband through the ages. Naomi cannot see beyond Obed to Jesse and then David and then the great Son of David, the true restorer of life.

Several things are striking about this story. First, it turns out unbelievably well. But God works like that. He accomplishes the impossible, the unexpected.

Second, I see that God's plan works itself out through small events. Every detail is in His hand.

Naomi and Ruth don't know the full significance of their story. Only in the New Testament, does it become clear that these events lead toward the coming of Christ. In God's plan, all things work together for good. Naomi, Ruth, and Boaz know that. But they can never fathom the depths of that truth. When I doubt God's control of a present situation, then I must admit that I cannot comprehend the scope of His plan.

Naomi finds renewal when she returns to the land of God. When her exile is over, life returns. When I seek His kingdom, everything else will be added unto me.

Ruth 1-4

And the Lord came and stood forth, calling (I Samuel 3:10).

In these days of the judges, there is no king in Israel; every man does what was right in his own eyes. The temple of God illustrates the situation. The priest Eli cannot or will not cope with the problems, particularly with the blasphemous behavior of his sons. His sons, Hophni and Phinehas, serve themselves, laughing at God and His Word. And Samuel, the child Hannah "prayed from the Lord" and then dedicated to His service, is too young to be of any help; he does not yet know the Lord.

The Lord might well turn away, but instead He calls. Samuel does not understand who is calling. But that does not matter. Gently, the Lord keeps on calling. He is in no hurry.

The Lord has not spoken to Eli for a long time. But when Eli realizes that the Lord is calling Samuel, he knows that something terrible is going to happen. Eli is resigned to whatever it may be. What a pitiful picture he makes! When the voice of God passes him by, all he does is passively accept God's judgment.

Although the temple is closed until morning when Samuel will again open the doors, the Lord gets in. The ark of His covenant is the symbol of His presence. He makes good the promise in the symbol; one day the promise will be fulfilled forever in Jesus Christ.

Now the time of the judges is over. Hearing that the Lord has made contact again, Israel finds new hope and security. During this very dark time, God's revelation has gradually faded. The judges and Israel have tried to follow God but stumbled in the darkness. Now the light starts to shine.

I know that the morning star has risen. The day of the fullness of God's kingdom is near. I must get to work.

I Samuel 1-3

What shall we do with the ark of the Lord? (I Samuel 6:2).

Needing help against their enemies Israel's elders bring the ark of the covenant of the Lord from Shiloh to the battlefield. But the results are disastrous. The ark is captured, Israel is defeated, Eli's sons are killed, and Eli dies.

What went wrong? Israel can move the ark of God, but they cannot put the Lord where they want Him. In the ark God shows Himself present among His people. But God is not in the ark. His laws have been broken, His temple service has been polluted with sin. When no one is really seeking Him, it is just superstition to take the ark along.

When I want God to be with me and to help me, I cannot point to a few drops of water on my forehead or to a piece of bread and a cup of wine in my hand and tell Him that He is now bound to be with me. God reveals Himself in tokens, but the tokens are not God. To have the Lord on my side, I must pledge Him my faith and dedication.

Now Israel knows that the Lord is not with them anymore, for the ark itself is missing.

Soon the Philistines confront the power of God in the house of their god. Dagon falls on his face and breaks to pieces. The people living around the ark are struck by a mysterious disease. In the end, no one knows what to do with the ark.

God did not do a thing for His people in the battle, but now He is confounding His enemies. He proves to the heathen that Israel's God is above all gods. Assuming His honor and greatness among those who think Him weak and defeated, the Lord makes people tremble before Him.

Furthermore, God is talking to His people from the land of the Philistines. He is telling them, "See, I am not dead and helpless. If only you would seek Me, you would know that there is plenty of help and power in Me."

God never stops calling His lost back to Himself.

I Samuel 4-6

*We will have a king over us, that we also may be like all the nations
(I Samuel 8:19, 20).*

The judges have failed to lead Israel back to God. Samuel's
sons are unfit to take over their father's task. Now Israel cries for a
king.

The Lord has always known that His people need a king. God
Himself commanded mankind to serve Him, faithfully, obeying
His commandments. And when they cannot reach that ideal, only
the King Jesus Christ can draw them back into God's fellowship.

So perhaps God should be happy about Israel's cry for a king.
However, Israel is not asking for help and leadership. Their pride
demands a king to lead them into battle. They see no glory in being
the people of an invisible God. They feel silly when other nations
stare at them and ask, "Where is your king?"

It is so hard to be different from the rest. How do I explain
that what counts in the world does not always count with the Lord?
I too sometimes desire to act like the world, setting the same
priorities and values as other people, blending into the crowd.

Israel's request upsets Samuel. He warns them that to have a
king like the other nations will not mean happiness. That king will
oppress them, demanding their taxes and their services. He tries to
make it clear that the joy of being God's own people far exceeds the
joy of being like the world.

Nevertheless, Israel insists on a king like the other nations.
Then, even though Samuel expects the Lord to say no, the Lord
says, "Give them their king." The Lord knows that they will never
admit their error without finding it out for themselves. So He
grants them their request. Soon, in King Saul, they will experience
how wrong they have been.

The Lord in His faithfulness can make me find out what I
should have believed in the first place.

I Samuel 7-9

Far be it from me that I should sin against the Lord by ceasing to pray for you (I Samuel 12:23).

Samuel has good reason to be bitter. In his old age, Israel tells him to retire because he can no longer lead them. They reject his sons, believing them unworthy to be his successors. Though Samuel has warned against taking a king like the other nations, the kingdom seems to be working well. Saul's initial actions are promising; well liked, he seems to prove Samuel's warnings unfounded. Perhaps this is the time for Samuel to withdraw grudgingly from the scene.

But Samuel remains a child of God. He reminds Israel about his near-perfect service to them and the Lord, and he warns them not to sin. And when the Israelites ask him to pray for them, he agrees to do so. He does not wish them misery. To stop praying for them would be a sin.

Samuel is right. An embittered refusal to pray for Israel would show that he considered himself more important than the salvation of God's people, and even greater than their God. The Lord is merciful; He never rejects those to whom He gave His covenant promises.

Therefore, even though Samuel's heart breaks when he sees how Saul and Israel turn away from the Lord, he does not take revenge. He keeps on praying. The Spirit of Jesus Christ is in his heart.

When Christ is nailed to the cross, He prays for Israel as no one else could. At the most impossible time, the great High Priest calls for mercy instead of judgment.

What do I do for all the people who have hurt me deeply? How do I react to those who laugh at me and my words? What shall I do when people reject my good intentions or do not respond to my love? If Christ lives in my heart, I will continue to pray for them. If that praying stops, I am walking in sin. I have to keep walking in Christ.

I Samuel 10-12

As Samuel turned to go away, Saul laid hold upon the skirt of his robe, and it tore (I Samuel 15:27).

Amalek was the first nation to attack the nation of slaves going from Egypt to the promised land. Now God tells Saul to punish them for what they have done to His child Israel. The love of God for His children is so strong that He will crush whoever bothers them.

But that burning love is not present in Saul's heart. He saves Agag the king of Amalek, for such a prisoner is a symbol of Saul's victory. Saul also spares the best of the cattle and all else that is good.

Wanting to get a little bit extra out of this victory, Saul disobeys the voice of God. But most of all, he does not share God's love and justice. His own desires dictate his behavior.

When Samuel confronts him with his disobedience, Saul tries to lie himself out of it. Explaining his sins away, he hopes that the Lord will understand. He doesn't realize that the real sin is unbelief. He is not with God. The branch that is not in the vine is pruned off and burned.

When Saul's excuses make no difference and Samuel turns away, Saul tries to hang on to him. When he tears Samuel's robe, he is told that the Lord has torn the kingdom from him. Again he begs Samuel to uphold his honor. If Samuel will stay with him, he may still be king in the eyes of the elders of Israel. Saul is concerned about maintaining his position when the Lord Himself is turning away. If Saul had returned to God in repentance, he would have found mercy.

What am I concerned about in my life? Do I desperately try to hang on to what God is taking away from me? I must remember that what God wants is obedience. And though my rebellious stubbornness may have to be punished, God will be merciful if I raise my hands in penitential prayer.

I Samuel 13-15

Saul said to him, "Whose son are you, young man?" (I Samuel 17:58).

Saul is puzzled. Who is this David? He *is* acquainted with him. When the evil spirit made Saul restless and upset, David played the harp to soothe his emotions. Now this young man has defeated Goliath, and the defeat of the Philistines follows. The women sing that David has slain his ten thousands. Saul makes the right deduction: nothing will stop this man from becoming king in his place.

Now Saul must know: What is the driving force in David? What is his secret? Therefore he wants to know who David's father is. His line of ancestors must include great and strong men.

Saul overlooks God's work. The Lord has simply chosen the son of Jesse. Jesse's sons who seem more eligible have been passed by in favor of David. Through David, God will show what He can do for His people. It is not important who his father is, what his abilities and talents are.

I cannot find explanations for David's rise to leadership, for there are none. Jesse could not have passed on all those qualities; the Lord gives them to whomever He pleases. David's courage is a gift of the Spirit. Love for God dominates his actions. His indignation at Goliath's defiant words is genuine.

When I accept God, everything else will fall in place. A slingshot will be enough to conquer the fearful enemy, for behind it is the power of my God.

The Lord calls all His children who are worried about their lack of talents. He gives them His strength; He fulfills His power in their weakness.

Saul's future is cut off by the evil spirits. He looks around in the world and finds no answers, for he cannot admit that the Spirit of God is the only answer.

Who is my Father? Whose son am I? I know.

I Samuel 16-18

And let his spittle run down his beard (I Samuel 21:13).

Afraid that Saul will kill him, David tries to be clever by finding protection among God's enemies. But the people of Gath recognize him as the general who defeated their armies. David's only escape is to act insane. What a sight! The man chosen by God to be Israel's glorious king acts the fool before King Achish. How did he get into this?

David wanted to give God a hand. God had promised to make him Israel's king; David should have known that the Lord would protect him. But David didn't trust the Lord much. He borrowed the big sword he had taken from Goliath. He lied to the priest of God in order to get bread, and then ate the holy bread dedicated to God. He sought protection from the heathen, but had to lower himself to posing as an idiot.

The results of David's actions are devastating. God's enemies have a good laugh at the fight between the old king and the new king. When Israel's hero asks for asylum, where is the glory of God?

That is not the only price being paid. The priests to whom David lied, who gave him bread and Goliath's sword, will be killed because of his actions. Saul will murder eighty-five priests who innocently trusted God's servant, David.

My unbelief has effects on the world around me. My own cunning may crush other people. As soon as I stop trusting God, things go haywire. One thing leads to another until I am standing there like an idiot, guilty of dishonoring my God and hurting other people.

I know that the Lord keeps His promises, even in the dark moments. In God's hands, David was safe, even against his own unbelief.

Who is the real king? David? Or I? Certainly not. God is the almighty and righteous King who cares to save an idiot.

I Samuel 19-21

And the Lord said, "They will surrender you" (I Samuel 23:12).

The people in Keilah are being harassed by the Philistines. However, since Saul is preoccupied with defending his own throne against David, he does not care about ruling and defending his nation. Therefore Keilah has to suffer.

But the Spirit of a compassionate Jesus Christ is in David. When David prays, the Lord tells him to go liberate Keilah. His men point out that this may be hazardous to his health. David is a refugee himself, under constant attack and in perpetual danger. Drawing Saul's attention with action against the Philistines will increase the peril. David double-checks with the Lord. But it is true: he may go, and he has the promise of victory.

The contrast between Saul and David grows ever stronger. David loves God's oppressed children more than his own safety, while Saul shirks his responsibilities as defender of Israel.

Not only Keilah benefits from this battle; David and his men profit as well. A negative approach to life defeats itself, but reaching out to help others is liberating. My task is to be a blessing. When I help others, I am too busy to see my own problems.

David hears that Saul is moving his army to capture him in Keilah and the Lord confirms that this is going to happen. But when David asks God if the people of Keilah will gratefully protect him, he is told they will surrender him to Saul. They are smart people. Saul's armies are bigger than David's, and they don't want to take any risks. Gratitude and love are abstract terms for them.

Could the Lord have changed their minds? Why should He? What I do must be done for my God and Father, not for myself. If I act for my own profit, I will be terribly frustrated. If I am trying to be an image of Jesus, the Lord guarantees my reward.

I Samuel 22-24

God has given your enemy into your hand today (I Samuel 26:8).

The most difficult temptations to resist are those which seem God-glorifying. Abishai goes with David to the place where Saul is sleeping. There he realizes that one thrust of his spear would end David's persecution. He even says that God must have given them this beautiful opportunity.

David must have been sorely tempted to kill Saul and call it God's work. But the Lord will give David the throne in good time. The Word of God never speaks of murder as a proper way to become Israel's king. David has to wait until the Lord opens up the way. Salvation will come only in the way of the Lord.

So many shortcuts are possible. On humane grounds, I may kill the unborn child, break up a marriage, "mercifully" kill people who don't have a chance for a full life anymore, steal to have more money to give to God's kingdom, tell little white lies. I can always find a good excuse to justify my actions.

But then, deep down, I am just using God for my own purposes and wishes. The way of the Lord is not an easy one, but it is the only sure way to salvation. I have to obey God's Word no matter what it may cost me.

Is there a blessing on David's attitude? When Saul hears about it, for one moment his blind eyes see, and he acknowledges the ways of the Lord. He realizes that he is wrong and that David is right. Though this doesn't last, David's witness *has* reached him and convinced him of his sins.

What more can I do? I cannot change people's hearts. But I can and must let the light shine in the dark world.

I Samuel 25-27

And when Saul inquired of the Lord, the Lord did not answer him (I Samuel 28:6).

Saul cries through the darkness of night to the Lord, but he receives no answer. Barred from God, he tries to consult a medium. But that experience is even more frightening: the voice of Samuel tells him to abandon all hope. Therefore, when Saul looks at the armies of the Philistines the next day, his heart trembles. The battle rages, Saul's army suffers defeat, and an archer's arrow finds its mark.

Defeat and darkness culminate in a night of suicide. Having lost his kingship and then his personal relationship to God, Saul attempts murder and finally kills himself.

But why was God deaf to Saul's cries? Doesn't God promise that I will never call on Him in vain?

First of all, Saul inquires of the Lord to know only what is going to happen. He seeks the future, not the Lord. I would like to shout, "Saul, repent! Seek the Lord and you will find Him. On your knees, beg for His nearness and forgiveness." But Saul must remain an unbroken man. Even in death, he must save his pride.

That frightens me. Stubbornness makes me unwilling to honestly confess my sins. Often I want to know of God and His ways. But do I want to know Him and be known by Him?

This story also shows us that there *is* a point of no return. The Bible speaks about the unforgivable sin, of the door falling shut with such force that it cannot be opened again. Used to Jesus' assurance that every sin can be forgiven, I may forget His words about utter darkness for those who don't go to Him. I cannot assume that I can return when it pleases me.

I deserve nothing but darkness. When I accept that fact, the light starts to shine.

I Samuel 28-30

*And David lamented with this lamentation over Saul and Jonathan
his son (II Samuel 1:17).*

This should be a great day in David's life. Saul is dead; the bitter persecution is finally over. But the soldier who brings David the
good tidings gets an unexpected reception. Instead of receiving a
warm welcome, he is killed. And instead of songs of joy in David's
court, lamentation breaks out over Saul's death.

When I achieve a goal, when I win a battle, I should be
grateful. But I never know pure joy. Here upon earth happiness is
always tinged with sadness. Saul is dead—but he was a child of God
too and his life ended in darkness. There has been a war in Israel
and when God's children fight, there can be only losers.

The spirit of Jesus Christ must dwell in my heart. He cried
over Jerusalem. He suffered under Judas' betrayal. He prayed for
those who crucified Him because He could not bear to see them go
into darkness.

Knowing victory means seeing the tragedy of the losers; when I
am victorious I still must struggle with tears. My life must be full of
mercy and prayer and deep concern for those who live in darkness.

But my concern should not be only for my neighbor. The glory
of God is also at stake. David knows that in the streets of Gath and
Ashkelon there will be unholy pleasure in the destruction of Saul.
They will celebrate a defeat for the God of Israel who let His
anointed King die. They understand the ways of the Lord, no more
than I can explain them. But they will laugh while I cry.

There is little I can do about the way the Sauls in this world
obscure the glory of God. But I *can* show that God is still victorious, because His Spirit is living in my heart and ruling my life.

II Samuel 1-3

And the anger of the Lord was kindled . . . And David was angry (II Samuel 6:7, 8).

The Father and the child are angry at each other. My first impulse is to take David's side. He has decided to bring the ark, the symbol of God's presence, to Jerusalem. That is good, for one cannot have prosperity and happiness without the Lord at the center of life. On this joyful occasion, thousands of people march along making music. The ark is moving on a new cart, and everything is in order. Then the oxen stumble, the ark slides, and when Uzza steadies it, he dies instantly. Why?

The Israelites have not followed the instructions of the Lord when transporting the ark. It should have been carried by the Levites. But the trip was long, and besides, the cart procession was impressive. David had good intentions, just as Uzza had meant well when he steadied the ark in the moment of danger.

Now David thinks that God is against him. In his anger, he puts the ark in someone's house and cancels the whole ceremony. The ark won't go to Jerusalem. Fear destroys love and dedication. Who can satisfy such a demanding God? Where is His compassion for people who want to serve Him, despite their shortcomings?

But even in His anger, the Lord shows love. The Lord is not angry simply because David and his men did not follow His instruction to the letter. He is angry about a sloppy attitude towards Himself.

God has come so close to me that sometimes I start to take Him and His commandments for granted. Then the covenant is no longer between the most holy God and His sinful child, but between equal partners. Only when I tremble in the face of God's majesty can I appreciate the way He stooped to me in Jesus. I may not lose sight of the greatness of His mercy.

II Samuel 4-6

David administered justice and equity to all his people (II Samuel 8:15).

David is a very busy man in the first years of his kingship. There are still many wars to be fought, not for the purpose of stuffing government coffers, though that is a nice side effect. But the enemies around are a real danger. They would love to destroy the glory of Israel.

I must not be satisfied with my life while blind to the hostile forces waiting to crush it. The church militant must continue fighting in order to have peace. As soon as my defenses are down, my life can be ripped apart by the forces which hate to see me happy. I must fight on in His power to protect my life.

However, while fighting off dangers around me, I may become an empty shell. Though all the devils be chased away, the house may be so empty that a seven-fold force of demons can come again and fill it.

David has seen that struggling against enemies is only meaningful when there is also building up of the kingdom. In David's kingdom, justice and equity complement arms and battles. In the justice of God, relationships must be healthy. Nobody may oppress the weak and the helpless. People are to live in peace, happy to be protected by the presence of their God.

I must listen to people who warn me of the dangers around me. I can even warn my children of the enemies. But have people seen in me God's peace in a human life? Do my actions speak of the Spirit of God dwelling in me?

II Samuel 7-9

Nathan said to David, "You are the man" (II Samuel 12:7).

The sin David committed was ugly enough: adultery, murder, deceit, hypocrisy. But worse, how can a man live with such guilt? David must have tried to hide behind excuses: every king does things like that (but am I different as a child of God?), the woman was not unwilling (is that my business?), the man was so stubborn and unwilling to cooperate (wasn't he in the right?), the Lord didn't react (is His goodness an excuse for my guilt?). David may be suffering some minor conscience pangs, but it takes a prophet to open his eyes.

Salvation begins when the Lord opens my eyes to what I have done. It is not true that the Lord comes when people repent. Instead, He comes with His Spirit to *make* people repentant. There is no part of salvation that is not the Lord's work.

After Nathan tells his parable, David becomes indignant, condemning a man to death for stealing a lamb without even a thought for his own guilt. I, too, condemn other people without feeling repentance for my own sins. Mercy for others must be born from the mercy I receive from the Lord.

The Lord can break through the hard shell around David's heart. A simple word of repentance and a simple word of forgiveness clears up matters.

A question remains: Why has the Lord come to David? Nothing can be done really; the man is dead, his wife married to David, and the child born. Why return to the sordid events that happened so long ago?

The answer is simple. The relationship must be restored. Not only human relationships are important. The Father-child relation is the source of every other relationship. Once that is restored, God can bless His people.

II Samuel 10-12

Carry the ark of God back into the city (II Samuel 15:25).

David is in deep distress. His son Absalom is rebelling against him, trying to become king in his place. Even worse, Israel is following Absalom with no allegiance to the man who has done so much for them. Worse still, in all the political tugs of war, the Lord's glory is forgotten. David and his men watch helplessly and shed their tears.

To comfort David, some of his people bring the ark to him, in essence telling him, "Fear not, we believe that the Lord is still with you." It is a nice gesture, but David does not want the ark to go with him. He tells them to bring it back to the city. Why?

First of all, David does not need this assurance. He knows that God is his Father. Psalm 3 proves that. No symbol can replace the presence of the Lord Himself.

A second reason David refuses is that he is not sure what the Lord has in store for him. A sinner himself, he may be the cause of this rebellion. Maybe he is not to be king anymore. What trust in God's rule!

There is however a third reason for David's refusal to take the ark of God along. The ark belongs to the people, not to him alone.

But those people have rejected King David, and thereby they have rejected their God and His covenant! They have shown no respect for the words of their God and His promises. The ark will be out of place with those sinful unbelievers.

Still, David insists that the ark be brought back to the city. For just when the people are rejecting God, they have to see that the Lord does not reject them.

One day there will be a cross and the people of God will shout, "Crucify Him." But over the cross a sign will show: You may reject me, but I am still your King. My Kingship does not depend on your acceptance.

II Samuel 13-15

The Lord had ordained to defeat the good counsel of Ahithophel, so that the Lord might bring evil upon Absalom (II Samuel 17:14).

The rebellion of Absalom against his father David promises to be successful. Not only are all the powers of Israel pitched against David, but a man whose wisdom David respects highly gives advice so good that Absalom *must* become king. "The counsel of Ahithophel was as if one consulted the oracle of God; so was all his counsel esteemed, both by David and by Absalom" (Sam. 16:23). Ahithophel advises that David must be pursued now while he is weary and discouraged, and that a quick execution must end his rule. It seems there is no chance for David to survive.

I sometimes find myself with no realistic hope; everyone may say it is senseless to look for a way out of a situation. I feel I should accept the inevitable. I stop praying; being a Christian shouldn't blind me to the reality of life anymore.

But then, unbelievably, Hushai the Archite, David's friend, is consulted. He gives advice extremely dangerous to Absalom and his group, but they all agree with Hushai and reject the counsel of Ahithophel. Why?

There is no logical human explanation. The only thing that can be said is that the Lord did it. Ahithophel must have felt that this was heavenly interference for he went home to commit suicide.

Suddenly the tables were turned. Now there was no hope for Absalom's camp, and David would be king again.

Despite my calculations and expectations, there is a factor that can disturb all logical conclusions. Who would believe that a dead Savior could rise to be my exalted King? I know God as the One whose wisdom is foolishness in my eyes and whose foolishness is wisdom. Of course, I must continue to think in a logical and orderly way. But the Lord can cross my straight way.

Therefore, there is always hope.

II Samuel 16-18

Then the king arose and took his seat in the gate (II Samuel 19:8).

To lose a child is bad enough. To know that he was killed while rebelling against his father is even worse. David is deeply sad and unable to rejoice in his victory. The price was so high! He cannot even organize the re-establishment of his reign over Israel.

Such familial love is valuable and beautiful, binding father and son together no matter how many sins are committed on both sides.

Joab, however, has a different opinion. He rebukes the king for just sitting there, weeping with heartbreak. David's kingdom is in danger. Now is the moment to retake the throne of Israel. If David waits, the chance may vanish and the kingdom of Israel may collapse. Joab tells the king that his love should go out to his servants and subjects more than to his own dead son.

He is right. If I love my son and daughter and father and mother more than Jesus, I am not fit for the Kingdom of God. Jesus even tells us that we should hate our own when we love Him. That sounds terrible.

What does it mean? Of course I may love my own, but when there is a conflict, I will have to make a choice. When David loves Absalom more than the Lord who has called him to take the throne of Israel, when he abandons his task because of his personal hurt, then he has demonstrated that he has no share in the kingdom of God.

It is not easy to follow Jesus. David rises and takes his seat in the gate. Now he has to deal with problems far from his mind while his heart is broken. He has to abandon the little kingdom of his heart and emotions for the great kingdom of God.

But that is not a bad choice after all. I too will find that out.

II Samuel 19-21

He would not drink of it; he poured it out to the Lord (II Samuel 23:16).

In one of his dark days, David wishes to drink water from the well in Bethlehem, the town where he was born and raised. But the city is in the hands of the Philistines. So three mighty and courageous men go out to Bethlehem and, right under the noses of the enemies, draw water from the well and bring it to David. But instead of graciously accepting this tremendous gift, David pours the water out on the ground. The risk taken and the love expressed by these men don't seem to count. It sounds harsh, this destruction in one moment of what courage achieved in hours of danger.

At this moment there is much of Christ in David. He did not come to be served but to serve. Though tempted to accept, David realizes that he is a servant of his God and that any achievements are work done for God. When I live close to God, I don't need compensation. Jesus was offered bread and protection and all the kingdoms of the earth, but He recognized satan in the offers. He had the courage to say, "Get behind Me, satan." The devil tries to lead David into the self-centered life of a worldly king, but David knows that in God's own time and way, he will drink from the well in Bethlehem. Christ did receive all the kingdoms of the earth in God's time, though the road went through Calvary.

At the same time David teaches his heroes a lesson. What is courage? It's not the glory of a feat to be storied among soldiers for years to come. Courage is doing what the Lord commands. These men have done that many times: they stood by God's chosen king when everyone else fled. But this time, they desired to satisfy not only David's wish, but also their own desire for glory. David recognizes this and says, I am not going to drink your blood. My blood may be given to the Lord, but never for a stunt.

Courage is following the Lord and striving for His kingdom. The rest is vanity. Please Lord, help me to see that!

II Samuel 22-24

Act therefore according to your wisdom, but do not let his gray head go down to Sheol in peace (I Kings 2:6).

From a dying child of God, one might expect gentle, encouraging words. However, in II Samuel 23:6-7, David has harsh words for all the ungodly, and in this chapter, there are very strange commands concerning specific people who went awry. David tells Solomon that he should take care of General Joab, who was a murderer, and of Shimei, who cursed David when he fled from his son Absalom. In his life, David could not do much about these people. He needed Joab and he had promised to spare Shimei's life. Now Solomon should punish these men.

Should revenge and judgment be in the mind of a dying man? Granted, David also speaks of people who helped him and should be rewarded. Still, this deathbed statement is hard to accept.

Of course, it is possible to say that David went wrong and that I should not follow his example. Yet something in these words hit me. So much is not right and I can do so little about it. People not only attack and hurt me, but, more importantly, they do not go God's way. And often it seems they get away with it.

There is a thirst for righteousness in every Christian's life, a thirst rarely quenched.

Can Joab murder innocent people and die in honor? Even though David accepted Shimei's curse as sent by God to humiliate him, still it was not right and was actually an attack on David's God. When David dies, he has the desire that someone will do something about it. Solomon is a wise man; he will know what to do.

Jesus, the merciful Savior, spoke of a judgment day and the Revelation reveals that God will find His glory also in judgments. In the cross of Jesus, I find mercy and justice in perfect harmony.

I must love my neighbor as myself, but I may not love them more than God. As a child of God, I must try to imitate not only His sense of mercy but also His sense of justice.

I Kings 1-3

So Hiram supplied Solomon with all the timber (I Kings 5:10).

David was a man of blood; Solomon, a man of peace. Therefore the Lord chooses Solomon to build His beautiful temple. Peace may need to be achieved through blood, but the Shalom of the Lord is the ultimate goal.

Now it is time to see who is able and willing to serve God in the building of His house. The hands of His own people should give expression to their deep respect and love for their Lord and Savior. But, strangely, Solomon invites Hiram, king of Tyre and Sidon, to prepare all the wood for the temple. Later he appoints another Hiram, an artist from Tyre, to take care of all the metal structures.

There may well be some disappointment among the Israelites about this decision. True, the men from Sidon are experts in these fields, and they will greatly contribute to the beauty of the building. But is it right to ask heathen artists to do the job? Should we not look for the heart rather than for the skill? Is it not better to have a simple church and unskilled voices to praise God, and to restrict the circle of workers for God to believers?

Solomon has looked around and discovered that this whole world is the Lord's. The pagan artists may not love God or serve Him, but they are God's creatures; as they use their talents, they will show who is the Owner of this world.

All the many people supplying my daily needs are in God's employment. Enjoying the products of their arts and skills, I can recognize the greatness of my heavenly Father in them.

Of course, there are certain limits. There may be things so clutched by satan, areas so defiled, that they cannot serve me anymore. But nothing can prevent the Lord from reclaiming His world. Revelation tells me that the kings of the earth shall bring their glory into the new Jerusalem.

This is my Father's world. Therefore it is my world.

I Kings 4-6

Behold, heaven and the highest heaven cannot contain thee; how much less this house which I have built! (I Kings 8:27).

The building of Solomon's temple is an achievement which I hardly can imagine in this technological age. With sheer manpower and human sacrifice, a house has been built for the Lord that costs millions of dollars and draws visitors from all over the world. At the day of dedication, Solomon might well offer this building to the Lord confident that the Lord will accept it and, of course, dwell in it. After all, the Lord should be pleased with the tremendous love that speaks through the gold and jewels and precious stones.

But Solomon realizes that this house stands on an earth defiled with sin. It has been built by sinful people who may have become proud of their achievement. Therefore Solomon sacrifices tens of thousands of oxen and sheep.

The Lord's presence costs. Pentecost and the indwelling of the Holy Spirit come only after Christ gave His life for the forgiveness of sins. Only then may my body be the temple of the Holy Spirit. God is present in my home and work and achievements, but only through His grace.

Just when everything seems right in my eyes, I must look through the eyes of my heavenly Father. Then I see such a small and filthy abode for God that I fall to my knees with the prayer, "Dwell in me, oh Holy Spirit." I am sure that He will do so, but not because He must. He chooses to dwell in and among His people.

But there is more involved than the fact of sin. The very idea that God can dwell upon earth is strange. Even the heavens, the highest heavens, are too small to contain the Lord. God is so much more than I can ever imagine. I can never confine Him to my small expectations. When Solomon sees the glorious palace he has built for the King of kings, he realizes that God's greatness exceeds all our thoughts.

I Kings 7-9

I will give one tribe to your son, for the sake of David my servant and for the sake of Jerusalem which I have chosen (I Kings 11:13).

No power on earth can resist the rule of the mighty King Solomon. Hardly anyone thinks of going to war with him. But the whole kingdom shudders and begins to tumble into a bottomless abyss, just because Solomon no longer serves the Lord with his whole heart. When he gets old, he cannot resist the demands of his foreign wives to build altars for their gods. He goes along, maybe half-heartedly, to serve those idols.

His sexual attraction for those women (who can speak of love when there are 1000 of them?) is not the cause of his downfall. His disrespect for the biblical concept of marriage is not the worst problem. His problem is weakness of heart. He cannot say "no" anymore. Then there is no stopping, one defeat leads to the next. And what seemed to be an invincible castle is suddenly nothing more than a house of cards, falling at the first touch.

There are many excuses. Solomon's personal supremacy may lead to his weakness. He is getting old. Wealth may have made him less alert to danger. The women misled him. Yet all the excuses don't matter.

I don't read that Solomon asked for forgiveness. Yet the Lord is gentle enough to promise him that the downfall will not come until after his death. That mercy may have led him to accept the judgment without protest or repentance. But is this life all that counts?

However, the Lord takes care of His own kingdom. He promises that David will still have a son on his throne and that Jesus Christ will reign. Jerusalem is protected by His promises, and one day, David's son will enter it as a King.

God's work cannot be thwarted. He is faithful to His promises.

I Kings 10-12

Jeroboam said to his wife, "Arise, and disguise yourself" (I Kings 14:2).

There is a Greek word for religion that means literally "to use the gods." Jeroboam is a master of this art. Because Jerusalem is in the hands of his competitor, the king of Judah, Jeroboam creates two new places of worship. To save political face, he manipulates the worship of God. And when the people want idols, he accommodates them.

Now his son is deathly ill, and he knows that the Lord is cutting off his house from the throne. Repentance may have saved the boy's life. Instead, Jeroboam tries to trick the Lord into curing the child. The prophet who appointed him years ago is still alive; he may be sympathetic to the king. But to be sure, Jeroboam sends some gifts to bribe him. And he sends his wife in disguise, just in case Ahijah, the prophet, may not be too friendly. If Jeroboam can only manipulate the healing powers of the Lord, he has won the gamble.

At the same time he is manipulating people. He gambles away the life of his child; he tries to trick an old, blind prophet into abusing his powers; he talks his wife into taking this sad journey. His wife will have to pay for it: she will never see the child alive again. His people will suffer grief and mourning because he led them away from God.

The story makes me uncomfortable, for it is so easy to understand. When in trouble, I can so quickly try to trick the Lord into helping me. Pray a lot, go to church, give offerings to God—it all may help. Maybe the Lord's prophets are still blind and will pray for me. Or perhaps the ministers will be sensitive to such bribery. The only way to restore peace with God would be to return to Him and humble myself. But I would rather gamble in order to save face. I would rather manipulate people to their own hurt.

Yet I know Him who came to serve at the price of His own life. He asks me to follow in His footsteps.

I Kings 13-15

The Lord, he is God; the Lord, he is God (I Kings 18:39).

Israel has traded their God for Baal. Baal is sun, rain, and harvest; money and jobs; sex, meals and drinks. It is much more fun to serve and trust those things than to rely on the Lord. But Israel doesn't see that such Baal-worship is slavery. Nor do they see that since Baal does not exist, he cannot do a thing for them.

Elijah demonstrates this. In his effort to win people back for their own God and Savior, he asks the Lord to close the heavens. Without rain life becomes miserable; obviously, it is God who gives everything in life. But that is hard to admit. So Elijah goes into open battle with Baal. Lightning must strike to show who is really the living God. Talk is endless; now action must show who is God. And strangely, Israel accepts this proposal.

Is it necessary for God to show that He is alive? So many wonders have given proof of His existence and power and love. Do I really need any demonstration that the Lord is my God and that He can do everything for me?

Baal's priests try first. They spend all day in a frantic effort to make their dead idol come alive.

In comparison, the quiet majesty of Elijah's approach is impressive. He simply prays, "God, show these people that they belong to You!" And there is the immediate answer. Fire falls from heaven to consume the sacrifice on the altar.

Now comes the moment in which Israel will have to admit that all their religion and sacrifices and service have been wrong. Admitting wrong is never easy. But the sight of the lightning striking the water-drenched altar leaves no more room for rationalizing. This is the end of the rule of Baal. The Lord, He is God.

How do I really know that the Lord is God? Not in the thunder of falling fire. God does not have to prove Himself in a spectacular way. But His saving love shown by the sacrifice on Calvary tells me He is the Lord!

I Kings 16-18

He lay down on his bed, and turned away his face, and would eat no food (I Kings 21:4).

God laughs at people who think they are important (Psalm 2:4). The great King Ahab, having made quite a show of his kingship, is lying on his bed, pouting like a little child. He turns his head to the wall and refuses to come for dinner, just because he wants something and cannot have it. Naboth's vineyard, the property adjacent to his palace, is not for sale. His wife makes his petulance worse by appeasing him.

This horrible story isn't funny at all. The king of Israel imagines that the people have to serve him and give him all he wants. When I don't get what I want, I too can be upset and act like a little child. That in itself is a terrible thing for me, a child of the greatest King who came to serve rather than to be served.

But then Ahab's pouting is translated into action. Naboth is accused of having cursed God and the king. In a kangaroo court, he is convicted of religious and political rebellion and put to death.

Sadly, nobody understands what is really going on. The people assume Naboth was wrong and stone him to death. It is often easy to keep up good appearances and go scot-free. But not in the eyes of God. Through the prophet Elijah, the Lord tells Ahab the terrible way in which he and his wife will die. It is impossible to escape the truth of God.

And this is frightening. When everybody respects me, and I think I can get away with a lot of things, God's laugh may be a horrible sound in my ears.

But I know that God does not want this. He loves to smile at me and put His arms around me. I am His child, but not by pouting and trying to have things my way. At the same time, in Christ Jesus, I may be a king or queen.

I Kings 19-22

The water is bad and the land is unfruitful (II Kings 2:19).

Elisha has seen the glory of Elijah's ascension into heaven. The lightning, the whirlwind, the chariot and the horses have impressed him deeply. Now he stands on the river bank alone, wondering what to expect next. A share of Elijah's spirit has descended upon him, as promised. But what does it mean?

A good question! I know that Jesus ascended into heaven and that the Holy Spirit has been poured out on me. But how do I translate that into the reality of my office and task? It is not easy to follow Jesus. He was so impressive and I am so unimpressive.

Must Elisha preach? Not really. The first people to approach him in his new capacity as prophet do not ask him for any word of God. They face him with a very real problem. The land is pleasant to live in, but the water is bad, causing miscarriages among people and cattle. Could the prophet do something about it?

Elisha could have been indignant that the people were more concerned with their water supply than with the Word of God. But Elisha, without a word, solves the problem by miraculously curing the water. And he claims that this is according to the Word of God.

How could this be? Because God's Word speaks to the practical problems I face. When bad water means death, in Jesus Christ the power of death can be broken. The power of Christ has been preached from the rooftops; it can also be shown in small acts of charity. God wants to defeat all death. In Jesus Christ He will. Since I have died in Christ, I can eat and drink again and be merry.

Here I see my task, too. God's Word means power to heal. If I cannot translate the gospel into the reality of simple life, I am not a real prophet.

II Kings 1-3

And he said, "Your servant went nowhere" (II Kings 5:25).

When Elisha asks his servant Gehazi where he has been, the man gives an answer that is prophetic. He went nowhere. How true! Gehazi contracts the dreaded disease of which Naaman was cured. Why?

The answer *seems* obvious. Naaman, the rich general from Damascus, is so thankful for his healing that he offers Elisha any gift he may ask for. But Elisha refuses to accept anything. Gehazi thinks this is pretty stupid. Why not accept a free offering of gratitude? Accepting it may make Naaman feel better. Nobody likes to be beholden to anybody; it would be more courteous to take the offered gift. So Gehazi secretly goes after Naaman and under a pretext demands silver and beautiful clothes. Gehazi lies to the prophet, is greedy, and steals by taking for his own what was given for his master. But is this enough to be punished by such a terrible thing as becoming a leper and being banished from society forever?

There is much more at stake. Gehazi is misrepresenting the whole character of the grace of God. Naaman is accustomed to the system "I will do this or that and God will respond positively with some blessing." This does not work in Israel; Naaman has only to bathe in the Jordan River. So now he reverses the system: "God did this for me and now I will do something outstanding for Him."

This is pagan thinking—making a deal with the gods. Naaman must learn that the God of Israel is not just a more powerful version of his own god in Damascus. The Lord is totally different; He gives His healing grace for free. The only payment for healing will be made by His Son Jesus Christ. We can only acknowledge and accept this deliverance. When Gehazi asks for and accepts Naaman's gift, he takes the gospel out of the gospel.

It is difficult to live from grace. I would rather do something, pay something. But to try to do anything is to claim that Jesus did not do enough, and that I earn at least part of my salvation. All I can do is accept His mercy.

II Kings 4-6

And the man of God wept (II Kings 8:11).

I am curious about my future. Wouldn't it be great if I could see what is coming my way? Not at all! God's love and mercy keeps the future from me. I can barely deal with the problems of today. I am not prepared for what is in the future.

Looking ahead with prophetic eyes, Elisha weeps. Hazael will become king over Syria by murdering the present king, and then he will harm the people of God. There is nothing Elisha can do about it. It makes him very sad.

One could resign oneself to "the will of God," and say that Israel deserves the punishment. Since there is nothing I can do about the future, I should just be brave and stoical. As a Christian, I see everything in the light of God's justice and holiness. The kingdom is coming and I should be prepared for anything that will bring it closer. Oh yes, I have an answer to all sorrow.

But Jesus cried when He gazed on Jerusalem. Jesus, don't you see that this judgment over Jerusalem is well deserved and that it serves the kingdom of God? But He wept. When His friends died, He wept. Isn't death a gate to heaven? And haven't I deserved it? Yes, but tears stream down Jesus' face.

Elisha stares at Hazael and then weeps bitterly. Even though the king of Syria will be an instrument in God's hand to punish His children and to lead them back to Him, his rule will be a sad story. The heathen will think that God is not able to help His children, that He cannot rule the world. To counteract this notion, Elisha tells Hazael about it all.

When God seems unable to protect His people, in reality He rules. That makes me cry. When I force the Lord into something He doesn't want at all, I suffer, and I deserve it. But God suffers too. I make this world a sad, sad world; for all that, I cry.

But because God could cry about it, He can also make me joyful again. The coming of the kingdom produces mixed emotions, but the joy will win.

II Kings 7-9

So all the people of the land rejoiced (II Kings 11:20).

It is disheartening to read the stories of the kings of Judah and Israel. Whole families are wiped out with a sickening disdain for the value of human life. Sometimes the murderers even claim that this all is done for the honor of the Lord. Not only do they shed blood and rebel against each other, but all this happens in the land to which God has chosen to reveal His glory. But just when I turn away from the kingdom because it shows so little of good in the eyes of God and His children, there is a break. For forty years, King Joash reigns in the name of the Lord, and the people are happy—a bit of heaven in the midst of hell.

It is hard to explain this. Everything is against Joash. His mother kills her own royal family in order to be queen herself. While the royal family is being murdered, Joash's life is spared by an unknown lady. A priest protects his life, sheltering him in the house of the Lord. King Joash is only seven years old when he is proclaimed king. His mother Athalia is cruel enough to murder him and he has only the protection of a few volunteers armed with the old weapons of David that were stored in the temple.

Nothing explains Joash's reign except the fact that the Lord wants to give Judah a breather. He wants to show, through all the doom and bloodshed, a ray of hope. To make His people happy, God gives them forty years of peace and prosperity. It is clearly His work.

In the life of God's church and also in my life, the Lord gives moments of comfort and joy in which I acknowledge His goodness in Christ.

The lady, the priest, and the volunteers armed with the old weapons teach me that the Lord always has ways. I must not despair. In my own small way, I may help Him make His people happy.

II Kings 10-12

You should have struck five or six times (II Kings 13:19).

The prophet Elisha is dying after more than sixty years of service, and King Joash of Israel is very upset. Israel is in ruin. As the prophet had predicted, Hazael of Syria has conquered Israel. Now Joash's last hope seems to be dying with Elisha. The Word of God seems to depart with him. Not that Joash is a very godly man; he does what was evil in the eyes of the Lord. But to lose this important servant of God is just like losing the Word of God itself.

Elisha tells the weeping king to shoot an arrow through an open window. As he does so, Elisha explains: victory is coming back for Israel. The dark years are over. The Lord will return in mercy to His people. What a joy for Elisha to be able to give this prophecy of hope!

Then Elisha asks Joash to strike the ground with the arrows. But the king does not show any enthusiasm. He is sceptical of the prophecy and not impressed. Three times he does what the prophet told him but without any fervor. And that makes the prophet very angry.

Joash's problem is not that he is losing the Word of God in the dying man of God. His problem is unbelief. Despite all the promises of the Lord, Joash cannot do a thing unless he faces the enemies in the power of faith. If he simply follows instructions, the victory will not be great. The prophet did not tell Joash how many times to strike the ground. Enthusiasm should have come from his believing heart.

It does not matter how much of the Word of God I have, but what I do with it. The total destruction of the powers of evil can be achieved only by a church that uses what it is given by the Holy Spirit. It makes no sense to pray and read the Bible diligently if there is no willingness to go out in the might of the living God.

Give me a heart that glows through the Holy Spirit. Then I will keep on striking.

II Kings 13-15

He broke in pieces the bronze serpent that Moses had made (II Kings 18:4).

It would have been wonderful to have some relics of the olden days: the ark of the covenant, the stone tables, Aaron's rod. But wear and tear, hostile actions, and negligence have destroyed all these objects. Yet at least one beautiful object could have been saved if it had not been deliberately destroyed by King Hezekiah. The bronze serpent had been the symbol in the desert of the saving power of God's love. Why did Hezekiah destroy it?

The people had started to turn to the symbol instead of turning to the Lord Himself. They burned incense to it. They had a special name for it, "Nehushtan," that is "the Great Brass."

There are things that slowly but surely take God's place in my life. "The old rugged cross" can become meaningless—or even dangerous. I can sing loudly of this cross, put it on the church steeple and walls, and even wear it on my body without realizing what Jesus did for me and without knowing Him. Religious symbols, rather than leading *to* God, may lead me *away* from the living God. I have a hard time admitting this; it seems sacrilegious to object to these accepted symbols.

Hezekiah might have warned the Israelites to stop their symbol-worship. Or he could have reasoned that it was at least better to serve Nehushtan, who at least had some relationship to the Lord, than to worship Baal and other gods. But Hezekiah had the courage to break this sacred object into pieces.

Blessed are those who have so much respect for their God that they can crush everything that takes His place. After warnings and sermons, there comes the point when the Lord wants me to be more radical: holy cows killed on the streets of my life, holy little temples destroyed.

Give me the courage, Lord!

II Kings 16-18

For he thought, "Why not, if there will be peace and security in my days?" (II Kings 20:19).

When the dying King Hezekiah begs the Lord to allow him more time, the Lord grants him fifteen more years to live. That puts Hezekiah in good spirits. When envoys from the king of Babylon come over to his palace, he proudly shows them all the treasures of his palace. His vanity is fatal, for now the king of Babylon is determined to capture Jerusalem. The Lord tells Hezekiah that his showing off will result in the total exile of his people and descendants. But the Lord also tells him that this will not happen in his lifetime. Hezekiah accepts this judgment with equanimity, apparently because it will not occur in his days.

His attitude may infuriate me. Doesn't it show terrible egotism and impersonal carelessness? What happens to other people, what happens to the next generation is of no concern to me. As long as I can enjoy life, who cares? This attitude has wasted the treasures of this world and polluted the earth.

But is there another side to Hezekiah's attitude?

Hezekiah detects an element of grace and truth in God's judgment. The Lord could have come down on him in His anger. But God shows love and mercy. The man who has done so much for the honor of his God finds out that the Lord remembers him, taking his obedience into consideration. The fifteen years granted by God will not be years of misery. The gift of an extended life, already given, will not be marred by the terror of exile to Babylon. Peace and security will be granted for the remainder of Hezekiah's life.

The Lord's justice is sure. Yet though he chastises His children, He loves them. My Father has only good in store for His children for the sake of Christ, His Son. I must acknowledge His love. There is mercy in His judgment.

II Kings 19-21

Still the Lord did not turn from the fierceness of his great wrath (II Kings 23:26).

The first surprise of this chapter is discovering all the ways in which God's people offend and insult their God. The list of sinful practices seems to be endless. The re-discovery of the Word of God in the house of the Lord is the most unbelievable event. How can God's Word be completely forgotten? Here is a most humbling truth: one can depart completely from the Lord without realizing it.

Now comes a reformation if there ever was one! All that the Word of God forbids is thrown out; all that God's Word commands is reinstituted. (When I get rid of all that is evil in the eyes of God, I must fill the emptiness with obedience.) So now the Lord will surely be very pleased about this reformation and turn away His great wrath.

But then comes the second surprise of the chapter. God's anger remains; His decision to deport His people into exile stands. Is it possible that I do everything that He asks me to do and He remains angry? Do I serve God in vain? Does He not even realize what I am doing for Him?

There are two answers to these questions.

First, I should realize God my Father is so upset about all my sins that He does not turn easily at the first signs of conversion. His justice requires that my sins not be flippantly shrugged off.

But there is another answer. This book tells of a supreme effort of a God-fearing king and an obedient nation. Hardly anything more can possibly be done. But all that is not enough. God wants to demonstrate that the best human intentions and hard labor are not sufficient to wipe out the anger of God. The hand of God is pointing toward the cross of Jesus and the Holy Spirit who will take hold of His church and save it. Not what I feel or do can give me peace with God; not all my prayers and sighs and tears can bear my awful load. Thy power alone, O Son of God, can this sore bondage break.

II Kings 22-25

So Sheshan gave his daughter in marriage to Jarha his slave (I Chronicles 2:35).

While the book of Kings gives us a description of all that happened in Israel and Judah, Chronicles limits itself to the story of David and his house. It tells us that the generations after David proved that a Greater One should arise out of the lineage of David to save God's people and the world.

As the royal tribe of Judah is inventoried, we notice certain situations that seem tragic. Some of the people who hoped to contribute to the future of Judah are left out because they are childless. They cannot share in the coming of Messiah; their line is cut off.

At the same time, I read about a man who is not going to accept this. Since he has only daughters, his name will die out in Judah. So he gives one of his daughters in marriage to his Egyptian slave. Since that slave cannot claim the children born as his own, they will bear the name of the family and so function as its future generation.

What a strange solution! What kind of marriage is that? How do the partners accept this arrangement? Can an Egyptian serve in the genealogy of Messiah? What is a slave doing among all the free children of God?

Despite all my questions, I still feel something of awe for these people who are not going to accept their problem as unsolvable. By hook or by crook, they will share in the future generations of Judah. All those involved make sacrifices; neither the parents nor the marriage partners can be delighted by the solution they found. But then, are there more important things in the world than my own satisfaction and happiness? Their desire to be a blessing and to be blessed goes far beyond their personal preferences. The Lord may have frowned upon this strange marriage. But I can also see a smile appearing on His friendly face. For Jesus' sake, I may do weird things, like cutting off a hand or ripping out an eye. What are my priorities in life?

I Chronicles 1-3

Jabez called on the God of Israel (I Chronicles 4:10).

Some people just don't have a fighting chance in life. Jabez is one of them. During his birth, his mother suffered so immensely that she gave this child the name Jabez, son of sorrow. Thereafter everyone believes that the child's future will be very gloomy, that suffering and pain and agony are going to be part of his life story. It's no use hoping for something bright, there is a predestination of sorrow.

Some people seem to have no chance at all. Perhaps the prediction of their doom is based on economical and social grounds. Or a person may have no good qualities, no home to give him the right start in life, no abilities to succeed. He may be born at the wrong moment in history or in a place in the world where nobody has any use for him. Sometimes I too feel that I am fighting against all the odds.

Jabez could have accepted these stark "facts of life." But he does not. When he sees how the roads of life are closed to him, he sees a road open to God. The Lord has made a covenant with him and he has received the sign of that; he believes that the Word of God is true and reliable. Knowing that the God of Israel is still alive and far stronger than all the forces in life, Jabez, in simplicity of mind, prays for a blessing, a share in this world, protection against harmful powers. Without knowing it, he, the son of sorrow, goes to Him who will become the Man of Sorrow, and asks Him to take from his shoulders the unbearable burden of predestination to suffering and defeat. He approaches the Lord as a God of love and mercy and his simple prayer is answered. He receives what he asks: a share in life, happiness, honor. And above all, he receives the knowledge that God answers prayers.

Blessed are the children who rely on their Father. Blessed are the poor in spirit for theirs is the kingdom of heaven.

I Chronicles 4-6

And Judah was taken into exile in Babylon (I Chronicles 9:1).

This one sentence about the exile reminds me that this whole book with all its names and details was written long after Judah had returned from Babylon. It was written much later than it happened. After the terrible experience of the deportation it would have been natural to say, "Let's never go back to all the sordid details. Forgive and forget." But Chronicles talks about the ten tribes that never returned from captivity. Its lists of former inhabitants of Jerusalem and genealogies do not mean a thing to us. Why did the chroniclers bother? Wouldn't it have been better to say, "Never mind what happened in the past. Only the future counts"?

No. God wants me to look into the past to find out what happened and why. The carefree-ness of "forgiving and forgetting" is not according to the will of God.

After a marriage breaks down, it is important to find out why and how. When I suffer defeat, it is essential to see the roots of the problems even though I may have to review details that I would rather forget. I must also know the history of schisms, mistakes, errors, and heresies in the church of Christ. It is not pleasant, but essential for facing the future.

When I review my failures, I experience forgiveness and guidance. My Father gives me power to face those problems that were once too much for me, and now in His power I see my way free to encounter them without falling again.

It is amazing how well all the names were preserved in these chapters. Nonchalance is not a virtue. My God takes me and my life seriously. He forgives, He wants me to know how good He is, and He gives me second chances.

I Chronicles 7-9

Then the Spirit came upon Amasai, chief of the thirty (I Chronicles 12:18).

The book of Chronicles recalls the glory of David's kingship and the deterioration of it that made Israel cry for the great Son of David to be born in Bethlehem. But it is also a book that adds many details left out of the books of Samuel and Kings.

One of these details is a problem which faces David while he hides in the desert. Many mighty warriors, frustrated by Saul's failures, join the army of David. But it dawns on David that this is a risky business. If they join him desiring to establish a better Israel, they are a blessing sent from the Lord. But it is also possible that they are traitors faking an affection for him and intending to undermine his position. It is extremely important to know which is the case. Without a united goal and purpose, a large number of followers is not in itself an advantage for David.

Unity among churches is good, and to see many people join in great numbers for the same cause is encouraging. But is it for real? I am too easily impressed by growth that has no meaning at all.

If David takes his chances, he might face disaster. A "wait and see" attitude is not the mark of a Christian. So David puts the man under oath before the face of their God.

Then the Lord Himself steps in; the Holy Spirit intervenes with a mighty action. The chief Amasai suddenly begins to prophesy. Filled by the Spirit, he recites a song that the people recognize as a genuine work of God's Spirit. A general is not supposed to make psalms. But Amasai does.

We can recognize each other only in the Spirit of the Lord. As God makes Himself known to us, He unites us. We recognize each other in Him. Only then we can talk about unity and power.

I Chronicles 10-12

. . . who should play loudly on musical instruments (I Chronicles 15:16).

Between all the serious business of government and religious rites and battles and politics, a bright note sounds. David appoints a director for the choirs who will sing at the home-coming of the ark. He also asks for an orchestra which will play loudly and joyfully. The director and the members of the choir and the band—all mentioned by name—are going to be dressed in robes of fine linen.

In our churches, the organ may be played—but not too loudly. A band is forbidden of course. Choirs are acceptable if they are very distinguished. When young Christians in our churches sing and play their music loudly, we wonder if they have lost their sense of decency. Would David have been too boorish for our refined tastes? Or are we lacking something?

Joy motivates David. The ark symbolizes the presence of God, and now the ark is being brought to Jerusalem. David knows that the most important part of his kingship is to be in close contact with his God. His joy about the presence of a merciful God knows no bounds. David realizes that the solid foundation of his own life and the life of his nation is safe in the coming of Messiah and in God's grace.

Isn't it right—David's command to play loudly and joyfully? God does not hold back. His music is in the singing of birds and in the roll of thunder. If He does not limit Himself to a whisper, why should we?

Art is important to David: the best director and the best players are appointed. But art is not valuable in itself. It is one way to praise the One who made this world so livable. All together we shout for joy.

It is a pleasant thing to serve our God.

I Chronicles 13-15

I declare to you that the Lord will build you a house (I Chronicles 17:10).

At first Nathan accepts David's proposal to build a temple for the Lord. Why not? Something done in gratitude to the Lord must be good. But the Lord intervenes to make it clear that He cannot accept David's good intentions. Why not?

The sudden realization that he was dwelling in a beautiful palace while the Lord was still in a cheap tabernacle has upset David; he feels sorry for the Lord. He wants to bring the Lord to the level he has achieved.

You can see the smile on the Lord's face when He replies to David's plans. Don't feel sorry, David, for the Almighty One. If it weren't for the grace of God, you would still be herding sheep. All that you are is the work of the sovereign God who chose you to be king. And besides, the Lord has never asked for a house, has He? He goes with His people everywhere, for the whole world is His. God is not really very concerned about a cedar palace or temple.

The Lord turns the whole thing around and promises to build David a house. That is the right order.

No matter how much I achieve in life, I am still the poor shepherd boy and the Lord is the King of kings. I am still the sheep and He is my Shepherd.

Then God adds a mysterious element to His answer. He promises David that his son will have the honor and privilege of building a temple for God. God can wait until Solomon gets around to it. However, unlike the author of Samuel, the author of Chronicles avoids identifying the temple-builder as Solomon (compare II Samuel 7:14 to Chronicles 17:13). His omission seems to say, "The true temple-builder is not really Solomon. It is the Son of Man who is the Son of God. Jesus the Messiah will build the real temple in His body and, through His Spirit, in His church."

That makes me humble but also very happy. Temple building is God's work in me.

I Chronicles 16-18

David built there an altar to the Lord (I Chronicles 21:26).

This chapter is a collection of the types of puzzling data which I find throughout the Bible. Satan incites David to count the people of Israel. But II Samuel 24 says that God did it. Against Joab's advice, David sins. How could he go astray so determinedly? God gives David a choice between three types of punishment. But can we decide what the Lord will do? David must be punished; seventy thousand men of Israel die. That will hurt David deeply of course, but do so many families have to be struck by disaster just because David sinned? David sees the angel of the Lord standing ready to destroy. Can I visualize that? Then, when the sacrifice is on the altar, the Lord sends fire from heaven to light the flame on the altar.

So much of this story I cannot understand at all. Perhaps my Western mind cannot grasp the thought and belief patterns of people in the Middle East. But then again it is not a local gospel which the Bible brings me; it is universal, meant for my mind too.

Too many questions of children and young people have no answers. All my efforts to resolve the contradictions and paradoxes are in vain.

However, I am not ashamed to admit that I don't have all the answers. My God and His Word are not the products of my intelligence. They are real, and therefore they boggle my small mind. In the cross of Christ, I find God and satan and my sins and my relationship to others and angels and lightnings; and I know that they are all interrelated in a mysterious way.

David indicates that the threshing floor of Ornan will be the place for the new temple. Within Thy temple, Lord, I see all the mysterious lines converge.

I Chronicles 19-21

With great pains I have provided for the house of the Lord. To these you must add (I Chronicles 22:14).

David is uneasy. How will his son Solomon, still in his tender years, manage to build a house for the Lord which will be renowned for its magnificence in every country? David started out with no more experience than any shepherd boy. But now he worries about his son.

Over the years, David has been taking booty from defeated enemies; he has traded and saved, and now he has unbelievable wealth ready for the building of the new temple. It was not easy, he admits. And so scepticism, even mild criticism, of the future generation colors an effort to give them the head start they need in life.

If I am genuinely concerned about the tremendous task facing the next generation, I should work hard to provide for it. The kingdom of God is moving on; if I do not move with it, I'll be left out. David's efforts will be preserved in the beautiful building that will rise after his death. I too can share in the future.

David avoids a trap. He could have said, "Solomon, here is the material you need. Use it well." However, the tremendous wealth which David has collected is not sufficient for the temple. Not that it would be impossible to build a temple with that material. But David does not want to say, "What I give you is what you will use." Solomon has to add to the materials for the temple, even if the adding be only a formality. In fact, he may find important things that did not belong to David's treasures.

I do not have everything ready; the next generation must add to the stores. I believe in the continued operation of the Holy Spirit. New treasures will be found. In every generation, God puts His children to work.

I Chronicles 22-24

All these were the sons of Heman the king's seer, according to the promise of God to exalt him (I Chronicles 25:5).

This chapter lists people who served in many ways in and around the temple. Not all the duties were terribly important. There had to be gate keepers, custodians for the treasuries, stewards, singers, musicians, those who did odd jobs.

It appears that the men do not apply for these jobs; they are appointed. Sometimes they are set apart for the service by the casting of lots. There is no record of protest. Everyone accepts the fact that he is needed, and he does what is expected of him.

The family of Heman is no exception. His fourteen sons are all members of an orchestra in the temple. Did they all have musical talents? Were they all willing to follow orders?

Where was their freedom? In the kingdom of God and in His church can you just assign people work and they obey?

In our society this is unheard of. We leave each other freedom and ask for volunteers. This way does not always work very well. But who would go back to the ancient way in which one's life was pre-determined? People were told whom to marry; they were appointed work they perhaps would not have chosen themselves. I am so happy that I don't live in a day and age like that.

Or am I?

I begin to realize that there is another side to the picture. Heman and his family felt that the Lord exalted them according to His promise. All those people who were appointed felt that it was an honor to serve God.

Of course, those days will never return and probably should not. But new light shines on the concept of freedom. Isn't freedom living, without protest, the life for which I am called?

I Chronicles 25-27

Direct their hearts toward thee (I Chronicles 29:18).

It is remarkable that in the chronicles of a king, so much attention is paid to his "religious" actions. Many chapters talk about his offerings and prayers and words of advice and his building of the temple for the Lord.

But isn't religion just a matter of the heart? Politics is not a matter of faith. Similarly, education is only giving people enough know-how to make a living or improve this world. In the social sciences, religion is not very practical. I have been trained to think in such terms.

David disagrees wholeheartedly. I may not separate my task in this world from my personal convictions. How can I act without being led by my deepest feelings? When I know that the Lord has given a law to guide me, how can I set that aside when I go about my business? Whatever I do is done by all of me, not just by a part of me.

David cannot be a king without being a child of God. How can I be a blessing for others if I am not blessed myself—if my selfish heart has not been broken by the tremendous love of God in Jesus Christ?

Not only my relationship to God is important; my relationship to others is also. As creatures of God, we belong together. I may have my task—even as a king or queen—but I cannot tyrannize others without breaking the rules for society as given by the Lord. David seems to be one with his people; only God's love can accomplish that.

No task in the world is in itself better than another. Children of one Father have to serve each other while serving Him. Instead of glorying in myself, I must feel that I am a servant.

I may try to separate religion from the whole of life. But David tells me to keep it together, for the problems of life can be understood only in the light of the Word of God. God knows what is good and profitable far better than I will ever know—so I had better listen.

I Chronicles 28-29

Give me now wisdom (II Chronicles 1:10).

If I could have any request granted, it would take me quite a while to figure out what to ask. Life is full of desirable things.

Solomon will be granted any wish. What a present with which to start his reign over Israel! His own long life would be good for the nation's stability. Wealth would keep taxes low and help the economy to flourish. The destruction of his enemies would have enhanced his security. Honor among the nations would make defense and foreign relations easier.

All these things would have been worth the asking. But Solomon decides to ask for wisdom.

I am not sure that wisdom would have been my wish. As an added gift, wisdom might have been nice. But it doesn't seem worth much in the world around me. Even the Bible tells me that wisdom is neither in demand nor respected. Wisdom seems to be a nice but highly impractical asset.

Solomon knew better. And we, too, badly need wisdom. Our possessions and inventions and know-how have made us very rich and at the same time very poor. The increase of knowledge without wisdom has brought this world to the brink of disaster. We can produce plenty of food, but millions are starving. Intricate communication systems abound, but we don't know how to reach each other; loneliness intensifies throughout the world.

Wisdom is the ability to apply whatever I can grasp to the well-being of this earth. I need wisdom in my church and in politics and social relations.

God promises Solomon that he will receive all the other things he did not ask for. And when I receive wisdom from my God, I can be a blessing. The little that I receive grows and is used so well that it becomes long life and honor and wealth.

The fear of the Lord means wisdom.

II Chronicles 1-3

When a foreigner . . . comes and prays toward this house, hear thou (II Chronicles 6:32).

In the dedication prayer for the new temple, Solomon intercedes for all those who will come and pray in this house of the Lord. He asks the Lord to be kind to His people and quick to forgive their sins. God and His children will meet in the temple; because of the sacrifice on the altar, they will be close to one another. Solomon then remembers all the needs, afflictions and sorrows that can live in the hearts and lives of those going to the temple or even stretching out their hands toward the temple. Finally he mentions something very unexpected. He asks the Lord to hear and answer the prayers of foreigners who will come to Jerusalem.

It is good to know that strangers will come and admire the temple and the God who lives in it. But isn't it far-fetched to expect that if they pray the Lord will give them what they ask for? What do they know about Yahweh? Their idolatrous minds may put Him on the same level as their gods. Certainly they may give honor to the God of Israel. But in no way should they expect to get something from Him.

However, Solomon's heart opens to embrace those strangers. He does not pray that they will go to confession class, be converted, say farewell to their own gods, prove for a few years that they can live a decent life, and *then* finally be taken into a class of "almost believers." He knows that his God has arms wide open. If the Lord accepts me and answers my prayers, why cannot He do that for anyone who comes to Him? The church of God is not exclusive but inclusive. The storm wind of Pentecost has occurred and the flames of the Spirit make God's church light and warm.

When the foreigners return home, they will tell their friends that the God of Israel treated them as kindly as His own children. They will learn to know God's name. The message of the Good Shepherd will spread all around.

II Chronicles 4-6

Solomon answered all her questions (II Chronicles 9:2).

When the Queen of Sheba comes to visit King Solomon, not only the riches and treasures of his palace fascinate her. She is especially interested in Solomon's wisdom. That is something nobody can buy for money. And she knows that this was the special present Solomon received from the Lord.

In those days, one of the most entertaining games people could play was to pose and attempt to solve riddles. The prizes to be won were not expensive gifts, but rather, deep respect.

Should Solomon play games with his God-given wisdom? Do I have the right to be entertained and laugh and enjoy myself in a world of so many problems? Solomon has no such qualms. He plays the game with the Queen of Sheba and astonishes her with his answers. There is room in the life of the Christian for entertainment and happiness. God never wanted us to act as if we were partly saved. In the complete care of our God, we may live a carefree life.

But this is not only a game. Asking for answers, the queen tells Solomon all that is on her mind. Behind the light-hearted approach lie deeper problems. Today, too, the church may have answers to many problems that are puzzling the world. At least, it should have the answers. It would be so easy to dodge my responsibility by laughing at the questions, or by saying that no one would understand the answers anyway, or by using big empty words. But God has entrusted to me His Word and Spirit, which answer practical questions. Behind the sometimes silly questions the world asks lingers a deep hunger for answers. Is God love? Why is there misery? What is the meaning of suffering? What happens after death? I hear many questions to which I should know the answers, for people are waiting to hear of Christ through me.

II Chronicles 7-9

I will chastise you with scorpions (II Chronicles 10:14).

The moment has come when the kingdom of David will be torn into two parts: Israel and Judah. God is punishing His people for their sin. Through His prophet Ahijah God has already informed Jeroboam that he will rule ten tribes.

But we must not forget the human elements here. Jeroboam returns from Egypt where he has been exiled since his rebellion against Solomon. After gathering people around him, he approaches King Rehoboam with a request to lower the taxes. This innocent request was really a cheap rebellious effort to attract the king. The older men advise Rehoboam to be friendly and take the wind out of Jeroboam's sails. But the younger counselors advise him to make it clear who is king. Actually, the younger ones are right: Jeroboam's rebellion against the kingship is resistance against the laws and the covenant of God. Rehoboam decides to be stern. Jeroboam does not accept Rehoboam's attitude; he rebels, and the division of Israel becomes fact.

What went wrong? It is easy to say that it was inevitable, or even that the Lord wanted it that way. But the main reason that things went wrong was Rehoboam's lack of love. To establish himself as the God-given king of Israel, Rehoboam does not have to tell the people that he will chastise them with scorpions.

I have to admit to division and even hatred in the kingdom of God. But I also have to remember that in the church of Jesus Christ, I am not first of all dealing with issues in which I may be wrong or right. My main task is to show that I live in the love of God and to deal with others on that basis. In my family and business, I fail when I isolate issues from the love of Jesus Christ. Is it my kingdom or the Lord's? Christ wants to show Himself through me.

II Chronicles 10-12

When Asa heard these words he put away the abominable idols (II Chronicles 15:8).

King Asa realizes that the only way to be fruitful and successful in life is to serve the Lord only. In his kingdom, he does what is right in God's eyes. But then, surprisingly, an unknown prophet comes to Asa and tells him that there still are matters which have to be cleaned up. Idols have to be removed; the altar of the Lord has to be repaired.

Though I am a child of God, I cannot take life easy. Some people say the key to life is to be born again and converted. But God tells me that if I am not finding new life every day, if I am not newly converted to Him every day, I will not see the kingdom of God. One of the most deceptive dangers in life is to rest in a conversion that once happened. Satan can use such rest to lull me into a sleep that serves his purposes.

There are two elements in Asa's life that may teach me something important. First, it is the Word of God which leads me back to the living God. It does not matter who the prophet is. A sermon, an article in a paper, a word spoken by a believer, a remark made by a child—all can be used by the Spirit of God. God has to come and show me what should change. I cannot assume that I am on the right track.

The second lesson: obedience knows no boundaries. In his zeal for the God of Israel, Asa removes his mother from the office of queen-mother because she made an abominable image for Ashera. If I love Jesus, I will find the courage to crucify my natural feelings and follow Him. To renew my service unto God, I may have to start thinking about my own home and other precious parts of my life.

Asa's people rejoiced with a loud voice and pledged their oath of allegiance to Yahweh with shouting and trumpets and horns. May I do the same, Lord.

II Chronicles 13-15

*How many times shall I adjure you that you speak to me nothing
but the truth in the name of the Lord? (II Chronicles 18:15).*

Ahab, the wicked king of Israel, invites Jehoshaphat, the God-
fearing king of Judah, to join him and fight against Ramoth-
gilead. Jehoshaphat is not unwilling, but before he goes to war he
wants to hear the Word of God. That causes some consternation for
Ahab, but luckily he is able to get four hundred prophets together
who all prophesy that the battle will be won. The chorus of voices
bringing good news is quite impressive. But Jehoshaphat is not convinced; it does not sound right. So they bring Micaiah, a prophet
hated by Ahab because he only gives bad predictions. Then the
miracle happens. Even this prophet of the Lord predicts victory!
But Ahab asks for the real Word of God. Now the truth is revealed:
there will be a terrible defeat and Ahab will be killed.

I learn a lot from this story. First, the unanimous message of
four hundred prophets over against one dissident is not necessarily
the truth. Even if the whole church with all its ministers and leaders
try to bring me a message, I must still think about it. The fact that I
like the message does not make it true. Second, I discover that even
when the good prophet goes along with all the liars and joins in
with the chorus, a doubt still arises in the heart of the king. The
voice of God speaking to the hearts of men cannot be silenced.
Ahab is a wicked man without any respect for the covenant of God,
but in his heart, God still speaks. When Ahab does not obey this
voice, he dies in spite of all his efforts to outsmart the enemy.

Through the clouds and fog of all the misleading speeches I
can hear in the theological arena today, I still hear the voice of
God. I will have to listen to God and follow His directions. It is
easy to deny God. But when He looks me in the eyes, I know better.

II Chronicles 16-18

When they began to sing and praise, the Lord set an ambush
(II Chronicles 20:22).

The Lord can help His people in many ways. He can keep problems away from us. Or He can make us strong as we fight evil
forces. Or He can show the deepest truth about Himself: that He is
the One who delivers us, no matter how He does it.

Jehoshaphat faces a hostile army that can defeat and destroy
his armies easily. He does the only right thing: he prays, proclaims
a fast, and humbles himself before God. Then the Lord gives an
unexpected answer. The Israelites will go out and stand, facing the
enemies, and do nothing. They will just wait and see what the Lord
is going to do. It takes a lot of faith simply to face the problems
and know that the Lord will deal with them. Jehoshaphat goes one
better. He commands the Levites and the singers to stand there in
holy array and to sing songs of deliverance. Before the Lord
answers their prayers and gives help, they are already singing,
"Give thanks to God." It sounds unreal. But when they start singing, something happens: the enemies attack each other and fight
until all of them are destroyed—without the children of God raising
a hand!

A Jericho victory can be repeated over and over again. I can
stand in a hostile world and still know that I can do everything
through Him who strengthens me. Or better: I cannot do
everything, but He can. To show the real ground of my salvation, I
must be ready just to sing and stand there in holy array. Even if the
Lord should make use of my labor and strife, I know that it is not
me but the Lord in me who succeeds.

When God's people stand there, singing and praising, the
heavens join in the song. For there is happiness when I trust God
and believe His word.

II Chronicles 19-21

All the people rejoiced and brought their tax (II Chronicles 24:10).

Is it really possible to pay taxes with a joyful heart? In God's church and kingdom, it can be done.

King Joash is having problems getting enough money for the restoration of the temple. What comes in is barely enough to keep up the temple service. So he tries a new approach. He has a box made and put in the temple. Now the money is pouring in, and people feel blessed themselves. Why? What made the difference?

First of all, Joash tells people to bring the tax that Moses levied (vs. 14). That was money God's children paid as "atonement money." When they gave it, they in effect said to God, "Thank You for Your mercy in saving our souls."

Every gift to God should be a matter of gratitude. It is because He took care of me first that I may take care of His temple. Therein lies the connection between the bringing of God's Word and the response of the congregation. When the gospel is not proclaimed, the well may dry up.

Secondly, Joash puts the box at the altar in the temple. People can only bring their gifts by going to the place where God dwells. I have to go and put my money into the hands of the Lord. I must make a personal appearance before His throne.

Finally, the money is contributed freely and joyfully because the people know what it is used for. It is not going to a general fund for some nebulous future use. Every day the money is brought to the masons and those restoring the temple. And every day the Israelites can see progress: a wall is repaired, a door can be used again, some art is restored. The results are visible.

Here are answers to the problems encountered sometimes in the church and kingdom of God. I may give my gifts happily to God when I realize what He has done for me. I must know that I am giving my gifts into the pierced hands of Christ; I must also understand what my gifts are doing.

The government may not care whether taxes are paid with joy or not. The Lord does.

II Chronicles 22-24

It is not for you, Uzziah, to burn incense to the Lord (II Chronicles 26:18).

Uzziah is a good king who reigns for fifty-two years and is highly respected. Then one day he enters the temple of God and starts to burn incense for the Lord. Eighty priests warn Uzziah that he is transgressing the law of God; when he gets angry at them, he suddenly finds himself a leper. At once he is banished from the house of God; he cannot come back for the rest of his life. It is a strange story. What went wrong?

Uzziah reasons that, as king, he may assume some of the rights of the priests. It seems good to want to be active in the house of God. So what is his sin?

He grew proud. Later, after Christ came, all kings and queens may also become priests of the living God through the Holy Spirit, but for Uzziah who lives in the Old Testament, this is not yet possible. Pride denies limitations and takes what is not yet given.

The Christian church is not a church triumphant yet, although that occasionally has been assumed. There are areas of life in which the church is not reaching its goals; it has to wait humbly until the Lord's time. I would love to know everything, to understand all, but the Bible tells me that I am only looking through a mirror into dimness. It is not easy to wait and admit failures. I would like to reach further. A servant of God, I would like to be a master. God's laws seem to limit my possibilities.

In reality the Lord is protecting me against myself. To walk behind Him and wait and trust is the only way I can be happy. The word transgression means stepping over the line. There I stand alone.

Uzziah has to stand alone the rest of his life. As a leper, he finds out that he reached too far. But Jesus came to heal lepers.

II Chronicles 25-27

Because the gods of the kings of Syria helped them, I will sacrifice to them that they may help me (II Chronicles 28:23).

King Ahaz is a very practical man, a pragmatist. Rather than follow principles, he asks the all important question, "Does it work?" If it does, it must be right and good. The Syrians have been successful in war; they have defeated the armies of Ahaz. So Ahaz switches allegiance from the God of Israel to the more efficient gods of Damascus.

Sound familiar? Despite Biblical principles, people have not become happier. The church is not succeeding, so let's try other systems. Scientific systems may contradict God's Word, but they give good results. Why bother with Biblical concepts? A new approach to morality, sexuality, and marriage may give better results. If necessary, I may even revamp my ideas about sin, calling them harmful for the development of humanity.

Pragmatism has convinced many Christians to try out what seems to be a more efficient system. The new god is success and achievement. In humble adoration, we bow down before it.

The only thing, however, that King Ahaz achieves is complete ruin. The house of God is closed and the doors shut. When Ahaz dies, he is not brought into the tombs of the kings of Israel; he is not counted among the kings anymore—and rightly so, for he has become a slave. Not only is he disobedient but he is blind to reality. He does not understand that it is precisely his disobedience to the God of Israel that causes the bad situation.

Human life is not destroyed by the Lord's commandments but by the neglect of them. I sink further and further into the marsh of sin if I become a pragmatist. Success cannot be my goal in life. The only thing that counts is my obedience to the Lord. That is what the church and all Christians should consider.

II Chronicles 28-30

He burned his sons as an offering (II Chronicles 33:6).

The world always tries to convince me that the service of my God is some kind of slavery. I have to go to church; I may not do a lot of things I would like to do; I have to give my money and spare time. In other words, I lose my freedom. With jealous eyes I watch the world around me where people can enjoy life.

It is time that I see things differently.

King Manasseh has decided that he is not going to serve the God of Israel. He wants freedom to make his own decisions. But the Bible reveals that this man does not find the good life at all. In his fifty-five years of rule, he has to find other powers to rely upon and to serve beside the living God. To overcome the powers in nature, he asks sorcerers to protect him with their magical powers. Because he wishes to know about the future, he employs soothsayers who will forecast and advise him. He deals with mediums and wizards, not because he likes to, but because he has to. Superhuman powers have to be used to ward off calamity and bring prosperity.

But the worst thing is Manasseh's constant fear that the idols will harm him. Too much luck and happiness is dangerous. One day the gods will strike. Therefore he tries to prevent their vengeance by bringing misery into his own life. He gives his sons as an offering and has them burned for those gods. Sons were a precious possession, especially in those days. But he sacrifices them to avoid the envy of his idols. What a terrible slavery! Would I like to serve gods that cannot stand to see me happy? It is unbelievable what people will do to avoid the love of God. They accept hardship; they bring sacrifices; they live in constant fear of danger and divine intervention in their lives. And then they accuse me of being a slave of the Lord!

I believe in Him who would never ask me to bring the supreme sacrifice, but rather brought it Himself. He gave His Son up to death so that I could live.

II Chronicles 31-33

Now in the first year of Cyrus king of Persia . . . (II Chronicles 36:22).

The wrath of God rises against His nation. He has decided there is no remedy anymore for His people. They have rarely listened to His messengers. Sometimes they have returned to God only to depart again. Simple medications have not been able to give healing; now major surgery in years of exile are the only way left to the Lord.

It is a frightening thing. Some of the tribes will never get back to Palestine and will be lost forever. Many of God's children will like life in Babylon so much that they won't want to return. The nations all around will laugh at the God who was not able to keep His children in line.

I do whatever pleases me, and whenever God does anything harsh, I accuse Him of being cruel and heartless. However, if the Lord decides that He needs strong medicine in my life to cure me, He Himself is hurt. His honor is at stake, and I am responsible for dishonor. I never suffer alone; my Father shares in this ordeal.

So the sad story about the deportation is told, and this period of Israel's history ends up in darkness.

But then a miracle happens. The last verses of this chronicle are the same as the first ones of the book of Ezra. They speak of the return to Jerusalem. That is not a mistake made by somebody who, when copying the Bible books, added the beginning of Ezra to the end of Chronicles. God can discipline harshly, but at once He speaks of His mercy. He cannot wait to tell us that after the years of exile, there is again the return to the city of God and the rebuilding of the temple. The Messiah will come, and there will be a new Jerusalem.

Almost before I suffer the misery that I inflict upon myself, God is reaching to the day when He can make everything well again. In the darkness, the light is already glowing at the horizon. The morning is breaking.

II Chronicles 34-36

*The people could not distinguish the sound of the joyful shout
from the sound of the people's weeping (Ezra 3:13).*

The tribes of Judah and Benjamin and the priests and Levites
have returned to Jerusalem to make a new start in the service of
their God. The unbelievable has happened: God has protected His
people from annihilation during exile and now He will proceed
again towards Bethlehem. One of the first things to do is to rebuild
the temple. God's people need a house of worship that is practical
and affordable.

When the foundation has been laid, a big celebration is
organized. The younger people shout for joy at the promising
prospect of the building. But the older people who have seen the
glory of the former temple weep. Remembering the beauty of that
building, they are disheartened by the sight of the small foundation.

What a common situation: the younger generation looks with
anticipation and resolve to the future while the older people look
back to see that new ways of worshiping God seem cheap and
gloryless compared to past greatness.

Their solution? When the older people start to cry, the youth
outshout them with their joyful songs. The seniors lost out to the
juniors.

But that is not really an answer to the problem. Too often I
hear people of God oppose each other, and the noise of shouting
drowns out the answers. Both sides are right. It is a shame that
because of our sins the service of God is not what it used to be. Yet
the younger generation may look at the past and be inspired to do a
better job. The fact that God moves on is undeniable. Thank God!

Ezra 1-3

*Artaxerxes, king of kings, to Ezra the priest, the scribe of the law
of the God of heaven (Ezra 7:12).*

When the children of God return to Palestine after the exile,
the glory is gone. The theocratic kingship is over. They are subjects
to the king of Persia. They will build a small temple, but no palace.
Nobody will come to admire the greatness of God's kingdom on
earth. Caesar Augustus, Nero the emperor—the great rulers of the
world will wield power. Tensions and complications will arise
because the church must live in a secular world.

There is, however, no reason to despair. When the king of Persia appoints a ruler for Israel, he is Ezra, a great man in God's
kingdom. There will be a subsidy for the church out of the state
treasury and an exemption for taxes for all kingdom workers. And
there will be freedom to use the money according to the will of
God. God, the supreme ruler, ensures a secure place for the church.

There will be many problems later. The government's interference in the life of God's children will be frequent and
dangerous. Nevertheless, Caesar Augustus will lead Joseph and
Mary to Bethlehem. The emperor of Rome will transport the apostle Paul to Rome to preach the gospel there. A cruel ruler will
banish John to an island where he will share his revelation to warn
and strengthen the church in Christian hope.

Should I play a part in politics? Is it right to pay taxes knowing
that the money will be used in sinful ways? Can I accept help from
the government? Answers are not easy. But towering over all my
concerns is the goodwill of the Lord. Ezra's appointment and the
help he receives speak of the greatness of the One who suffered
under Pontius Pilate to become the King of kings.

Ezra 4-7

On the first day of the tenth month they sat down to examine the matter (Ezra 10:16).

The many years in exile have not been able to thwart God's cause. The kings of Persia help Israel to settle and to restore the service of God so that poverty and problems of immigration are not obstacles to the growth and security of the church. Only sin can destroy the beautiful new start. And it nearly does.

Among those to return from exile are many who have married women not belonging to the people of God. It is quite understandable. There is not too much choice among the Israelite women. It is more practical to marry a girl who knows the area and the language and can help build up a new home. No doubt, the usual promises are made. The man says he will convert the woman and she says that she will leave her husband free to do what is right in his eyes.

But Ezra is appalled when he hears about it. Such marriages are clearly against the Word of God. All practical considerations have to yield to the most important one: How can I serve my God? In the past Israel was not willing to give herself completely to the service of the Lord. Now, a new start would be futile without total dedication. So Ezra and the leaders of Israel, knowing that this is not a time for half-hearted attitudes, demand that the foreign wives and their children be sent away.

But there is one condition: a committee should be appointed to investigate all the different situations in those families. It is ruthlessly easy to see matters as black and white. But God allows exceptions to the rules, situations where love must overrule law. There may be hardship so great that the Lord will show mercy on the wives and children. Justice and mercy are one in my God.

Ezra 8-10

Come, let us build the wall of Jerusalem (Nehemiah 2:17).

Ezra and Nehemiah take different approaches to the rebuilding of the nation of Israel. Ezra begins by rebuilding the temple. A church of the living God must worship to be alive. The people grant him their wholehearted support. Nehemiah, on the other hand, proposes to rebuild the walls of Jerusalem. It is more difficult to support that approach; to build walls seems so negative and fruitless, just an attempt to keep certain elements out.

The surprising fact, however, is that Nehemiah gets support just as easily for his undertaking. People seem to realize that there is also value in the wall-building. There are enemies who want to attack the church and destroy it. The prince of darkness hopes that I will be naive enough to deny that fact. If I let down my defenses, there may be a moment in which I stand helpless.

I hear enemies mocking the message of the Bible, pointing out how stupid it is to believe a book like that. I know that I can never prove the truth of God's Word. Yet without becoming apologetic, I try to show them how rich and true and strong the message of my God is. When they accuse me of believing sheer nonsense, I point out that the only answers to the problems of life are to be found in what my God teaches me. While knowing that I cannot convince anyone who does not want to believe in my heavenly Father, I will stand and show that I care. I may provide some protection for young people by warning them against dangers around them. And I may look around myself for powers that try to take my strength away.

To build and to defend what is being built are not opposites. They belong together.

Nehemiah 1-3

Ought you not to walk in the fear of our God? (Nehemiah 5:9).

While the walls of Jerusalem are being built, it appears that an enemy has entered without Nehemiah's noticing it. Social injustice is found among the workers. The rich people can work on the walls without having to sacrifice. But the poor people have to borrow money, sell their children as slaves, and take high mortgages on their small farms.

Why did this problem come to light now? The tremendous gap between the rich and the poor became apparent when they began to work together on the walls. The rich can live splendidly isolated from the poor in their ghettos. But in the church of God, they meet and get to know each other. In the Lord, we are equals building the kingdom. At the table of the Lord, we sit side by side. We call each other brothers and sisters. The church of Christ should be in the front lines in the fight against social injustices. How can we profit from the need of others?

Nehemiah calls the rich people together to discuss the problem but apparently gets no response. It is so hard to part with riches! At last he gathers the whole crowd, and there he finally finds a solution to the problem. The rich swear an oath that they will return to the poor their lands, their slave-children, and the interest on their money.

How is this amazing response achieved? First, the Word of God is on the side of the poor. Secondly, the rich have been exposed in their greed before the whole congregation. But perhaps most important is Nehemiah's example. He has freed slaves in Babylon with his own funds; he refuses to accept payment for work that others do for free. He practises what he preaches. I can so easily shout about injustice, criticize others, talk about Christian love. But have I set an example?

Christ became poor to make me rich. People will only listen to me when I follow in His footsteps.

Nehemiah 4-6

The joy of the Lord is your strength (Nehemiah 8:10).

To be more holy, I should be more serious. If I would listen better to the Word of God, laughing and joking would not find a place in my life. When I go to the Lord's Supper, I should feel sad about my sins.

That is the way people in Jerusalem react when Nehemiah and Ezra read the law of God. Realizing how far they have strayed from God's words, how sinful they are, they begin loud wailing and lamenting. This response to the preaching of the law would have impressed me.

However, the leaders of Israel protest that wailing and crying. That is not the response the Lord wants. As a Christian, I deplore my sins and repent, but I must also realize that my sins are forgiven. At the Lord's table, I can eat and drink and be merry because in Christ I have died and am alive again. God does not like to see His children sad. Our crying is only the road to joy. We may not get stuck halfway down that road.

So the people are ordered to celebrate. Sharing the good gifts of the Lord, they have a beautiful celebration that lasts for days. The joy of the Lord is their strength. The devil cannot harm someone who lives in the joy of Christ's victory.

Still, this text does not mean simply that joy is our strength. It is the joy of the *Lord* that makes us strong. He is happy when He knows that we listen to Him and want to follow Him. He is our bulwark, our defense. When He is angry, nothing can protect us.

It is a glorious thing to know that the Lord is not moaning under the load of my sin. Salvation is accomplished. Now I should join Him in songs of deliverance and celebration.

Nehemiah 7-9

I contended with them and cursed them and beat some of them and pulled out their hair (Nehemiah 13:25).

The actions of Nehemiah shock me. He throws a man out of the temple building, furniture and all, because he may not live there. He argues with people, determined to make them act as he wishes. He starts beating and pulling hair, and worst of all, he curses. There is no need to defend his actions. Even when I mean well, I can get carried away and act in a way that does not reflect the love and rule of my God.

However, Nehemiah is not just facing sinners. He returns to Jerusalem after a stay in Babylon to find a rebellion of sorts going on. Tobiah and Sanballat are enemies of God who have laughed at the work in God's kingdom (chapter 4) and have plotted against it. The high priest of God is their willing servant; he allows Tobiah to live in the house of God, a terrible desecration of the temple. Those who should be the holiest of all are plotting against the cause of God! They are willing to ruin the beautiful work of building Jerusalem in order to promote their own welfare.

Sometimes it angers me to see that, under false pretexts, things are going on in the church which destroy much that is being done by faithful children of God. No wonder young people turn away from it in disgust. Admittedly, I should remain calm and try to reclaim for God those who oppose the work of the Lord. But sometimes I cannot take it anymore. Strong protest may be the safety valve of my Christian concern. Even if the way in which it expresses itself is sometimes clumsy, I must not be afraid to show my ardent love for the holiness of my Savior.

Nehemiah 10-13

Haman sought to destroy all the Jews (Esther 3:6).

The strangest aspect of the book of Esther is not that the name
of the Lord is never mentioned. Many times in my life I see and feel
God's presence without having to refer to Him by name. This is the
strangest riddle: Why was God willing to save *this* group of Jews
from the hands of their enemies?

The Jews involved are the ones that stayed in Babylon. They
are of no importance to the coming of the Messiah. There is no
reason for His own cause and glory that the Lord should come to
save them.

It is also hard to admire stubborn Mordecai. Nowhere in
God's Word can I find any excuse for his proudly defiant attitude
toward Haman. A defiant man asks for persecution.

His using Esther as a means to get ahead is disgusting. Apparently he rejoices to see her become one of the many wives of the
king. Esther herself is not reluctant. Nowhere do I find a protest
that a girl in God's nation is being defiled.

But even if I do not judge Esther and Mordecai harshly, I cannot find legitimate grounds for the Lord to intervene. That is my
problem with this book. Why should God help them?

Why should God help me? I am not the person I ought to be. I
ask for trouble. The kingdom of God does not stand or fall with
my salvation. Surely the Lord must have more pressing concerns.

Then it strikes me that all this does not stop God from being a
Savior. To show His mercy, to be kind, to help those who get
themselves into trouble appears to be His delight.

I'm certainly happy to belong to such a God—a Savior who
lifts a drowning Peter out of the sea, who heals Malchus' ear in
Gethsemane, who keeps His church secure through all its heresies
and schisms.

I ask for trouble and He gives me His love and protection.
Hallelujah, what a Savior.

Esther 1-3

If I perish, I perish (Esther 4:16).

These words of Esther impress me deeply. Apparently she is
risking her life with courage and dedication. What an example of
self-denial and concern for others!

Then I realize that this is just not so. Behind Esther's words is
Mordecai's theology. He is not sure of the Lord's willingness to
help, but it may be worth a try. Faith does not always work, but it
is a possibility. God cannot be counted on, but He may help this
time. In a similar way, people who are not sure there is a heaven or
a hell become church members, just to be on the safe side. (You
never know!)

Admittedly, Mordecai believes that the hand of God may bless
his scheme. But it is all very vague and far removed from the
psalmist's songs of faith. It is and remains a gamble.

Then there is Esther's attitude. She gives in to Mordecai's proposal only after she is convinced that she too cannot escape death.
If she does not act, there will be no hope. Only by taking chances
may she come out on top. There is no joy in her words, and she is
preoccupied with perishing. She tries to improve her chances by
fasting with her maids. No word arises about prayer; God seems to
be far away.

When people say that this is a book in which God is not mentioned, there is a deeper truth to their statement. Living without experiencing God's closeness brings uncertainty, somber feelings, and
vague hopes, but no songs.

What a surprise, then, to see that the Lord uses Esther in His
plan of salvation! His mercies exceed my wildest hopes, for when I
trust Him, and even when I don't, He will not let me perish.

Esther 4-6

There was gladness and joy among the Jews (Esther 8:17).

The reason the Jews were in danger was none too glorious. Mordecai and Esther's actions are not to be admired. And now even the solution to their plight is not very acceptable according to Christian ethics. When the edict that all the Jews have to be murdered is contravened by an order that they may defend themselves, they turn their imminent massacre into bloody revenge on their enemies. After Haman's plans are shattered, he is hanged, along with ten of his sons. Mordecai becomes second in command, but there is no mention of him being a blessing for the nation which he helps to govern. Of all the many gory stories in the Old Testament, this is one of the worst, especially since it shows so little of the glory of God and the coming of the Messiah.

It is said that there was joy and gladness among the Jews. But was there blessing and gratitude and faith and dedication?

Still the hand of God is clearly in the events. Strange reversals, memories of things that happened in the past, the sleepless night of the king, his favorable moods—the events are not without divine intervention.

Suddenly I understand. In the half-hearted life of the church, in my small pleasures, in my so-called Christian life, in the emptiness and meaninglessness of it all, there is still a God who does not let me go. He knows that my gratitude will be small, that I will abuse His gifts, and that I will be less than a blessing for the world around me. And still He gives me more than I deserve.

Why? Because His love is limitless. But also because He still calls me. His hands remain stretched out to stubborn humanity.

When I feel good, when there is gladness and joy in my life, I must hear His voice.

Esther 7-10

He still holds fast his integrity (Job 2:3).

In the book of Job, God does not try to justify Himself; He doesn't have to. He does not try to explain what human suffering is all about; He would not be able to make that clear in all its complexity. It is not a story about a man who was brave—Job wasn't. In the book of Job, the Lord proclaims that He is the one who keeps me in His hand, no matter what happens. There is no power on earth that can separate me from His love.

Satan tries hard enough! He uses the powers of nature, of nearby enemies, of a bereaved wife who in a mistaken show of love tries to lead her husband to suicide, of friends who mean well but make life unbearable for Job. Yet the worst danger is not in the outside world. Deep in his heart, Job thinks of defending himself even though it would mean denouncing God.

In Job's life I see how the Lord triumphs. Job first proclaims that the Lord has given and the Lord has taken away. Later Job says that what the Lord has given him is bad, but he will endure it. Finally he curses the day he was born. His faith has diminished; there is hardly anything left of his profession of the love of God.

Then the Lord shows how He keeps His children in His strong love. Through His Spirit He hangs on to them even when they are sliding away from Him. Jesus says, "Nobody can snatch them from My hands!" This is certainly not our doing. Soon there will be the cry, "I know that my Redeemer lives!" And in the end there will be the peace that passes all understanding.

The Lord is the only one who can be proud. It is as if God smiles when He says, "Have you seen My servant Job who holds fast to his integrity?" But the Lord does not smile, for He suffers along when He uses His children to His glory. He tells me, "You invite satan into your world and life. But I never give up. And My love is victorious." His life is a mighty comfort.

Job 1-3

A spirit glided past my face (Job 4:15).

Job's friends come to comfort him in his desperate situation. Why are they not able to alleviate the suffering of their friend? One reason is that their philosophy of life is so terrible that we sigh with relief when Job refuses to accept it. But a second reason is that they want to sell their ideas with force. This high-pressure comforting is doomed to failure. One can say, "With friends like that, who needs enemies?"

Because Eliphaz knows that Job may be wary of his words, he tells Job that he has received special revelation from the mouth of a spirit. In this way he tries to eliminate Job's resistance. Who can refute a message from the great beyond? He even suggests that it would be very dangerous for Job to reject these words: hidden powers could hurt Job even more. What a terrible approach to suffering!

People who are not too sure about their own insights often try to give themselves some kind of authority by hinting at divine and spiritual powers behind their words. A church that teaches more than is in accordance with God's Word tries to convince me to accept those teachings by showing hidden powers. Parents who cannot answer the questions of their children because they don't base their education on the clear Word of God frighten the children into obedience by hinting at divine powers.

Do I myself want Jesus to speak through me? Or do I want my words and ideas to prevail? The first thing I should do is accept the possibility that my views are not the Lord's. And then I must humbly realize that even if I speak His words, I can only witness, not convince. As a simple witness of Jesus I am a friend to those who suffer.

Job 4-6

If your children have sinned against him, he has delivered them into the power of their transgression (Job 8:4).

Telling the truth is not always easy. When Jesus speaks to the crowds, they consider His words harsh, and they turn away from Him. The Sanhedrin sentence Him to death because He hurt them deeply with the truth. So we are in good company when we do not spare our friends the hardship of discovering their mistakes and misconceptions—*if* we intend to heal, not to hurt.

Such love is completely lacking in Job's second friend, Bildad. He has the evil courage to suggest that Job's children have died because they were terrible sinners. Bildad is trying only to break Job's heart and spirit. Wanting Job to bow before the logic of his theories, he hits Job where it hurts. On the occasion of his children's birthdays, Job brought sacrifices to the Lord so that their sins would be forgiven. In a deeply touching display of parental love, Job always prayed that his children would have peace with God. Now Bildad denigrates Job's love and prayers with harshness and complete absence of love.

Why do people hurt each other so deeply? Accusations and harsh judgments spring up where Christ's love does not rule hearts. I tremble when I hear words and see actions among Christians in which there is not the love of Christ. Schisms have seldom occurred because of difference of opinions; lack of love and understanding have done the harm, even though they were veiled in piety. If God Himself ever hurts people, He does so out of love.

Teach me to love as You have loved, my Lord!

Job 7-9

You will be secure and will not fear (Job 11:15).

Job's friends try to force their theories about his suffering on
him by different means. Eliphaz clothes himself with divine and
magic powers. Bildad makes a cruel effort to rip his fatherly heart
apart. Zophar seems to be much kinder. He appeals to Job to give
in so that he may enjoy life again. Job may not be convinced that
his friends are right; he may even strongly object to their strange
way of comfort. Still it would be wiser to confess his sins and in this
way find peace with God and men. True, it is not easy to accept
such compromise, but the world depends on our bargaining, wheel-
ing and dealing, giving and taking.

Of course, there is some truth in these words. I cannot always
have things my way; I do have to deal and give and take. I cannot
maintain that I am right and everybody else is wrong.

But when it comes to compromising my deepest feelings and
convictions, I have to draw the line somewhere. Even if the prize
will be peace and security, the price of this false peace is just too
high. Even if compromise means that I will be accepted and
respected, I cannot prostitute my deepest self.

Jesus had the courage to say no to all attempts to bring Him
into line with His enemies. The apostles preferred to go to the cross
with Jesus than allow the truth of their message to be lost. Luther
said no, he would not recant.

It is not easy to determine when I am being a stubborn person
or a witness of the faith. But as soon as it is clear to me, satan's attempt to lead me to a compromise should be met by a "Get behind
me." The peace he offers is not the peace of Christ.

Job 10-12

Make me know my transgression and my sin (Job 13:23).

Job's friends explain his misfortune with this theory: when we live obediently God will bless us, and when we sin God will punish us. Therefore, since Job suffers badly, he must have sinned badly. If he confesses his sins, he will receive mercy.

Job does not accept this explanation. He knows that there is no special sin in his life that would support the theory of his "friends."

I hear people around me proclaim the same message. They preach a harsh God who punishes sins, and they tell me to call myself a sinner and to face hell and damnation.

Job's answer to the accusation is beautiful. He says, "Well Lord, if there is something the matter with me, why don't You tell me that, instead of hitting me with misery?" The father-child relationship requires talking things over, not just punishment.

Job is correct. If he had sinned as his friends suggest, the Lord would have spoken to him and corrected him. The friends may be satisfied with a God who works anonymously, but Job is not. However, God cannot tell Job that He is showing satan that he can never break Job's genuine faith.

There is a lot the Lord cannot tell me. But I can be sure that whenever something is really wrong between us, He will come to me and make it known.

God has been so kind to me. He has given me the first chapters of the book of Job as a comfort in my trials. He has given me Christ Jesus to make it clear that He does not want to punish me for my sins. He gives me His Spirit to talk to me through His Word and maintain our relationship.

There are no mysterious messages hidden in frightening events. When something is wrong, God will tell me. Otherwise life remains as it ought to be—Father loving and caring for child.

Job 13-15

Even now, behold, my witness is in heaven, and he that vouches for me is on high (Job 16:19).

    Job's friends continue to accuse him of terrible sins. But when they preach a cruel God who, without admonishing him, crushes him, Job rejects that theory fiercely. He has no special revelation to support his protests. He has no arguments to contradict their airtight reasonings.

    When I deal with God things are not simple and logical. God is so great that I cannot comprehend Him. Therefore, I should be very careful when someone presents attractively simple ideas and doctrines to me. When examined very closely, they may prove to be merely the inventions of a sharp human mind.

    Job feels that his companions are replacing his living God with a dead and deadening doctrine. He cries out that he would rather have a living Father whom he cannot understand or explain than a dead network of logical and reasonable ideas. He does not want to see "Him" replaced by "it."

    This determination to retain a personal Father rests on nothing but faith. Job experiences a God who seems to hate him as no father would. Still, he knows God and His name: I am who I am. I am the faithful God of the Covenant.

    And because Job believes this, he shouts to his friends that there must be someone in heaven to intervene between himself and his estranged Father. There must be a person who is with God and with man, who is God and man, who restores the broken communications. This witness, my Mediator Jesus Christ, proclaims God's love in spite of everything and also vouches for Job when Job seems to have no access to God's throne. There is a personal connection.

    What a comfort to know that Jesus the Mediator is my witness in heaven to vouch for me.

Job 16-18

For I know that my Redeemer lives (Job 19:25).

When satan leads me into problems he does so to bring out the worst in me. When God does the same, He does so to bring out the best in me.

Satan tried to separate Job from his God, but the Lord in triumph shows how He is victorious over all the evil powers of darkness. Tried by fire, Job's faith shines with such beauty that it is hard to believe that we are still in the Old Testament. Job confesses his faith in the Mediator; he knows for sure that someone leads Father and child together. These words of faith come from one who has suffered without parallel.

It must be true (I too have known it from experience) that suffering can lead one closer to the real essence and meaning of life in Christ. That is how God turns the evil to the good.

But there is more. For awhile, in all his struggles, Job lost hope and trust in the future. He could see no light at the end of the tunnel. He was speaking of death and what comes after it in dark and hopeless terms. But now that he has discovered his Redeemer, he also knows that there is something to look forward to. He is not hoping for heaven, or explanations, or a reward for all his deprivations, or a better life. He just hopes to see his Father. The rest will be granted as well.

What I am looking forward to is not something but someone, and not someone untouchable and mystical. In his flesh Job will see God; it will be for real. There is a resurrection and his own eyes will behold his Father. Out of deep love for his God, he is crying out for that great moment when his love will be satisfied.

When God pushes me away, He draws me at the same time irresistably unto Him. When I am about to give up, He shows that He never gives up. In this mystery I live!

Job 19-21

God pays no attention to their prayer (Job 24:12).

It is a well-known fact that suffering can make a person self-centered. Accounts of sickness and its symptoms, long stories of the horror of sudden death in a family—such things are understandable, but they obscure the fact that other people are suffering too.

Job does not have this problem. Though afflicted himself, he knows what is going on in the world. He sees the oppression of the rich and the hardship suffered by the poor.

Sometimes I lack the courage to see injustice and oppression. This unpleasant world is rife with corruption, greed, and crime. Ten percent of the population of this world are eating and drinking ninety percent of the world's riches. If I ignore all this, maybe it will go away: so the Christian church has said, more often than not.

Job is honest about it. If injustice is hidden, nothing can be done about it, and the power of darkness will get stronger.

But Job has another motivation for recognizing oppression. He accuses the Lord of seeing evil and doing nothing about it. That is strong language, but again Job is right.

The church, for centuries, has said "sweet nothings" about God which have little to offer the masses that suffer. "We should understand that everything has a special meaning. The Lord is doing the right thing. Everything will work out in the end. He comforts and helps."

Such solutions are too cheap and easy. Job would rather wrestle with apparent paradox than listen to the flowery words of his friends who obscure the problems. Only when I have the nerve to say that God does not seem to listen, am I ready to hear the "Why" that was spoken on Golgotha. When God, through Christ, performs surgery on this rotten world, I can say, "Thank You, God, it was about time."

Job 22-24

What is the hope of the godless when God cuts him off? (Job 27:8).

Job has just stated that he is not going to agree with the theories of his friends. But his language sounds like theirs. Both talk about the terrible things that happen to godless people. However, the friends postulated that since Job must have been a godless man, he was cut off. That was where they went wrong. The text they used was fine, but their sermon was fallacious. They spoke about the greatness of God; now Job does too. But again Job has more valid application for it.

My use of the words of God can make a mockery of what the Lord really wants to say. That's what makes reading of the speeches of Eliphaz, Bildad, and Zophar so interesting. Often I am inclined to say, "Well said." But then it hits me that their implications are not correct at all.

Such misinterpretation is a problem in the Christian church. Bible texts can be arranged to construct a theology that sounds Biblical but is, in fact, contrary to the thrust of the Bible as a whole. There are scores of children of God who are tricked into a heresy or sect by this strange way of quoting Scripture. Satan tried to tempt Jesus by quoting the Bible—what power there can be in the abuse of texts!

Only a mind disciplined in the whole Word of God and a heart willing to question any conclusions in the light of the Biblical message can discern the real message of God's Word. To compare Scripture with Scripture is a long and tedious method of Bible study. But it is the only way to avoid manipulating the dynamic Word of God.

To silence the Bible-abusers I should know the Bible well. But above all, my heart should be willing to listen to a voice which is not always pleasing to my ears, but is the only medicine for my heart.

Job 25-27

I put on righteousness and it clothed me (Job 29:14).

Job looks at sin in two ways. On the one hand he admits many times that he is a sinful man, needing forgiveness, needing to bring sacrifices for the sins of himself and his children. On the other hand, Job will not admit he is a special sinner. He tells his companions that he is a righteous man and always was.

His words shock me. I am used to saying that I am altogether sinful and cannot do any good in my life. It seems awkward to say that my righteousness covers me like a cloth. I am more used to the confession that Christ's righteousness must be the clothes that cover me.

Can God be pleased by these words of Job? Certainly. God's work in me must show in a life dedicated to God. There can be hypocrisy in my lamentation that I am completely sinful and deprived and wicked. By the grace of God this is not so anymore. The Holy Spirit who works in me must have done something good! It is not my own work, but I must not deny the Spirit His harvest, even if I sound humble in the ears of other people if I do deny goodness.

In the Psalms, people call themselves righteous. Paul says that he has obtained the victory in the struggle of faith; he says he wants to do good even though sin is always around him. John says that when I am a child of God, I am not sinning anymore, at least not from the heart.

The glory of God shines through my life, and I should have the courage to say so. Falling into the trap of dishonest "humility" is sin against God.

Job put on righteousness; righteousness was not his own body, just the clothes that covered him.

I don't live, but Christ lives in me. I may and must glory in that.

Job 28-30

Then man prays to God, and he accepts him (Job 33:26).

Elihu has heard Job say many times that there is no iniquity in him which would warrant his present plight. It is true that suffering is not necessarily linked to particular sins. But Job's self-justification has almost become an arrogant claim. Elihu becomes angry at Job because he continually tries to justify himself (vs. 8-11) rather than God. Elihu reminds Job that God is still greater than man.

Job has also accused God of not answering any of his questionings (vs. 12) and again Elihu has to show him that he is wrong. God speaks to man in two ways. First, God sends warning to men in night visions so that they may turn away from evil deeds, strip themselves of their pride and avoid death and destruction. God can also chasten His children through physical pain to prompt fasting and a reexamination of their relationship to God. Elihu concedes, however, that neither dreams nor bodily ailments in themselves carry the Word of God to man, but merely prepare man to listen.

There is yet another way that God reaches out to His creatures. He provides a mediator or interpreter who not only shows man what his duty is and where he has gone wrong, but also pleads man's case to God. He prays for man's deliverance from death. He is intercessor. But He also provides the ransom: He offers the price of man's atonement.

Elihu has unwittingly pointed to Christ. I need someone to go between my great God and myself. Someone who will help me understand my role and duty and who will lovingly point out my inherent shortcomings to a just God. But this Intercessor will go one step further—He will offer His life so that I may be forgiven.

Unfortunately, Elihu still believes that submission brings forgiveness *and* physical restoration. The reality of life teaches me that the effects of sin cannot yet be put aside. But if I know that redemption is real, then I also know that God will restore all things to wholeness soon.

Job 31-33

I have yet something to say on God's behalf (Job 36:2).

What arrogance! The Almighty who created man from dust will find a lawyer in the man He made! Elihu complains that Job has not sufficiently justified the Lord.

That ridiculous attitude has existed in the church of God. Answering questions and accusations, people defend their God, and sometimes even apologize on His behalf. Books have been written to protect the good name of a God who seems to have given an imperfect Bible. They come to the conclusion that God's work is pretty good after all. When people suffer, I hasten to tell them that the Lord does not make mistakes. What I show is an insecurity about God. Perhaps not so convinced that everything is well, I shout to drown my own uncertainty and doubts. Yet what kind of a God needs me to protect Him?

On the other hand, is it fair to speak only of Elihu's arrogance? He *loves* God; he speaks out angrily because he cannot stand all the talk about God's wrongdoings. A child, he strikes out against those who offend and insult his Father.

I am not wrong to become angry with people who so easily say, "Is that a God of love? How can the Lord do a thing like that? Why cannot He stop all that misery?" Even though I know that I cannot give the answers and I know that God does not need my help, I still may express my deepseated affection for my Savior. When a man says, "I want to say something on behalf of God," certainly the Lord hears the love in his voice.

Job 34-36

Then the Lord answered Job out of the whirlwind (Job 38:1).

Job has thrown all his "Why's" into the face of God and now his Father is ready to answer them. Surprisingly, the Lord does not say a word about satan and his doings. That is not essential to His answer. Instead the Lord speaks from a whirlwind about His greatness. When the Almighty One speaks, Job humbles himself and lays his hand upon his mouth.

But silence is not what the Lord wants to hear. He goes on to make the right response clear to Job. Does Job trust his Father in heaven? All right then, should God not be allowed to use His children in the great struggle of His kingdom?

Sometimes God has to sacrifice something beautiful (and so do His people) in order to achieve an even better result.

We are very small and see only our brief part of the struggle. God rules the ages and knows exactly how to handle it all. I don't get the answers in detail because I cannot understand them anyhow. Life is a matter of trust.

Do I really believe in God as my Redeemer? Then I must say, "Take my life and let it be consecrated, Lord, to Thee." And when that means hardship, I know that I have communion with Christ in suffering.

In fact, it is an honor when God takes my life in His hands and moves it to achieve the victory. I am not a useless bystander and passive receiver of His grace. He has appointed me to a task, even when that task is to suffer and to praise His name with a song in the night.

Now I know what my sins are: not the sins Job's friends were talking about, but my reluctance to abandon myself to the glory of His coming kingdom. I am afraid to take God at His word.

Job says, Now my eyes see Thee. My eyes have seen the glory of the coming of the Lord. And He uses even me.

Job 37-39

And the Lord restored the fortunes of Job (Job 42:10).

What a happy ending! The friends of Job recognize how they have sinned against the Lord and Job by trying to replace the living God with a dead philosophy. The hurt which one does to God and one's fellowmen cannot be undone, but it can be forgiven. Job's friends bring sacrifices, restoring communications with God and man. Then Job starts praying for the men who have done so much harm to him; he prays in love for those whom it is hard to like. And that love best expresses itself in intercession, in prayer for their conversion. I can pray for those who live in darkness, but I can only do that when I am rich in God myself.

And Job receives double restoration for all he lost in the catastrophe. When he receives seven sons and three daughters, he even has double the number of children, for children lost are still safe in the Lord.

His is now a joyful and happy life. Brothers and sisters and friends who clearly had paid no attention to him in his evil days return, and in kindness Job accepts them. When I am rich in the Lord, I can hardly be ungracious; the goodness of God shines in my gentleness. Then Job lives 140 years, sees four generations and dies, full of days, satisfied with the mercy of his God.

This all sounds like a fairy tale: "They lived happily ever after." But why not? Isn't my whole life in Christ a story of unbelievable events? Don't I know wonders, miracles, and joy that passes understanding? The Lord loves to make us happy. He does not like to see His children in distress. As soon as satan can be defeated, the Lord returns with His arms full of gifts. I am rich already, but the greatest part is still to come.

Job 40-42

Thou, O Lord, art a shield about me, my glory, and the lifter of my head (Psalm 3:3).

It seems that the psalms give no revelation about God, but rather a mirror of the Lord's words. And the reaction of the author to God may be a private reaction, quite different from mine. Does that mean that the book of Psalms does not belong to the Word of God? No. The book reveals that the Lord is able to work in the hearts of men to create responses, faith and prayer, love, and even hatred. Christ speaks through this book as surely as He lives in me.

In this psalm, David feels he should be helpless and downcast. Everybody has given up on him. Tens of thousands of people have set themselves against him. Because of his flight from Absalom, the possibility of his returning to the throne is small. There is no hope, even in God.

But then the Lord reveals what He can do in His children. David knows, with no external proof, that the Lord is his shield. Nobody can really hurt him because his heavenly Father watches over him.

Furthermore, the Lord is his glory. There is nothing glorious about a man fleeing from his rebellious son. But the God of life gives him back his dignity, his worth. God remains faithful; He lives in my heart, He has a task for me, and He speaks to me. This dignity nobody can take away from me.

Above all, the Lord is the lifter of my head. Here I stand, looking down at my shoes, tears streaming down my cheeks, with nothing to look forward to. But then a gentle hand touches my chin. It lifts my head upwards slowly but firmly until I look into the eyes of my Father. Through my tears, I see His smile and then my smile breaks through.

Now that my head is lifted, I see more light. I can look around and discover that nothing is impossible anymore. Hope has returned.

Psalm 1-6

Arise, O Lord; O God, lift up thy hand (Psalm 10:12).

David is faced with a predicament. The wicked of the world oppress the poor and live in luxury themselves. The evil ways of the ungodly are very successful, and the Lord does not punish them.

How do I as a Christian approach a situation like that? I could deny the deeds of the wicked; pretend I don't see. Or I could explain that they may fit into God's plan. Or perhaps it is "educational" for the poor to be oppressed; it may strengthen them in their patience and faith. Or I could point to the future when the rights of the poor and the sins of the ungodly will finally be brought into the judgment of God.

But precisely because of such wishy-washy, pie-in-the-sky approaches to sin, the church of God has lost its credibility in the world.

David does not deny the oppression and injustice and hurt and arrogance in the world. Nor is he willing or able to defend God's inaction. Nevertheless, he does not accept a rotten world, simply because God did not accept it. In Christ, He came to make it a better world.

So now David calls upon the Lord to do something. "Arise! Please don't just sit there. Lift up Your hand! Take Your hands out of Your pockets and go to work." That is strong language, but that is the way a child can speak to a Father he trusts.

God is pleased when I do not try to talk away problems, but rather call upon Him, knowing that in Christ He started a good work. Of course, I know that it may take quite a while before everything turns out well. But when I love God I do not defend Him. I cry to Him because I trust Him.

Psalm 7-12

The fool says in his heart, "There is no God" (Psalm 14:1).

When the psalms mention wicked people, they are not referring to people who commit sin. The fact that I am not sinless does not make me a wicked person. This term is reserved for those who are fools.

The fool says in his heart, "There is no God." He is an atheist in practice. He denies God's effective control over the world and makes himself god.

The fool is not a simple-minded person but a coarse, brutal, self-centered rogue who loves only himself. The fool may know about God and even argue about Him, but he doesn't know Him personally.

There is a definite and basic difference between children of God who do wicked things and the wicked themselves. I don't constantly have to fear that I could be rejected by God because I sin. In all my struggles and failures, I can still call upon the Lord, and know Him, and realize that I am not independent, and desire to give more love to God and my neighbors. It would be false humility to call myself wicked, for in Christ, I am a new creature. Thank God!

There is also comfort in the fact that God calls practicing atheists "fools." When the wicked declare that men are the only gods, that the Bible is a book of lies and that life can be so good without God's commandments, I say they are wrong. But I still fear that with all their knowledge and influence, they may be right. However, God tells me that they are the idiots, not I. When I know God, my knowledge is a greater wisdom than anybody in the world possesses without Him.

I must pray for wicked fools, but I should not be one of them.

Psalm 13-18

My God, my God, why hast thou forsaken me? (Psalm 22:1).

It seems difficult to find texts that clearly speak of the Messiah. Some may or may not allude to the suffering of Christ. Here, however, is a most obvious and undeniable prophecy of the Man of Sorrows. Jesus Himself used the words of this psalm at the time of His own death.

I should be careful though. This song was written by David. Was David really forsaken by God? Or was he speaking in a vision about the future? It must be true that David is speaking of more than his own problem.

In my suffering and tribulation, I can speak of my problem. But another One takes over for me. The deepest of suffering, the agony of being forsaken by God, should have been my share in life. But Christ took it upon Himself.

Now the song of David goes on to the greatest happiness. Because Another One has taken over the hellish agony, he is more joyful than he can describe. I should have gone through the distress of hell, but Christ did it for me. The text of Psalm 22 should have been my words, but the Lord took them away from me. This is Messianic!

I don't have to search the Bible for words that perhaps vaguely relate to the coming of the Messiah. The whole Bible, and especially the book of Psalms, speaks of the glory that Christ came to deliver. God has mercy and compassion. He does not deal with me according to my sins. I can call now to the congregation to praise God with me for my narrow escape.

David is struggling with this mystery for which he has no explanation. The expectation expressed in this chapter of a Messiah not yet born is very similar to the expectation of God's people today of a second coming—a time when God will not forsake His own but invite them to share in the joy of His kingdom.

Psalm 19-24

Wait for the Lord (Psalm 27:14)

The word "wait" is beautiful. It means that the Lord will certainly come to help and comfort. The only thing unknown is His timing. Confident expectancy is included in the word "wait."

This is Christian hope at its best. I *believe* that I shall see the goodness of the Lord in the land of the living.

It may be surprising that this passage does not mention a future after death. It is not often that I find any mention of that in the Old Testament. Of course not: my future is in Jesus Christ. Heaven is not just nebulous happiness and glory. It means to be with Christ. Only after Christ came can there be hoping for that life which will be the fulfillment of life upon earth.

Nevertheless, David knows quite well that it is good to live with a God of mercy. The joy David found in the land of the living is the joy we know, having begun eternal life with God on earth.

So I can have Christian hope. I am on the lookout; my heart can take courage. Great things are going to happen: the Lord will not give me up to my adversaries, but will lead me on a level path.

Meanwhile, I should not be in such a hurry that I run ahead of the Lord. Waiting also means watching God, following in His footsteps, and obeying His commandments. I need strength and courage to follow; it is not easy. But it pays off. Just wait—and see.

Psalm 25-30

Then thou didst forgive the guilt of my sin (Psalm 32:5).

Sin and forgiveness are terms used so often that their real meaning can escape me. Of course, everybody is a sinner; of course, there is forgiving grace.

David talks about his guilt in a different way. He has tried to conceal it; he hasn't had the nerve to mention it in his prayers. But not telling the Lord doesn't help either. Guilt makes David's body groan. His strength is wasting away, dried up as by the heat of summer.

In contrast, how casually I often deal with my sin. If Christ really lives in me, won't my sin disgust me?

Then in an honest confession, David finds complete forgiveness. It is all over, not gradually but immediately; joy returns and is stronger than before. The more thoroughly I know how my sins offend God and my neighbor, the happier I will be in the knowledge that they are washed away by Jesus' blood.

But David does not stop here. If forgiveness is real, something else must happen. He is going to tell others about it. Honestly confessing that I am a forgiven sinner is not easy. I can only rest in Christ, letting go of false pride and self-respect.

But even confession to others is not enough. Now David has to know which way to continue. So that David can avoid sinning again, the Lord must instruct him and teach him the way to go. This is not easy either. I have to realize where I went wrong as I learn what direction I should have taken. Only by following the directions of Christ through His Holy Spirit can I avoid falling into the same trap again.

When I take sin seriously, I find true happiness in my forgiveness.

Shout for joy, all you upright in heart!

Psalm 31-36

My lifetime is as nothing in thy sight (Psalm 39:5).

David is afraid of death. He seems to be sick or in danger or perhaps just aware of the fact that he will not be around much longer. Suddenly, for no special reason, I suddenly may be shattered by the knowledge that I must die. My execution may be postponed for a short time or for many years. But it is unavoidable. Death comes to all.

But David keeps silent about his fear. He is afraid that the wicked will find out that even faith in God is not strong enough to assuage this fear. It would be terrible if unbelievers would lose their respect for my God because they see me trembling in the face of death.

But David cannot go on in silence any longer; the fiery question has to be spoken. How about death? What is the meaning of life?

Once David opens his mouth, he understands. He does not have to cope with life and death in a vacuum. He may speak to the Lord of life and death. In communion with God, he begins to sense the relationship between sin and death. There must be a solution for the problem of death because God's forgiving grace is an answer to the burden of sin. There is hope!

Beyond the river Jordan, there must be something of that same communion with God that I experience here. To depart and to be with Christ will be by far the best. Jesus will be there when He calls me into His glory.

That does not solve all my questions and problems. But I need not fear the tunnel, knowing that I will see light again. He will be waiting there and He is the Light.

Is David a happy man now? No. It is nonsense to assume that the gospel of hope immediately obliterates problems. In spite of the hope he has found, David still sees death as "being no more." But he is talking and praying. With God, he and I will get there.

Psalm 37-43

There is a river whose streams make glad the city of God (Psalm 46:4).

Little is found in the book of Psalms about the individual futures of God's children in heaven, while much is found about the tremendous things that will happen when the Lord comes to judge the world. The coming of the kingdom is far more important than my own interests, especially since they are incorporated in that kingdom.

There will be a series of catastrophic events when the world comes to its end. The chaotic waters of the underworld will break forth, shaking the mountains and overwhelming the earth. What could be more stable than a mountain, more changeless than the sea? I can make gods of my certainties, but when the Lord comes, He will show who is God Almighty.

Then shalom will be found only in the city of God. Through the whole ordeal, the church of God will stand in glory and gladness. There will even be a river whose streams make glad the city of God.

An abundance of water was very important for a city in the Middle East; water meant security and fertility for a city. But Jerusalem never had a river. Water had to be brought in from wells. The city's water shortage became acute in times of drought and war. Therein lies the paradox of the image. Though there never has been a river in Zion, the poet describes the city as green with plants and flowers, and as secure against all enemies.

This could be called poetic liberty: the singer is describing Jerusalem poetically to convey his vision of the new Jerusalem. Does that mean that his vision is less than accurate?

What is reality? The hard facts which my western mind can describe? Or what my spirit, enlightened by the Holy Spirit, can see? Blessed am I when I discover the real things that eyes have not seen and ears have not heard.

What I see in faith is very real: the city of God in the midst of the chaos of the world, shalom while the storms in the world howl around me.

The Lord of hosts is our refuge.

Psalm 44-49

O that I had wings like a dove! (Psalm 55:6).

The suffering of Christ illumines my sinfulness and selfishness. Peter denies his Lord, Judas betrays Him, the Jews abandon their King and crucify Him, Pilate seeks the easy way out of his problems, the disciples flee in unbelief . . . each person portrays an aspect of human nature as it seeks itself instead of God.

In the Old Testament, David's suffering has the same effect; it points out the sinfulness of man. The man who is called to serve as king is being persecuted by a mad king Saul. Later David's own children turn against him. People betray him whenever betrayal profits them. Worst of all, his friend, his equal, his companion with whom he has had sweet conversations and with whom he has walked in the house of God in fellowship has turned against Him. Breaking a covenant with a friend is the lowest and meanest sin in Israel. Once Jesus too had to admit, "One of you shall betray Me."

David feels that his problems are too much to bear. At times I feel like running away from pressure and strain. Oh, that I had wings like a dove and could fly away and be at rest. And again I hear the words of Jesus, "My Father, if it be possible, let this cup pass from Me."

People do try to escape. The obvious escape routes are alcohol, drugs, fun, sex, and sometimes even suicide. But there are more subtle ways of trying to escape unbearable strain. I may lose my temper, be mean to other people, or become philosophically aloof. I see in the Bible that the desire to escape is not sinful in itself. The lives of David and Jesus tell me that tensions and frustrations can become too much to bear. Still, I know that escaping is not solving. The problems will still be there.

Finally, David gets to the point where he casts his burdens on the Lord. Jesus takes them; He accepts the cup that cannot be passed.

I can do everything in Him who strengthens me.

Psalm 50-55

Thou hast kept count of my tossings (Psalm 56:8).

David has never known as we do how close the Lord came to us in Jesus Christ, how He became one of us, and dwelt among us. He has never received the indwelling of the Holy Spirit through which the Almighty God lives in my heart. David's God should have been remote and beyond comprehension. And yet David understands the closeness of the Lord better than I do. I may call God my Father in Jesus Christ, but David understands what "Abba, Father" means.

This is not an easy time in David's life. At night he tosses in his bed and in the daytime he cries about the way men oppose him and the kingship of his God. But he never feels forsaken and alone. He claims that the Lord sits at his bedside and everytime he turns in his bed, the Lord makes a note of it. Whenever he cries, the Lord catches his tears in His bottle. This sounds as silly as that expression in the Bible that not a hair can fall from my head without His sovereign will. Isn't that exaggerating things? In the first place, who cares about the number of my hairs? Likewise, the tossings in my bed and the tears I shed are of little importance. I try not to pay attention to them and I try to hide them from loved ones.

But David says that the Lord cares. David makes me understand the care and presence of my heavenly Father. He may not automatically make right the miserable circumstances, but He is there, all right. When He asks His children to make some sacrifices for the coming of His kingdom, He stays at their bedside and walks with them in the darkness.

New Testament Christians can learn from David's faith.

Psalm 56-61

Thou crownest the year with thy bounty (Psalm 65:11).

This psalm starts so nobly with talk of sin and forgiveness, of prayers heard and vows made. How blessed to live in the courts of God! How joyful to live the Christian life!

But towards the end of the psalm, nobility falters. The poet looks at fields, crops, flowers, sunshine, and rain, and he so enjoys the sight that he cannot keep silent about it. That is understandable. What a beautiful day! Good crop and lots of money! What a meal it was! Got a good deal and am doing fine! Such talk sounds frivolous, compared to the serious start of the psalm. Are the good things in life frivolous?

Luther reckoned that the body did not count for much. Calvin didn't look like a man who enjoyed the good things in life. Many people have assured me that earthly joys are the lower values in life. The body is just the wrapping for the soul.

Is that true? Of course not. The Lord wants me to be abundantly happy and to enjoy the life He gives me. He attacks sin so that He can be my God again; so that He can restore something of the lost paradise. Satan tries to make this world a valley of tears, but God is starting the recovery. And when David sees an abundance of flowers and crops, he sees that one good thing—forgiveness—leads to another—the restoration of life.

Restoration cannot be total yet. Brokenness is still all around me. But when I see and feel and taste the beauty and riches of life, I can say, "Lord, we are getting there,"

God is not happy about people who neglect their bodies. Sloppy figures and downcast minds do not please Him. Neglect of the body shows spiritual poverty. Christ makes life whole.

I *must* go out and look at the marvels of God's love in nature. I *must* enjoy the gifts of my Creator. The meadows and the valleys, the birds and the flowers shout and sing together for joy. Sing along!

Psalm 62-67

Do not cast me off in the time of old age (Psalm 71:9).

Is old age a hard time in life? Well, the problems of age cannot be denied. Yet nowadays many provisions are made. Organizations, pensions, and programs attempt to meet the needs of the senior citizens, sometimes so thoroughly that the dignity of older people is threatened.

There is no doubt, however, that in the days in which the psalms were made, old age was a time of bitter hardship. There was no social security, no pension, no homes where the aged were welcome and could live among understanding peers. The old could not make a living; therefore they often had to beg for handouts.

One thing those ancient "ancients" did have in common with today's aged: the feeling that nobody needs the old, but they need everyone else. An old person longs to continue to build his own life, but now others often decide what will happen.

This situation is especially hard on the poet of this psalm. Enemies make life hard for him. He needs friends to help him, but there are none. I can sense his feeling of helplessness. To whom can he turn? He is forsaken.

Indifference and callous unconcern are often disguised. The good humanist is offended by the hardships the weaker suffer and so lobbies for new government programs for the underprivileged. Christians occasionally feel guilty about the situation and make their token gestures as well.

But it seems that underneath a thin veneer of tokenism, there lurks the cruel nature of man. The Bible speaks of tripping a blind man, of cursing the deaf, of preying on widows and robbing orphans. The old man in agony in this psalm shows me what I am *by nature*—cruel and mean and selfish.

This old man turns to God and he knows that the Lord will not forsake him. But his cry reaches my ears. Is my heart really made new by the Spirit of Love?

Psalm 68-72

We will tell to the coming generation the glorious deeds of the Lord (Psalm 78:4).

"The children will have to make up their own minds about religion. I cannot pass on faith to them."

"I can only reject or accept what I know. I need information before I can make up my mind."

Such common sense notwithstanding, it is impossible merely to "pass on" God. That kind of neutrality just does not exist. If I speak about the Lord in a cold, matter-of-fact way, I tell my listener that He has not moved my heart and life. No, the information I pass on must be a witness of what God means to me.

Psalm 78, speaking about the glorious deeds of the Lord, is full of joy and excitement. The history of Israel is told as a series of mysterious "dark sayings." God has done so many things that are sheer wonders of His love!

Throughout the history of His people, God has surprised them by His help and goodness. But His children sin and turn away from Him. And then the real mystery occurs. God does not turn away from them. He always comes back to them, sad and terribly disappointed, but with love that endures. He always overcomes the obstacles that they put up against Him. The mystery is that I cannot sin God out of my life!

Understandably, children don't like to think of a God who is righteous and demanding and always watching them. But if children see God as a harsh, overbearing super-parent, perhaps their own parents have not been touched by the mysterious love of God.

It is vitally important that the next generation be able to carry the torch in a dark world. Therefore I must see to it that I am able to pass on to them the truth of the glorious deeds of the Lord. They must see God's love, speaking through me.

Psalm 73-78

O Israel, if you would but listen to me (Psalm 81:8).

What is unique about the Christian religion? Don't all religions have the same basic characteristics? Perhaps there are many ways to serve God, or perhaps all the various gods are versions of one God.

Not so. The God of the Bible actually comes to human beings to ask for their love and dedication. Now when I look around at other religions, I don't find such a God. There are silent gods who do not reveal much about themselves, and those who look angry at unbelievers and punish them; there are those who act as tyrants who must be pacified, and those who are just super-humans with human fallacies and shortcomings. But all these false gods wait for me to rise to their level so that I can satisfy their laws. Perhaps I will get to some kind of heaven, but I will have to work hard for it, struggling with the laws of Islam, the meditation of Buddhism, or a heathen fear of taboos. Despite tremendous struggle, I will never be sure that I will be close enough to the god to know peace and happiness. Many religions hallow the struggle to reach the top of the ladder and make much of people who claim that they have (almost) made it.

What is unique in Christianity is that God came to me in Jesus Christ. I do not struggle to get high; He stoops low. What a difference! I cannot be proud, for I have not found; I am found.

This is not a weakness of our God; it is His strength. He is not a silent god, watching his creatures struggle to climb a ladder and then tumble down. Instead, He stretches out His hands to me. He prays me to listen to Him and love Him. Only a great God can do a thing like that.

Psalm 79-84

The Lord records as he registers the peoples, "This one was born there" (Psalm 87:6).

This psalm must have sounded strange in the ears of the Israelites. Salvation is for the children of Israel! A few may be adopted into their company, but not with the same full rights as native citizens. This is understandable. The Lord must keep His hands around the small flame in a dark world. Since the Holy Spirit has not yet been poured out, there is not enough power in Israel to allow them to take other nationalities into their midst. It is hard enough to keep the candle burning in Israel itself!

But in Psalm 87, the Lord extends His arms and calls other nations into the glory of His presence. It is as if He cannot wait until Pentecost; already He writes with eagerness the names of other tribes and peoples in His records.

The gods of the other nations have always challenged the God of Israel to meet their strength. The Lord replies by quietly taking their children away from them and incorporating them into His own family. The church can prove its strength by taking outsiders into fellowship with Jesus Christ.

The church is not an exclusive but an inclusive communion. God does not hesitate to write in His records people who come from the most hostile tribes and nations. I should overcome my hesitation to call on certain groups of the population who are, in my opinion, not open to the gospel. The very rich and the very poor, the intellectuals and the minority groups—they are all written into the book of God.

The most shocking revelation is that the Lord records them as being born in Zion. They are not second-rank newcomers. They do not form a group that should be patronized by the older and "more genuine" group of Christians. They have the same birthrights as all other Christians. By God's mercy, we are *all* adopted as His children.

Psalm 85-90

They still bring forth fruit in old age (Psalm 92:14).

In the olden days, old people elicited respect. Since most knowledge was achieved through experience, older people were the wise ones. This has changed drastically. Today it is assumed that the complications of our society demand young and bright minds to understand things and to give advice and direction. Still, there is a truth in what the Bible says about older people. Wisdom is not the same as knowledge; there are matters that can only be learned through trial and error.

But now this psalm puts a limiting condition on this whole concept. Older people are valuable and beneficial only as long as they are green and fruitful like a good tree. The elderly do not deserve respect just because they are old. Interesting museum pieces do not contribute much to the enrichment of life. Ruins can be admired but do not give shelter to anyone. No, the old must be like old cedars and palm trees; they must show unexpected greenness that can be only the Holy Spirit continually nurturing the roots of their existence. As soon as I believe that I can survive easily on what I received earlier in life, I will put out no more green leaves. I must constantly feed on the Word of God; Jesus must live within me.

But the fruits are also important. Green leaves may look nice, but fruit proves that there is sense and meaning for a tree's existence. But many older people ask, "What can I do? I used to be fruitful; now I am only a burden." Age has its own sweet fruits: prayer for the younger generation; patience and kindness, learned through the hardship of life and the realization of personal failures; gentleness in dealing with other people who are not so kind to me; speaking out of experience, not about the experiences.

The big question in my life will always be, "What fruits does Christ find in me?"

Psalm 91-97

Make a joyful noise to the Lord, all the earth (Psalm 98:4).

A choir of young children had been singing during the worship service. After the last note, somebody in the congregation gave one clap and then thought better of it. In this congregation, one did not do a thing like that. But a word from the pulpit changed that. When "Clap your hands, all ye people" was quoted from the Word of God, applause sounded through the church building. Some still felt uncomfortable with this swerving from tradition. Others felt that this was more in line with the worship of the people of God through the ages.

To sit silently in church except to sing a song has become acceptable; silence is regarded as pious respect. The silence at the Lord's communion table is so thick it can be cut. Nobody would dare chime in during prayer.

Now listen to the Bible: Make a joyful noise! Break forth into joyous songs! Sing praises with the lyre, trumpets, horns—all quite loud instruments. Let the sea roar! Let the floods clap their hands!

Worship in Israel was a noisy and boisterous celebration which one could hear from miles away. It was as if people wanted to bridge the gap between heaven and earth; as if they knew that they could make themselves heard in God's dwelling place if they only tried hard enough.

Why are we so quiet now? Has this "piety" infiltrated our churches through monasteries and the meditations of hermits? Why do I hesitate to express myself? Do I believe that the Lord would rather have me keep my mouth shut? Or is there no urge to make a joyful noise because there is not much life in me?

The psalms admonish me to make the kind of noise that is pleasing to the Lord. When my heart is full of thanksgiving, then my heavenly Father loves to hear my joyful noise.

Psalm 98-103

I will sing to the Lord as long as I live (Psalm 104:33).

There are several accounts of the creation story. In Genesis, I find a rather sober, straight-forward narrative of creation. Job gives a more emotional picture of the great things that happened when the Lord made heaven and earth. And here in Psalm 104, there is an enthusiastic song about how God made this universe.

Obviously, it was never God's plan to give an account of creation which would satisfy my scientific mind. The tone of this psalm is far from scientific. These poetic songs are about the joy of knowing who made this beautiful world in its splendid setting of the universe.

In the psalmist's days, other religions claimed their gods were the makers of all. Nowadays similar claims are made. Evolutionists want me to believe that God had nothing to do with the formation of the cosmos. They would have me think that one thing simply led to the other and God, if He existed, had only to watch it all evolve. The powers of nature are the new gods who get all the honor; the survival of the fittest is the cruel replacement for the upholding care of a Father in Heaven.

I have never heard any evolutionists singing songs of adoration. Evolution is a drab and impersonal affair. But the church of God sings, "How great Thou art!" God's creation and providence, His care for what He made is so impressive, that I can scarcely take it in. I will sing to the Lord as long as I live!

Creation means that my whole life makes sense. If I just evolved, then I just happen to be here. But because I was made by the hands of the Father of Jesus Christ, my whole life must have meaning and purpose.

I will not be robbed of this joy by semi-scientific oracles. Listening to this song of creation helps me to know that God made me to glorify Him in all I do. That is worth a song!

Psalm 104-108

The Lord says to my lord: Sit at my right hand (Psalm 110:1).

Portions of this psalm are quoted in the New Testament at least 21 times. The sheer number of such quotations suggest something strange and fascinating in this and several other royal psalms.

When this psalm mentions the lord or king, it seems to refer to more than an earthly king such as David. This king seems to be ascribed more awe and respect than would be appropriate for a human king, even though the kings of Israel were the leaders of the people of God, and, as theocratic rulers, the representatives of God on earth.

A second point: Would the Lord God invite a simple human king to sit at His right hand in the place of honor and power? Finally, the king mentioned in this psalm appears to be both king and priest, just as Melchizedek was the king-priest in Jerusalem at the time of Abraham. But the kings in Israel were not priests, for the priests since the time of Aaron had come from the tribe of Levi.

(And who was Melchizedek anyway? He was a mysterious figure, almost mythical in dimension. As king he ruled and blessed Abraham, yet at the same time he acknowledged Abraham as the head of God's covenant.)

I conclude that this passage must point to the Son of God who far excels all the Israelite kings and even the mysterious Melchizedek. I am amazed that Jesus Christ is mentioned and predicted in the Old Testament with a glow of mysterious glory around His head. Nobody can fully understand all the nuances of this passage. That is why the scribes cannot answer Jesus' questions concerning this passage in Matthew 22:44.

When I find questions in the Bible that I cannot answer, when the meaning of a passage eludes today's most scholarly methods of exegesis, I do not become frustrated or unhappy. Rather, I am proud that I cannot comprehend my great God. Jesus sits at His right hand. And I may sit with Him.

Psalm 109-115

Oh, how I love thy law! It is my meditation all the day (Psalm 119:97).

The length and repetitiveness of this psalm may discourage me from reading it. But a closer look reveals that it is quite an intricate piece of poetry. It is divided into twenty-two sections, each of which begins with a different letter of the Hebrew alphabet. Furthermore, within each section, each of the eight lines has the same opening letter. However, this special feature of Hebrew poetry is lost on me. Besides, doesn't such a tight structure make the writing stilted and destroy the spontaneity of a song from the heart?

Is this lengthy, elaborate poem really to the glory of God, or to the glory of a clever, imaginative poet? God must be pleased when people spend years creating something special for Him. God did accept a beautiful temple from the Israelites. Could not my effort to make something nice for the Lord be a way of saying, "I love You"?

Not only is this psalm terribly long, it also speaks of a forbidding subject: the Law. Law may appeal to a scribe but not to a New Testament Christian. But again, a closer look reveals more. Almost every line has a synonym for the law: testimonies, words, commandments, name, promise, precepts, statutes, etc. It becomes clear that the poet is not speaking of a law that condemns and whips into action. Law and promise, commandment and name are different ways of saying the same thing.

Obeying the law of God gives life. As a Christian, I may find joy in serving my Father. The scribes and Pharisees never found that joy because they did not accept the love of God in Jesus. But as soon as I accept Jesus as my Savior, the law shows me the road to walk with Him.

Psalm 116-121

He gives to his beloved sleep (Psalm 127:2).

The translation of this text leaves something to be desired. A better translation is, "He gives to His beloved in their sleep." The meaning then is not that God's people have no need for sleeping tablets, but that the good things of life are not the fruit of toil and human effort, but rather, that they are gifts of the Lord. While I am asleep, God is providing for me. The Lord can give to those He loves more good gifts during a night's sleep than they can accumulate in a life of anxious toil. The psalm tells me that my house, my family, and all that I have are not the product of my care and efforts but blessings from my heavenly Father.

Now these are marvelous and soothing words. But then I go off to my job, or I toil in the household; I study in school, or I attend city council meetings, and the business of life nearly kills me. It is nice to say that all my toil does not provide for me. But meanwhile, I cannot sit with my hands in my lap and do nothing. So does this psalm not turn into a nice but empty thought?

Here is the "conflict" of the Lord's providence and my activity. Actually they are not in conflict with each other at all. Putting both truths into practice is like rowing a boat. The two independent oars must be used simultaneously; if I use only one oar, I will go in senseless circles. If the two are used with the same strength at the same time, the boat will go straight.

On the one hand, there is my activity. In my house, family, city, I am called to act in a responsible way. But then there is still the other oar. It is the Lord who does everything. And this is equally true. If ever I consider my work to be the determining factor in life, I lose sight of my God.

My God and I work together. That is the joy of His covenant. What I accomplish, He gives to me as in my sleep.

Psalm 122-135

Do I not hate them that hate thee, O Lord? (Psalm 139:21).

There are elements in the Bible that I would rather overlook. I would rather overlook the psalms such as this, which express hatred against all those who hate God. The poet hates them with a perfect hatred. Psalm 137 includes that awful statement: happy will be those who take the children of their oppressors and dash them against the rocks. I, as a New Testament Christian, don't want to hear such emotions anymore. Hatred seems to be in conflict with the love as God has revealed in Jesus Christ.

But there are also expressions of this kind in the New Testament. Paul said that he delivered a sinful man to satan for the destruction of his flesh. Revelation speaks of the imminent torment of the Antichrist and all his followers. Jesus speaks of those at His left hand who will go into utter darkness. The epistle to the Hebrews speaks of God as a consuming fire; it is a fearful thing to fall into His hands. It is not easy to overlook these texts.

The man who made this psalm speaks of a God who knows everything and who is everywhere. He extols God's creative power. This great God is so precious to him that he cannot possibly imagine anyone not loving his God. He declares himself one with his Creator and counts as his enemies, not the people who have offended himself, but those who have offended his God. Blessed are those who are so close to their Father that they cannot accept any insults to His name.

At the same time, the psalmist realizes that he is not God. I, too, must be aware of depths in the human mind that I cannot explore myself. It is often hard to determine my deepest motives. Therefore I should pray that the Lord will purify my heart.

Psalm 136-143

He has not dealt thus with any other nation; they do not know his ordinances. Praise the Lord (Psalm 147:20).

People who do not know the Lord have an assortment of other gods. It is hard to believe that all things come from the hands of one God. Because of the contrasts and paradoxes of life it seems more likely that various gods each take a part of the universe to govern. This psalm describes some of those contrasts. The Lord is concerned about the outcast, the broken-hearted, the wounded. But He is also the one who determines the number of stars and counts them by their names. So almighty and strong that He takes care of all the powers of nature, still God does not delight in strength. He sends peace and makes people happy. But He also sends the frightening winter with its snow and ice. I cannot put Him in a category; I can be unhappy because I cannot figure Him out.

This psalm expresses the opposite feeling. One of the "Hallelujah psalms," it approaches the paradoxes in God, not with suspicion, but with complete acceptance and happiness. Why?

First of all, because His great love is clear. In all His doings, He cares for the afflicted. He is not a God who toys with His creatures. Whatever His actions are, no matter how strange they may seem, love governs them.

But the main reason for the joy in this psalm is that God has given His Word to me. In His covenant, He speaks to me and deals with me according to His ordinances and statutes. Furthermore, the Word He declared to Jacob is Jesus Christ, the Son of God, through whom I know God.

All the contrasting actions of my God find their center in my Savior. In Christ, I can see the coming of His kingdom. Taught by the Spirit, I can accept the astonishing things He must do. Praise the Lord!

Psalm 144-150

In all your ways acknowledge him, and he will make straight your paths (Proverbs 3:6).

"Books of wisdom" are often hard to read. Full of deep sayings and thoughts which appeal to an intellectual elite, wisdom literature is not exactly for everyone.

But the Bible offers me a whole book of Proverbs that can reach every mind. Instead of proffering deep confusing philosophies, it gives straightforward, practical advice concerning areas of life in which I need guidance. It is so simple and down to earth that at times it seems somewhat vulgar. I don't like intellectuals to tell me what they think and see from their ivory towers. It is good, then, to meet my God, who bends to meet me and speak to me.

Every nation surrounding Israel had wisdom literature written by wise men who were expected to share their insights. Some of their proverbs may have found their way even into this book. Children of God never stand in perfect isolation, and not all that is found outside the church is nonsense. But the deepest wisdom is the fear of the Lord. That is the heart of the matter. Jesus Christ is the wisdom of God given to me. God's wisdom tells me simply to acknowledge Him in all my ways.

There is not always a rule, a law, to tell me exactly what to do. But I do have to go through life in consultation with my God. That involves prayer and honest listening for answers. When I make decisions I should ask, "Lord, what do You want me to do?" What does the Lord require but that I earnestly *try* to serve Him? When I do so, He will make my paths straight.

That does not mean that there will be no winding or difficult stretches. My way may not look straight to me. But—what wisdom!—I know that He will straighten out what I make crooked. This is a philosophy of life; it is the gospel; it is the highest wisdom.

Proverbs 1-3

The path of the righteous is like the light of dawn (Proverbs 4:18).

According to the book of Proverbs, there are basically three groups of people. There are the righteous or wise who understand God's Word and accept it. Then there are the fools, those who are beyond reach because they have turned away from God. And finally there are the simple, those who are confused but still can be taught. To these simple ones goes out the cry to listen and learn.

This proverb tells me, "The path of the righteous is like the light of the dawn." Strangely enough, the word *path* or *way* is used often to describe the wise life of God's child. The book of Proverbs makes clear that wisdom is not introspection, or toying with nice ideas. Instead, Proverbs calls all people who have any insight to *follow*. Such wisdom cares about the well-being of my neighbor. It calls to the world, "Don't perish in your folly."

It may not always be pleasant to relay this call to the world; I feel embarrassed and silly when it is thrown back in my face. But Jesus gave His life to save fools, so I should be willing to run the risk of being scorned for the sake of Wisdom, Jesus Christ.

Now the word *path* or *way* comes into focus. I am not just sitting; I am going somewhere. The kingdom of God is not words; it is power. I don't have time merely to tinker with ideas; I have work to do.

"The path of the righteous is like the light of dawn." In those days, light was very important. Without artificial lights, it was very hard to find a pathway in the dark. Wisdom, the understanding of God's will, shows me when it is safe to put my foot forward. John calls me to walk in the light as Jesus is in the light.

The light upon my pathway will improve. Dawn preceeds the full day. In that light of life, I'll walk till traveling days are done.

Proverbs 4-6

He does not know that it will cost him his life (Proverbs 7:23).

Proverbs is very concerned with adultery; several passages deal with the topic. In the cultures around Israel, a marriage was less than idyllic. The wife was the property, sometimes even the slave, of her husband. Within this framework, adultery was just a matter of stealing an item of some value and not much more offensive than other forms of theft.

But in Proverbs, the wife and husband are called companions (Proverbs 2:17). Proverbs describes the true meaning of love and affection: marriage is a God-given bond that should never be broken.

Then Proverbs gives a revealing view of adultery. Often people hold only the man to blame for marital infidelity and adultery. He is supposedly the prowler seeking prey, while the woman is the innocent victim of lust and passions. But this passage shows a lady enticing a shy man, and using all her wiles to get him. Here is an honest admission that the blame for marital breakdown can lie with either party or, more likely, with both parties.

I also notice that this chapter does not emphasize the sexual aspect of the problems that cause marriage break-ups. The woman in this chapter is not after sexual satisfaction. Sexual desires can be satisfied very cheaply, even for a mere loaf of bread (Proverbs 6:26). Rather, this woman wants to score a victory. She has no concern for her intended victim who, by the way, is just as guilty as she. Her motives seem to be thwarted pride, a seeking of revenge for other defeats in life, a desire to prove to herself and others that she is somebody. The issues are not simple when a relationship breaks down. God Himself reveals this to give guidance to the wayward.

But most of all, He warns that their unfaithfulness will cost them their lives. What seems to be fun is actually gambling away life. How utterly stupid to sacrifice life, and to go as an ox to the slaughter. The Lord wants me to live, fully, in Him.

Proverbs 7-9

A man who is kind benefits himself, but a cruel man hurts himself (Proverbs 11:17).

I live in a cruel world. People will do anything as long as it serves their own purpose. The invention of more powerful weaponry is cause for deep alarm. But who cares what will happen to my neighbor as long as my own interests are defended? In building up a life and future, everyone has to fend for himself. To quiet my conscience, I can give some alms and charity to victims of the rat race, and from there, go on to an even more selfish pursuit of my own advancement.

The culture in which the book of Proverbs was written was perhaps even worse than today's society. Our culture is still somewhat Christian, and we have certain norms that exercise some restraint over our actions. But in those days, cruelty was unadulterated. And not only that, it was praised and honored. The stronger a person was, and the more harshly he ruled, the more respected he was. Grab and lie and hurt and see that you get the world in your power!

Now, Proverbs brings a message contrary to this whole philosophy. The kindness of my Lord and God should be reflected in me. The Lord hates cruelty, the work of satan.

These are strange statements even today. Isn't it dangerous to be kind? Isn't that losing your life? Yes, says my God. But he who loses his life will find it, while he who tries to save it will lose it. The proof of this statement is Christ Jesus, who gave Himself humbly and has received the highest honor in heaven and earth.

When I am kind, I share in His victory, and when I am cruel I gain nothing but death. The poor in spirit, the peacemakers, the meek, and the merciful will inherit the earth and receive the kingdom of heaven.

Proverbs 10-12

The heart knows its own bitterness (Proverbs 14:10).

Words of wisdom are cruel and sterile unless spoken in the spirit of the Good Shepherd. Some people in the world who feel they know it all always have a ready solution for everyone else's problems. But their easy words can hurt other people deeply.

One of the first things I learn from my Shepherd is that people often suffer more sadness and bitterness than meets the eye. They may hide pain by a brave effort to bear a burden alone. Perhaps it even seems that there is no problem at all. But Proverbs reminds me that even in laughter the heart can be sad. A sensitive Christian is aware of this. Not having found a partner for life, not receiving a child, struggling to get through life with less than adequate gifts, bearing the load of broken ideals and unreached goals—all are hard burdens to bear.

Hidden bitterness is bad enough. But the bitter one's courageous fight not to let on should not be rewarded with an insensitive remark. As a child of God, I must be gentle and kind, observant and careful.

Then a second admonition is given by my Shepherd. I have to accept that I cannot understand what another is going through. The worst remark to receive when faced with suffering and sadness is, "Oh, I know what you are going through. I know, I know." That is a lie. Relating all *my* troubles helps no one but myself. It shows that I am not listening and trying to understand. What I can do is point to Him who really knows what is living in the heart. Because He knows, He can help and heal.

Proverbs 13-15

He who forgives an offense seeks love, but he who repeats a matter alienates a friend (Proverbs 17:9).

"To err is human; to forgive, divine." This secular proverb echos what God says in Proverbs. One of the hardest things in life is to forgive completely. In fact, only God in Jesus Christ can do that.

Perhaps when I cannot forgive, it's because I want to hang on to my dignity and somehow keep the upper hand over the offender. "I forgive, but I can never forget." "The scars are too deep; you hurt me so terribly." Such sentiments have nothing to do with pardon.

Perhaps I have never received real pardon myself. To repent of sin and to admit failure to God is extremely difficult; I prefer to rely on explanations and excuses. But to accept the fact that God has erased my sins from His books is harder still; it is, in fact, impossible without the Holy Spirit's work in my heart.

Now the book of Proverbs reminds me that there is another danger in this whole matter of forgiving. Many times, people react charitably, yes, Christianly, towards those who have violated them. But later they come back to what happened. They repeat the matter, as the text says. Marriage partners do not really want to rub salt in wounds, but still they rehash a painful episode, just to make sure it is over. Children ask for forgiveness, and receive it. But later they are reminded of the snares they met. Such behavior only means that I am not willing to give my neighbor a chance. Such behavior can only alienate a friend. This is not the type of forgiveness that God teaches.

One of the most glorious texts in the Bible states that God throws my sin behind His back and never comes back to it. Do I learn from Him?

Proverbs 16-18

It is a snare for a man to say rashly, "It is holy" (Proverbs 20:25).

This text seems to kill all the joy of enthusiastic giving to the Lord. A man, in a moment of gratitude or pure love of God, makes a vow: he declares something in his possession to be holy, separated from normal use, and dedicated to the Lord. But a few moments later, he discovers that this tremendous promise he has made will be very difficult to keep. Unforeseen complications arise. Then he has to take back his promise.

The lesson here is that it is better to think first and then to act. Jesus tells me not to start building a tower until I have figured out how expensive it will be, and not to start a war before I have counted the soldiers of the enemy.

All this is true, I suppose, but it seems such a damper on spontaneity. Wouldn't it be better to get people to pledge themselves more enthusiastically to the service of God and their neighbor, even though their promises may not always work out? To overcome their natural reluctance to act, it is perhaps necessary to make people pledge quickly and rashly; otherwise nothing at all may come. Why must wisdom moderate spontaneous decisions? I need somebody to get me going, not to slow me down.

Still, this word of God is calling me to order. Of course the Bible demands that I stand up and act. But here I see that there must be a balance between enthusiasm and wisdom. A vow given to God but not paid will be a snare. On the one hand, if the person breaking the vow remains lighthearted, the vow becomes meaningless. On the other hand, broken vows may generate guilt which hinders one's relationship to God and other people. What's more, one failure is the seed for the next.

Balance between zeal and wisdom is far harder to achieve than thoughtless, spontaneous action. The Holy Spirit is able to guide me to such a balanced faith.

Proverbs 19-21

If you say, "Behold, we did not know this," does not he who weighs the heart perceive it? (Proverbs 24:12).

Verse 11 of this chapter calls for charity and mercy. Help the helpless; love the oppressed, save those who are dying. Surprisingly, service to man seems to be stressed more than service and worship of God.

This is, of course, a false dilemma. God wants to be served through the little ones who have no helper. He tells me that what is done unto them is done unto Him. And in the day of judgment, my attitude towards the Lord will be revealed by what I have done for my neighbor.

Then this chapter mentions an excuse that is heard many times in the world and in the church: I didn't know there was so much suffering; I did not realize what was going on.

The One who knows our hearts will be the judge of what we knew. When God's eyes pierce my mind and heart, He may discover that I knew too well what the problems were, but that I just did not want to make a sacrifice and help.

But what if I indeed am *not* aware of the problems that existed around me? Is that a good excuse? Sometimes not. Often, I could have and should have known. It is quite convenient not to investigate, to remain safely in my own pleasant neighborhood. Do I do so because I am afraid of the reality of life? Or do I fear I may discover an urgent need for my time and money? If this is the case, then these words really hit hard: "God weighs the heart."

I need not fear that the Lord is watching me like a great spy in the sky. But I must know that I do not have to give account of my life to a jury of my peers, but to Him who weighs the heart.

Proverbs 22-24

It is better to live in a corner of the housetop than in a house shared with a contentious woman (Proverbs 25:24).

Many times this text has been used as a joke. Blessed are those who can joke about it! Too often it is the grim reality of life. Fights and quarrels sour the life of the family; children suffer as innocent victims. When husband and wife cannot get along, marriage is hardly an image of Christ and His church.

This text refers to a home where the woman is quarrelsome. Apparently this woman has never understood that there are ways to improve her situation in the house and her relationship with husband and children without harsh words and fights. When a wife takes the place entrusted to her by God, she must also use tact to contribute to a healthy family life. The husband may act stupidly, but a comment which shows understanding will do much more to correct the situation than a stinging critical comment. The wife may not do harm to the God-given harmony of the family. In fact, many wives and mothers have endured personal inequities and injustices because, rather than fight for their rights, they fought for the well-being of their families. Happy is the family in which both partners are willing to deny self and to sacrifice themselves for the good of their family.

At the same time, this text implies an accusation for the husband. How did the situation get so out of hand? What was there in him that caused all the quarreling and shouting? Only a coward lives on the housetop. A man must face reality and seek the causes of the discord in his home. Together, the marriage partners must work at restoring the harmony and unity of the home so that it once again reflects Christ's marriage with His bride, the church.

Proverbs 25-27

Her children rise up and call her blessed, her husband also, and he praises her (Proverbs 31:28).

Ideals can change considerably through the ages. Perhaps few women nowadays can identify with the description of a good wife as found in Proverbs. Many mothers and wives may look down irritably upon this "antiquated" praise in the Bible. However, they may not if they give this passage a second and more honest look.

First of all, God gives honor not only to all the great men with the familiar names. Here we see that the Lord is proud of those women who contribute so much to the coming of the kingdom through their more anonymous efforts. His Spirit works through these women, and He acknowledges their contribution to His cause upon earth.

Secondly, this woman is more than a money-maker. She is praised for her care for her workers, her love for husband and children, her kindness to strangers, her trust in the future, her wise teaching, and above all, for the fear of the Lord which is reflected in all her actions.

This woman is not just a worker for her husband, but a partner on equal footing. Apparently her task is not limited to the chores; instead, she has to handle responsibilities that require insight and determination. She considers fields and buys them; she buys and sells merchandise to the merchants. The claims that women should be confined to the kitchen and the bedroom find a strong antidote in this passage.

But the greatest reward for all her efforts comes when her family recognize and appreciate her contributions. The children stand there, a bit clumsily, searching for words, and say: "Mom, you are great!" The husband compares her to other women and announces that, whereas other women have done excellently, his wife (in his opinion) has surpassed them all.

When I am a blessing for others, isn't that a blessing?

Proverbs 28-31

There is nothing better for a man than that he should eat and drink and find enjoyment in his toil (Ecclesiastes 2:24).

Ecclesiastes has been called the sad and somber book. "All is vanity" does ring with the bitterness of frustration and broken ideals. The author seems resigned to the fact that nothing means much in this gray world of ours; he will try to make the best of it.

What this book is doing, however, is a glorious thing. It says "No" to falsely grounded optimism and idealism. Those who do not accept God as their Father have to take refuge in beliefs that will never stand up to the test of life.

As a child of God, I must start by admitting that, yes, all is vanity. In itself, life does not make sense. In God I find meaning in life, but I can only accept that after I have seen how vain and nonsensical life is without Him. I must admit that fun, learning, power, riches, sex, alcohol, drugs, work, and knowledge can never give real meaning to my existence. I must ask the ultimate questions: What do I live for? What is my work all about? What is my place in society?

In this particular passage, the writer laments that the results of his prudent and steady toil will someday have to be passed on to someone else. What if the successor is a fool? What if he mismanages so badly that the results of my toil quickly come to nought? What if the next generation does not see things the way I do, does not share my vision, cannot join in my dreams?

The writer has tried to find joy in the fruits of *his* labor. But God says, "No, you must enjoy life as *I* give it. Realize that all good things came from *My* hand. Do not try to establish meaning by the work of your own hands, for that indeed is futile."

As the wisdom writer discovered, the real and full answer to my quest for meaning can never be found in life itself. But when I find meaning in Christ, I may rest and enjoy the beauty of life. Faith helps me relax and eat and drink.

Ecclesiastes 1-3

He who loves money will not be satisfied with money (Ecclesiastes 5:10).

The Bible speaks positively of money. God's Word does not say that money is the root of all evil. I need funds to sustain my life and to enjoy what the Lord gives. I read about the wages that should be paid to the workmen. Jesus put the prayer for daily bread with petitions about forgiveness of sins and protection against the devil. He fed the hungry crowds. All spiritual talk that ignores the importance of bread and money is pietism, not the gospel of the Bible.

On the other hand, God's Word warns many times against the wrong attitude toward money. Even though I need it, I may not love it. Ecclesiastes says that I may not assume that the meaning of all my toil and labor is the earning of money.

If I start to love money, I will lose the real meaning of life. First of all, I will find that the money I love has become my master and tyrant, for my desire for more will never be satisfied.

Lust for money is one of the worst ailments of modern society. So many people will sacrifice their health in order to get more. They will hurt other people by striking or withholding a fair wage. No longer brother's keepers, they develop into brother's murderers. This is utter foolishness: because of their hunger for more earthly goods, they will never really enjoy life. The main message of Ecclesiastes—that it is good to live out of the hand of God—is lost on them.

Money can be a gift used for many purposes. But if I *love* money, I cannot love God's kingdom and my fellowman. What I get from God's hands should return to Him in gratitude. Gratitude will satisfy my heart.

Ecclesiastes 4-6

Be not righteous overmuch . . . be not wicked overmuch (Ecclesiastes 7:16, 17).

This really sounds ridiculous! How can I ever be *too* righteous? In all my struggling, I can only see that I fail to live up to God's standards. Should I be careful now not to "overdo" righteousness? And I should not be *too* wicked. Can this be God's Word? Of course not. Such confusion happens when I take God's Word out of context.

Ecclesiastes puts down the idealism which claims that all the problems here on earth can be solved. The author speaks in the name of the Lord who does not want me to reach too high and then to fall flat on my nose. I should know my human limitations and realize that only a real Savior can redeem this evil world. I should quit trying to act as if I am God. Of course I should fight to correct the evils around me and to restore wholeness. But being too righteous means that I take everything in my hands. My pride could destroy me and ruin my happiness and effectiveness.

On the other hand, I should not be too wicked either. If I assume that what is wrong around me cannot be changed, and therefore give up trying to make this a better world, I am equally wrong. Being too wicked means that I am lazy and untouched by the urgent cries for the improvement of our society and church. I cannot use the claim that I cannot save anyone as an excuse to withdraw from my task in this world.

I have to realize that I am not a little god; I cannot do miracles. But neither am I a person without a calling. The great comfort of my covenant with God is that I may work as if I had to do it all, but know that He is doing it through me.

Ecclesiastes 7-9

Remember also your Creator in the days of your youth, before the
evil days come (Ecclesiastes 12:1).

This verse may sound like a stern reprimand to frivolous
young people who live it up, forgetting that they will be judged by a
God who takes matters more seriously. But it isn't. Rather, here is
an admonition to young people to rejoice, to live the good life and
taste the goodness of your Creator before it is too late. God's sunshine radiates all through life. You are His child and live out of His
hands. The result is joy and happiness.

Our Father does not want to see us with sad and bewildered
faces animated only by tedious conferences on the meaning of life.
He may well protest the way we encumber our children. They have
to study and cram as much knowledge as possible into their weary
heads. We teach them to fight, to scrap and to compete and when
they take time off for games and play we look concerned. The Lord
is a better Father for them. He tells them to love life, His gift. Of
course, they will be judged for what they do, and they should live
responsibly.

Just as the Lord sheds His light on the young, He smiles on the
old. Old age, like youth, can be described in poetic terms. The eyes,
the sun and moon, cloud over. The hands, keepers of the house,
tremble; the legs, strong men, are bent. Then comes death: the
silver cord is snapped; the golden bowl is broken at the fountain.
The spirit returns to the God who gave it.

So as a young person, I may revel in the goodness of life and
living, knowing that my Creator lavishly pours out His goodness on
me. And as an older person, I may relax in the dignity and serenity
that comes when God sheds His light over me.

Ecclesiastes 10-12

My beloved is mine and I am his (Song of Solomon 2:16).

There are various explanations for the Song of Solomon: either Solomon is singing for his bride, or he is trying to seduce the bride who holds fast to her beloved shepherd, or the book is just a collection of songs about love in general. It is remarkable that all three views posit the same basic idea: there is a love relationship important enough to be described at length in this book of the Bible.

The love relationship described here reflects or symbolizes the love God has for His people and the response of His bride, the church. Paul's teaching that marriage is a reflection of the relationship between Christ and His church has its Old Testament counterpart here.

No other religion describes the bond between God and His people as a marriage. God gave Himself to me so completely that He can speak of His love for me as the affection a bridegroom has for his bride.

There is no theology that can explain fully how God's redemption works. I may have glimpses of understanding about various parts of redemption: regeneration, calling, atonement, and faith. I may even present these glimpses in logically formulated doctrines. But then it hits me. God loves me so much that He calls me His bride. He made a universe which seems to stretch for ever, yet He says to me, "You are Mine and I am yours." It sounds absurd, but it is true. The mystery of God's love is the mystery of marriage; the unity between Him and myself is as between two lovers. It's hard to believe, yet He tells me it is so.

Song of Solomon 1-3

I had put off my garment, how could I put it on? (Song of Solomon 5:3).

Faith is not swallowing dogma. Faith is to personally accept the love of God. Faith is difficult; it is so hard to believe that God could love me so much that He would give His Son for me.

In this passage, the bride describes how she reacts to this miracle of love. At her door, the bridegroom calls to her with all the tenderness of his heart. It is late, and a miserable night out; the bride answers that she is not willing to get out of bed, put on her clothes, and open the door for him. But when she hears his hands trying to open the door, she thinks better of it. She gets up and goes to the door, only to find that her lover is gone. Now she goes out into the city looking everywhere for him, but she cannot find him. Sick with love, she hopes desperately to be reunited with him.

What a beautiful description of the love relationship between God and His people, His bride! He stands at the door and knocks. He wants to commune with me, but He will not break the door open. Our relationship must be a mutual love affair.

But I don't want to respond to His call for I am comfortably in bed. He can stand in the dew of night and wait. Going to Him is too much bother. It can wait. Other things in life are more important than His love and mercy. So it seems to me. But my real problem is that I have never fully understood the miracle: He has loved me with an eternal love!

Then God goes on to show that my reluctance does not break the relationship between us. His Spirit pours love into my heart. As He seems to go away from me, He wakes up my love which sends me after Him. That is love divine!

Song of Solomon 4-6

Make haste, my beloved (Song of Solomon 8:14).

Generally, there has not been much calling and praying for Jesus' return in the church. There are songs in the hymnals about His second coming, but there is not much real waiting and looking for Him. When at the dedication service of a new church building, a pastor prayed that God would soon destroy the beautiful edifice in the final fire, the congregation was stunned and certainly not pleased. Jesus may come back, but He does not have to hurry. First I want to achieve and receive a lot of things. He can wait.

This verse from Solomon's Song disagrees wholeheartedly with this attitude. "Make haste, my beloved" is the same cry heard in the Revelation of John. "Come back soon, Lord Jesus."

Why does this prayer disappear from the minds of God's people? Probably because the love relationship is not as real as it should be anymore. God has become a stranger who showers His gifts upon me, but is not close to my heart. The gifts have taken my attention away from the Giver. Jesus' return is described as the end of this world, rather than as a reunion of lovers. This world is so precious to me that the thought of its end means more to me than the thought of reunion with my God.

But most of all, I forget how God badly wants to come and end this sin-broken world. The world still hates Him; satan still destroys the purity of His work; sickness and poverty and death are still blemishes on His creation. He loves this world so much that He longs to renew it. If I really love my Savior, I will realize that the process of salvation and redemption is not yet finished.

The fact that I do not long for the final reunion with Him shows how much I need such a reunion. The more my love for Him grows, the more my prayer will be, "Make haste, Lord Jesus; come soon."

Song of Solomon 7-8

Come now, let us reason together, says the Lord: though your sins are like scarlet, they shall be as white as snow (Isaiah 1:18).

Much in the world around me and in my own life should be improved: unholy lives, the neglect of the oppressed and the poor, the half-built kingdom of God. "Prophets" point out what must be done, and urge me to do it. But they often forget that my willingness to obey and my good intentions are not enough. A real prophet should point out that human failure is so pervasive that my own efforts can never succeed.

Isaiah certainly does not share in the optimism of pseudo-prophets. He calls Jerusalem Sodom and Gomorrah. Its sin is crying to high heaven. Worst of all, nobody seems to mind. The people still worship the Lord and bring sacrifices—but these actions are mere formalities to buy God's grace. The Lord is disgusted. Isaiah cannot yet call God's people to action. He tells them instead that God has to give a new start; He must forgive their sins.

Forgiveness does not seem to fit into the normal chain of thought: "I am bad; God wants me to be different; I will do my best to change." Without God's mercy, all my efforts will be in vain. My willingness accomplishes nothing.

God says, "Let us talk it over." He is not going to lay the whip over His people. God understands that when I am deep in debt, sheer despair may lead me to become more and more irresponsible. What is the sense of doing my best?

So God gives me a new start, new hope. He wipes out my debt completely and asks me to start all over again. The scarlet sins become the glorious white of freshly fallen snow. How that can be done is God's mystery. But in Jesus it has been done.

This passage calls for a daily reasoning with God. Then, in the mercies of my Lord, I can find the power to start all over again, each day again.

Isaiah 1-3

What more was there to do for my vineyard, that I have not done in it? (Isaiah 5:4).

In the entranceway of a German church stands a very simple statue of Christ. With His hands spread out, He looks into one's eyes, and the inscription underneath reads, "What more was there to do?" The statue almost makes a sermon redundant.

In this passage, Isaiah starts to sing a love song. People then, just as now, are always ready to hear a nice song of love. The love relationship between a bride and her bridegroom, between God and His people, is often described as a well-kept vineyard. Isaiah describes the careful cultivating of the vineyard in detail. The keeper has carefully chosen fertile soil, cleared it of stones, and then planted choice vines. He has built a watchtower from which to observe the gradual maturing of his vines and, in anticipation of a rich harvest, he has built a wine vat. But the end of the song has a terrible twist: the vineyard yields wild grapes. Literally, the words mean "stinking things." The conclusion is so unlike a comforting song of love. And that is exactly what Isaiah wants to make clear.

In relation to the love of God, my sins are stinking things. In the light of the love and constant care of the vineyard keeper, of my bridegroom, there are no words to describe my lack of faith. There is only the pathetic, imploring question, "What more could I have done?"

What more could the Lord do for me so that I would be compelled to worship Him in all my life? Jesus gave His blood for me; why am I not willing to give of my time and resources to His kingdom? If He forgave my sins, how can I be so harsh on others who have wronged me?

He filled my life with His goodness. Now I must yield good fruit.

Isaiah 4-6

Of the increase of his government and of peace there will be no end (Isaiah 9:7).

What does one do when the church of God is falling apart, the world is going from bad to worse, morality is deteriorating, and the anger of the Lord is growing? Perhaps the best one can hope for is that a small group remain faithful and try to survive.

Isaiah has every reason to despair. People don't listen to the Word of God anymore. Soon they will go into exile and they don't seem to care at all. The real church of God is shrinking. Darkness covers the earth and there seems to be no hope.

Then Isaiah, as God's prophet, speaks a message for the people. The message is not only that there will be a faithful remnant. That is part of his message, but that is only a small hope, a temporary comfort.

That hope is the seed of greater things. God, through His prophet, is looking forward to a glorious future. He will re-establish the kingship of David over all the earth. Righteous government and eternal peace will rule after the victory is won.

It may seem that the kingdom of Christ is shrinking, and that at best we may be able to retain some territory. But God says, "No, you have to see it differently. The world is still mine and someday it will realize that I rule. I am not giving up any area of life. I am not admitting defeat." It may be a terrible stage we are going through, but it is only a stage.

The prophet says that the old Davidic ideals will return in full glory. That is not just a dream. The Messiah is coming; in Christ, the dream becomes reality. He is the Wonderful Counsellor, the Mighty God, the Everlasting Father, the Prince of Peace. He is going to rule victorious. God has a claim on the world, His world.

Isaiah 7-9

There shall come forth a shoot from the stump of Jesse (Isaiah 11:1).

God's kingdom does not come steadily. It is not like a tree which gets taller and wider and more impressive by the year. Often God cuts down the tree and, when nobody expects anything anymore, new growth springs forth. Abel, the child on which the future depends, is killed, but Seth is born. The waters of the flood extinguish all hope for the world, but in the ark there is a new start. Abraham has a promise but not a son by whom it can be fulfilled. But when it seems most hopeless, the child is born. God's people die in Egyptian bondage, but the strong hand of God leads them out. The sea attempts to swallow them, but the Lord makes a path. The exile nearly extinguishes the hope for a continuation of Israel, but once again a temple is built in Jerusalem. When nobody expects anything, Jesus is born in Bethlehem. The stone is rolled in front of the tomb, but life is victorious over the power of death. When satan and antichrist celebrate their victory over the corpses of the witnesses slain in the streets of the world, Jesus will come back and show who really won.

Human hopes always fail, but God gives hope to the hopeless. Indeed, the "narrow escape" may be called the Lord's trademark.

Isaiah has discovered this in the light of God's Spirit. The kingship of David is destroyed. Jesse has no son. The tree has been felled, and only a stump remains. But there will be a new son born to Jesse. Out of the roots a new branch shoots forth.

God's work will end in glory, not because of our achievements, but only because of its grace. What a miracle! What a comfort!

Isaiah 10-12

I will make myself like the Most High (Isaiah 14:14).

The prophet's task is to reveal to his people that which can be seen only in the light of God's Word. Isaiah has to unmask the powers of the world to show how weak and ridiculous they are.

An exile in Babylon is the instrument by which God will purify His people. Babylon's power over Israel goes only as far as God deems necessary; Babylon becomes strong *because* of the will of God. God's children should always know this.

But listening to Babylon's boasts, I would never know! The rulers of Babylon call themselves the God of the Morning. They see themselves sitting like gods on the high mythical mountains of the north country, discussing matters and planning the fate of the world. To rise above the clouds; to call themselves equals of the Lord, the Most High, such aspirations motivate all their actions and views.

Such motives are still prevalent today. Science and technology's boasting resembles Babylon's claim to be like the Most High. Sometimes I even want to push God from His throne and occupy it myself, or use other powers to be my gods.

It is hard to believe that I would do such a thing. God in His mercy has given Himself to me, and now I want to remove Him from my scene? Here is another proof that sin is foolishness.

When I shout that I am the Dawn, the Light of the world, I hear His voice, "Walk in *My* light and all your days will be bright."

Isaiah 13-15

Though you plant pleasant plants . . . yet the harvest will flee away (Isaiah 17:10, 11).

Israel has forgotten the God of her salvation, the Rock of her refuge. Yet her people's lives seem pleasant and satisfying. It is nonsense to think that all the people who no longer worship God are experiencing gnawing spiritual hunger.

Isaiah describes life without God as the planting of pleasant plants. They grow as soon as I plant them. In contrast, life with God seems complicated; the process of sanctification takes such an agonizingly long time.

The process of forgetting God has been described by people as a kind of liberation. One can forget the obligations and restrictions of the law of God. Such forgetting can occur even among those who remain in the church. The strict preaching of Biblical truth is often a hurtful and painful experience. But when sermons remove the sharp edge from the gospel, people feel relieved and can relax. When the heavy yoke is off their shoulders, they feel better.

Isaiah does not deny that the easy plants are pleasant; he says only that they will never yield a harvest day. Weeds grow beautifully and have attractive flowers, but they are and always will be weeds. They not only are worthless, but they can even prevent the real harvest from yielding fruit. The only harvest for those "liberated" from God will be a day of grief. Eventually I will have to face my Maker, and on that day I will have no more time to produce a harvest for Him.

I must resist the blossoming, alluring attractions of a life without God. Such a life will never lead anywhere; it will never come to fruition. God invites me to live in Him. By bearing fruit, my joy may be full.

Isaiah 16-18

*In that day there will be an altar to the Lord in the midst of the land
of Egypt (Isaiah 19:19).*

Egypt is the super-power from which Israel escaped, centuries
ago, and Israel still remembers with awe the tremendous strength of
their God who led them out of the house of bondage.

But that escape years ago is not the greatest thing the Lord can
do. Isaiah has a dream. He envisions the Lord riding a cloud to
Egypt and conquering it. Everyone trembles in fear before Him.
Egypt, that awe-inspiring nation, has become a helpless slave, crying for mercy.

But the dream becomes even more beautiful. Instead of
revengefully punishing Egypt, the Lord turns their hearts to Him.
The conqueror will not put His foot on their necks; instead He will
win them over into His service. They will build an altar for the
Lord; they will worship with sacrifice and burnt offerings. And
God will heed their supplications and heal them. Furthermore,
Israel will be the center of the world powers. A highway will lead
from Egypt to Assyria through the territory of the Israelites and the
children of God will rule this earth.

Now, this is a beautiful dream, but it is only a dream.
Throughout history, nothing has happened that could even remotely be considered the fulfillment of this prophecy. Is it then a dream
that deceives God's people? By no means.

So far the church of God has been saved by God and has
found help in Him. It has been led out of the bondage of sin. That
is all well and good, but it is not God's ideal. He is using me to
achieve the *full* victory of His kingdom over all the powers of the
world. God claims Lordship over His church, but also over the entire cosmos. As His Lordship comes to pass, I, with my Lord, am
more than a conqueror.

Isaiah 19-21

I will place on his shoulder the key of the house of David (Isaiah 22:22).

This story seems rather meaningless. I know almost nothing about either Shebna *or* Eliakim. Shebna had the highest position in the nation under the king. He executed the king's decrees. On his shoulder was the key of David; he opened and none could shut, and he shut and none could open. This position was so important that in Revelation 3 Christ uses the same words to indicate His power under His Father.

Now I am told that Shebna loses his office and that Eliakim is appointed in his place. What revelation of God is in that?

This mini-story makes sense only if I read it in the context of God's dealing with His people. Shebna assumes that he is entitled to ride through the streets in splendid chariots. He is hardly aware of his role as a servant of God's people. He has even planned his burial. No cost will be spared to make a monument that will remind people for centuries of the tremendously important man Shebna.

The Lord gets very angry with him. Shebna's actions are typical of Israel in those days. Selfish striving for power and glory count more than humble obedience to God. God singles out one man to demonstrate how He thinks about this widespread attitude. He thrusts Shebna out of office and appoints an unknown man. God can do His work just as well through Eliakim.

God *does* use me in the ushering in of His kingdom. But the kingdom does *not* depend on my efforts. That is a humbling reality but also a great comfort. I can go ahead with my tasks boldly, knowing that when I fail, God will pick up the pieces.

Isaiah 22-24

They are shades, they will not arise (Isaiah 26:14).

A missionary attended a celebration: a shrine which housed the bones of a holy man was carried through the streets. The holy man was believed to be responsible for all the good fortune which the tribe had experienced. They pointed out to the missionary that he did not have any such thing around which to build a celebration. The missionary admitted that there were no bones to be carried around in the Christian religion. "Our Master rose from the grave and is alive" was his simple reply. "We do not carry a dead Christ around. That is the glory of the Bible."

In these beautiful chapters of Isaiah, I am told that God cannot be compared to anything upon earth. In Jesus Christ, He is the One who conquered death and lives forever. The rulers of this world, the lords that frighten me, the tyrants that make me cry are all dead. They are just shades; they will not arise. There is no longer any substance to them. Looking back, I can see that tyrants such as Hitler rule for only a short time. So, looking forward, I know that there may be terrible oppressors, but that there will be an end to them. Time passes, and they pass on with it. What remains is the kingdom of God.

Throughout history, various scientific theories have appeared to pose fundamental threats to Christianity. But now many of those theories are dead, and people laugh at some of the things once believed to be truth.

The art of living the Christian life is to maintain a sense of humor and see things as they really are, to realize *now* that all these forces will eventually pass away. This will enable me to do what Christ wants me to do.

My labor is not in vain in the risen Lord. It may not look like much, but in the end what is done for Jesus will remain while everything else turns to ashes.

Isaiah 25-27

For the bed is too short to stretch oneself on it, and the covering too narrow to wrap oneself in it (Isaiah 28:20).

Why should I bother to bring the gospel to people who try to live without it? Better to leave them alone; they have happiness and peace.

Religion is a very personal affair: if I want to live according to my belief, that is my business, but there is no need to push my belief on others. I should not bother with foreign missions or even with evangelism in my own neighborhood.

The Lord denounces such points of view. He tells me that only those who trust in Him can know real joy and peace. When people try to sleep through the Lord's calling, they will discover that the bed is too short. Having finally found a position of minimal discomfort, they will try to wrap themselves in a blanket against the cold of the night, but then they will find that the blanket is too narrow. No matter how they turn and twist, they will find no warmth or rest.

God loves to see people well cared for. And He knows that there is no rest apart from Him. When I see primitive tribes living in fear of their cruel gods and evil spirits, I know that they will never find rest. They may not be crying out for the gospel, but they are tossing and turning. In my own neighborhood, I see people claiming that life is good without God. Believing God's Word, I cannot take their claims too seriously. I cannot prove it, but I know it is so. So I will continue to go out and call and call.

Isaiah 28-30

Your eyes will see the king in his beauty (Isaiah 33:17).

Nobody knows exactly what Isaiah had in mind when he spoke these words. Was he referring to King Hezekiah or to some other king? Was he speaking of the Messiah? Was it God their King whom they would see in His beauty? It is not clear. But without a doubt, God's children will see their heavenly Father as their king who protects and rules them.

Isaiah 33 is a remarkable chapter. In the middle of sixty-six chapters of prophetic admonition and comfort, I am asked to look up and see my God.

Sometimes all these chapters seem repetitious and monotonous. But even an earthly father knows how many times he has to tell his children the same thing, over and over again. With patience and goodness, he calmly but firmly goes on to lead his sons and daughters on the right path. This is the way my Father in heaven deals with me. When I feel irritated or bored, He goes on speaking to me. I want something exciting, but He knows what matters most: His eternal love and patience with me.

It is comforting to know that the same message is not brought in vain. That is encouraging for ministers of the Word but also for parents, teachers, and all who spread God's good news.

And the same message can be brought in so many different ways. These sixty-six chapters show that the gospel is as varied as life, and that God's clear light is comprised of many different colors.

In the middle of the stream of God's words, I look up and see the King in His beauty.

Isaiah 31-33

The king's command was, "Do not answer him" (Isaiah 36:21).

Shouldn't I always be ready to answer those who question my relation to the Lord, ready to defend my beliefs? Not always.

The Rabshakeh of Assyria is assaulting Jerusalem with words. In the Hebrew language, he shouts propaganda that he hopes will undermine the Hebrew spirit. How can Hezekiah and his people hope for a victory over the almighty king of Assyria? The Rabshakeh knows that Israel trusts in the promises of the Lord, but he insinuates that they have more faith in an alliance with Egypt, which indeed is senseless. On the other hand, if they really trust in God, they are certainly in trouble. Look what happened to all the gods of the other peoples whom Assyria has conquered. Besides, all altars in the nation except the one in Jerusalem have been destroyed; their God must be angry with them—for aren't the more altars, the better.

When he shouts these words of ridicule, there is silence in Jerusalem. No comment. Because the Rabshakeh is trying to undermine their faith, an answer is pointless.

Sometimes I have to point to God's greatness with silence. When people ask questions that could bring them closer to God, I must always talk with them. But when they come to challenge my beliefs, hoping to shatter them, then, as John said in his epistle, I should not give them even the time of day. The majesty of God requires such a response.

When Jesus is accused by His enemies, He does not argue. He simply looks a person in the eye. His silence speaks volumes. I should follow His example.

Isaiah 34-36

Now Isaiah had said, "Let them take a cake of figs, and apply it to the boil, that he may recover" (Isaiah 38:21).

King Hezekiah has been suffering from an infected sore. Eventually it becomes clear that nothing will heal it. There is no medication for this boil; death seems imminent.

The king knows that help is available in his God and Father. Yes, the Lord has said that he will die. But Hezekiah also knows that his God is not an impersonal fate or destiny. One can talk as a child with this God. And he does not think it strange when God says that He will change His verdict and add fifteen years to his life.

Do I find this story hard to accept? In my scholastic doctrines, is there room for a Father who listens to His child and does the opposite of what He predicted? Hezekiah has no such problems. He believes that it can be done, and it happens. That is the simplicity of faith.

Then, as a sign, the Lord makes the shadows cast by the declining sun on the dial turn back ten steps. How could this occur? A small landslide, a tiny earthquake, a breaking of the sunlight in a different way? Who knows? Who cares? The Almighty One uses His creation to comfort His child.

My faith is sick if I don't believe in miracles. They are happening daily; if God deems it necessary for His kingdom and for me, He will do things that astonish me.

But then Isaiah also requests a cake of figs and puts it on the infected boil. That common, old-fashioned remedy is used to show that the Lord can also work miracles through medicine and surgery. That fact does not diminish God's greatness; it makes it even more awesome.

Isaiah 37-39

He will gather the lambs in His arms, He will carry them in His bosom (Isaiah 40:11).

This verse is a touching description of God's care for His people. The shepherd carrying the lamb in his arms has always appealed to children. Sculptors and painters have time and again portrayed God as the Good Shepherd. That emphasis is good, as long as it does not become sentimental.

Isaiah is describing how the Lord will bring His people home after the long years of exile. This part of the book is his great announcement of the end of the misery in Babylon, and of the imminent return to Jerusalem. The exiles must be heartened and comforted so that they can assume with joy the task of rebuilding the temple of God. They must be aware that their exile ends not just because of political actions. They have to recognize, in their return, the power and care of their God.

It is hard to describe God's actions as carrying lambs in His bosom. These are people who have sinned badly against their Father; they are stubborn and rebellious children who had to be punished severely in order to save the future of God's kingdom. Lambs? Bucking rams might be a better description.

Am I a lamb? Yes. I, the proud builder of my own destiny, the ruler of my own empire, am in God's eyes just a helpless lamb. He sent His Son to save me; to lead me and carry me. I struggled to get out of His arms, but through His Spirit, He did not let me go.

The other part of the picture is just as hard to visualize. God has hit His enemies hard in order to get His people free. To lead His nation back to the promised land, He had to use the strength of His hands and arms. Now with His almighty hands, He gently takes the lambs and carries them.

I am the lamb and my Father is the gentle Shepherd. Sometimes things are not what they seem.

Isaiah 40-42

And the rest of it he makes into a god, his idol (Isaiah 44:17).

Israel spent years of misery in Babylon because they turned and returned to idols. Now, when they return from exile, it is most important that their whole hearts be turned to the Lord in faithful service. This nation exists to make Bethlehem possible, and eventually to make possible the new Jerusalem in Jesus Christ when the worship of idols will never again lead them astray. Therefore, Isaiah hammers away at idolatry.

In this passage, Isaiah ridicules those who make idols. After long toil and labor, they have carved out an image that they will adore and worship. The shavings serve as kindling, and the remaining parts of the tree will be used as firewood. In other words, the idols are no better than any other wood that is burned to ashes in the fire. In fact, the wood that goes into the fireplace is *more* profitable than the rest. It at least provides warmth on a cold day, whereas the idols give no relief whatsoever.

Now I see: money, luxury, sex, social position, fun, entertainment—all have their place. They can bring warmth into life. But as soon as I make them an idol and start to worship and serve and trust them, I am doing a ridiculous thing. In themselves, these things are absolutely nothing; all the efforts and services pledged and given to them are good for nothing. How utterly ridiculous that people bow down and worship what has no value at all.

In my pride, I can make idols myself. But God has made me, and to Him belongs all honor.

Isaiah 43-45

For my own sake, for my own sake, I do it (Isaiah 48:11).

This does not sound good. I like the idea of a God who is always willing to help me, who loves to see me happy, whose whole activity can be described as salvation. To hear that the Lord does everything to His own glory seems a contradiction. Suddenly I see a God who is just as selfish as I sometimes am. As long as I give Him the glory He needs, I serve His purpose. But am I just His instrument? Where is the God of love? Surely His love is more than self-love.

Such reasoning shows a misunderstanding of the Biblical concept of the covenant. Certainly the Lord works for His own glory, but when He is my Father and I am His child, we share that glory. The idea that I am only one insignificant creature belonging to a far-away God is contrary to the Biblical message. I cannot be happy without a God who glorifies Himself. And He cannot glorify Himself without letting me share in His joy.

God says that He does *it* only for His own sake. *It* means the exile and the return from it, a triumph over Babylonian power, and the building of the new nation and temple. But above all, *it* means His loving return to His people. After all their sin, He still hangs on to them and wants them to hang on to Him.

God wants to make clear now that all this is done for His sake. I cannot just relax and say "Thank you." I must seek to glorify Him. Every gift He gives me is also a mandate. And in this way God honors not only Himself but also me. He emphasizes the fact that, through His regeneration, I am useable again for His kingdom. He employs me; He grants me a goal to live for. I must see to it that everything in this world conforms to His will and to the glory of His name.

When it is not my desire to honor Him, I will know no joy of salvation either. They both rest in my God.

Isaiah 46-48

The Lord God has opened my ear, and I was not rebellious (Isaiah 50:5).

Speech is a great gift. The prophet tells me in this chapter that the Lord God has given him the tongue of those who are taught. That means that he is well-spoken. He is able to speak as if he were a rhetorician trained in effective communication. That is very important: the best message, conveyed to my neighbor in a crude, unpleasant, or a hesitant way, will have little effect. A word of comfort to the weary and discouraged fellowman must be carefully planned and gracefully expressed. It is easy to hurt someone when I use the wrong words to express good ideas.

But perhaps it is even more important that the Lord gives an ear to listen. I have to listen to God before I speak. It must not be my own ideas that I bring to others. What is the will of God? What is His message? I cannot help anyone unless I speak the words of the Lord. What God tells me to pass on may not please me. But I must not rebel; I cannot question the Lord's message. I have to be faithful to His Word. Only then, only after I have given my ear to Him, can the Lord use me as His mouthpiece.

But I will not be prophetic without one more element. I have to listen to the weary, as the prophet says, and understand their problems so that the word I bring them may be appropriate to their needs. I would not go to a doctor who writes a remedy for me before he has heard and seen what is wrong with me. I must listen first. The Lord must give me that patient ear, for often the wounded soul needs someone to listen.

People must hear something of Jesus in me. God's Word is a balm to make the wounded whole.

Isaiah 49-51

The Lord has laid on him the iniquity of us all (Isaiah 53:6).

Isaiah 53 is not hard to understand. Most people grasp it at once, but then wonder how the Old Testament can so accurately prophesy the events of the New Testament. Whom actually did the prophet have in mind? Was it a king or another person in Israel's history? Was it Israel itself? Or was the Spirit of prophecy really so strong that he could see the dying Christ on the cross already? Biblical scholars are still contending this point; however, in Acts 8:32-35, Philip tells the eunuch that the passage speaks of Jesus. What the prophet had in mind is immaterial. What the Holy Spirit meant is sufficient.

But what really puzzles me is how my iniquity can be laid on another. How, after I hurt God and my neighbor, can this guilt be lifted from my shoulders and put on the shoulders of the Son of Man? This substitution goes against all my inclinations. *I* should suffer for what I did.

Besides, atonement hurts my pride. I myself should pay for what I did. Isn't it cowardly to let someone else bear the burden of my ruined life? Am I so helpless that the Son of God has to step in and suffer in my place?

Unbelievers, challengers of the faith, say that it is easy to be a Christian: you can do anything you want and then simply put your iniquity on the shoulders of Jesus Christ. And then you can start living it up again. Such religion is too cheap to be attractive.

Others have blamed the confession of this verse for inaction in the Christian church. If I can give my sins away, I don't feel responsible anymore for the well-being of my neighbor and for the honor of God.

But as soon as I humble myself and put my iniquity on Jesus' shoulders, such problems disappear. My only salvation is that Jesus stands in my place. And then I ask, "Lord, what may I do for You?"

Isaiah 52-54

My house shall be called a house of prayer for all peoples (Isaiah 56:7).

Two groups of people were not allowed to enter into the house of God even though they believed in Him and were willing to serve Him. Foreigners could join themselves to the Lord, but their status remained different from the native Israelite's status. Israel's ethnic purity had to be protected. Foreigners had to accept the fact that they could believe in God but still did not share in all His benefits. No doubt, though, they longed to mingle with the crowd in the temple grounds and to minister unto the Lord.

The second group excluded from the temple were the eunuchs. Because their job was to look after the harems, these people were forcefully deprived of the ability to enter marriage and have children. God's covenant is made with His people and their children; the coming of the Redeemer required procreation, and they had no part in that. So for them too the temple was a forbidden area. And they too felt left out.

It is debatable whether Israel was obeying God's commandments concerning foreigners and eunuchs. Perhaps they were. Or perhaps it was just their exclusivistic pride that barred these groups from full fellowship.

But now the prophet speaks comfortingly to these forgotten groups of believers. The Lord says, "My house shall be for all kinds of people." As long as they love the Lord, worship on Sabbath days, and hold fast to the covenant, they may enter and serve God just like anybody else. The eunuchs receive more than sons and daughters; they receive an everlasting name. And the foreigners feel at home.

What about the lonely and forgotten people on the fringes of my church, those who are different and perhaps hard to understand, those that are somewhat foreign to our customs? Jesus opens His arms wide for them. Can I then bar them?

Isaiah 55-57

He who departs from evil makes himself a prey (Isaiah 59:15).

The angels in heaven may sing for joy when a sinner departs from evil, but he should not expect the same response on earth. The prophet describes what happens when somebody decides to follow the Lord's commandments. In a "dog-eat-dog" society, I will make myself the prey if I don't want to be the hunter.

This message is very discouraging. First of all, the situation described is so bad that it must infuriate anyone who loves the Lord. How can this sorry condition exist in the people chosen by the Lord to serve Him? Just where one should find shelter against the sinful practices of the world, the prospective "do-gooder" is threatened.

But secondly, this discouraging message makes it harder to choose Christ. I can assume that if I follow the Lord, people will not praise me. It will be an uphill battle. In a degenerate society, perhaps there is no room for Christ-imitators anymore.

Similarly, a nation may find it hazardous to stick to God's laws. For example, it is not easy to reduce nuclear arms, even if a nation feels that the use of nuclear arms is wrong. When every nation has them, it is risky to do without.

Should I still depart from evil and choose the dangerous path? If I want to follow Jesus, I have to. He became the prey of evil powers and did not hesitate to face the hostility that made life impossible for Him. He knew that in the end the evil powers will lose *because* He became their prey.

Now I can take whatever will come. I would rather depart from evil than from my Savior, even though I am warned that it will be hard for me—but just for the time being.

Isaiah 58-60

Take no rest, and give him no rest until he establishes Jerusalem (Isaiah 62:6-7).

Something is unusual about these words of Scripture. I know that I have to pray, "Your kingdom come." But at the same time, I know that God will take care of that anyway. He must be happy to hear that I agree with His plans and work, but do they really advance His cause? Shouldn't I leave the establishing of Jerusalem to Him?

The prophet uses strong language to wake me up; he says "Give the Lord no rest." Just as a child nags his parents until they finally get around to filling his demands, so I have to go after the Lord. What a strange metaphor. It suggests that the Lord wants to take it easy, but I have to disturb His quiet peace.

Is this a true description of the situation? Of course not. But as a warning against all the laziness in my prayers, the Lord says, "Don't take it easy on Me. Insist in your prayers; pray without ceasing; never give up." I should keep on hoping and asking in spite of disappointments and frustrations. In Gethsemane, Jesus prayed three times. Only after three prayer sessions did the Lord tell Paul that he should accept his thorn in the flesh. The Lord wakes me up by telling me that I should wake Him up.

The other strange idea in this text is that I should not take a rest until the Lord establishes Jerusalem. Yes, I can see that the Lord builds His church and I should also build it. But that is not what the prophet says. He tells me I have to work hard so that the Lord can do the work. There is no reason for me to feel any satisfaction about what I have done. When I am working, God is doing the work. On the other hand, when I despair of my own efforts and successes, I know that all is in His hands.

Isaiah 61-63

The lion shall eat straw like the ox (Isaiah 65:25).

Jesus said, "I thank You, Father, Lord of heaven and earth, that You have hidden these things from the wise and understanding and revealed them to babes." Scientists will smile condescendingly when I, in my childish naiveté, tell them that the lion shall eat straw like the ox. They will make it clear that a lion is a carnivorous animal whose digestive system cannot utilize straw. They will point out that the balance in nature requires animals to devour each other. And if they are somewhat "religious," they may also add that this is the will and intention of the Creator.

When I see films or pictures of lions, I admire their beauty, strength and dignity. But when I see this kingly beast attack, kill, and devour a graceful deer, I feel sick. Even though I know all the "natural" reasons, it still hurts to see it.

Now God uses this feeling of repulsion to point out what He is going to do at the end of time. He tells me that He will change things so that cruelty and hurt will disappear from His creation. Perhaps in His new world the things mentioned in this chapter will become a reality; it is not beyond Him to do it. But God is not giving details of what the future will be like. Rather, He wants to assure me that there will be nothing offensive in the new heaven and new earth, nothing that will hurt me or revolt me.

There are so many other things in life that I have learned to accept, though they disgust me. Now God says I don't have to accept them. They may be necessary preparation for the shalom that is coming. But God will heal all brokenness; He will create wholeness once again.

The future is not determined by my romantic feelings about lions and lambs grazing together and a child leading them by the hand. But I can smile, knowing that God will restore that pastoral quality, that wholeness, that shalom to His world. And only babes see it.

Isaiah 64-66

I see a rod of almond (Jeremiah 1:11).

When the almond tree is blossoming, the winter is over and the beauty of springtime is just around the corner. Its majestic white flowers promise renewed life long before leaves appear on the tree. When Jeremiah envisions a blossoming almond branch, he knows that the long winter of God's waiting is over and that once again the Lord is going to do great things in Israel. The almond tree has been called the waker tree because it wakes up the spring. So the Lord tells Jeremiah that He is wide awake and ready to perform His Word.

But unbelievably, the Lord has called a mere youth to be His messenger. Jeremiah was probably not more than 14 or 15 at the time. What would I say about a young boy who claims to be a prophet of God? Shouldn't he first learn to show respect for his elders? Won't he lack the wisdom to bring the message so that it will be accepted?

Jeremiah's youth and inexperience show. He speaks fierce words and warnings. He is quite temperamental and easily upset. Furthermore, his message is revolting. He tells his people that the Lord wants them to discontinue their resistance, accept their exile, and through the darkness come to the light. He warns them of doom, but also says that they cannot and should not evade it. Therefore, he is locked in prison several times, and his work seems ineffectual.

If only the church would speak more comfortingly, if only its leaders had more wisdom, if only the approach were more appealing, the church might have more influence on the world.

But the Lord tells me that He works through the unexpected. If I can hear His voice, even when brought by a 15-year-old boy who speaks of unpleasant things, then I know the Lord is working.

As surely as the almond flowers are there, the springtime of God will come.

Jeremiah 1-3

Break up your fallow ground, and sow not among thorns (Jeremiah 4:3).

I can hardly believe that any farmer would throw his seed upon rock-hard soil in the spring without first plowing the fields or would seed a piece of land that is full of thorns. A child would know not to expect a harvest.

In this text, Jeremiah instructs the people to let the land lie fallow for a year. When the harmful elements have died out, they can plow and cultivate and start building toward a good crop. Before starting the positive work, they have to do a lot of negative work.

This lesson is not, however, directed to the farmers, but to the leaders of God's people. Busy trying to build a new future for Judah, they organize everything conceivable and call the people to action. But Jeremiah tells them in the name of the Lord that this is the wrong approach. They must first try to find out what was wrong and remove it. It is not so bad for the soil to lie fallow for a year. Examine your hearts and your deeds, remove the sinful thoughts and actions, and *then* go on to more positive actions.

Jeremiah's advice is not well accepted. I hate to first look into problems, and do preparatory work, and plow, and kill weeds, and rip out thorns. Such labor shows no easy results.

Perhaps I am continually frustrated because I have not gone to the roots of problems. Hasty patchwork is all that I can show—and no results. In church and state, in labor and science, the lesson must be learned. Without a good foundation first, the whole structure will tumble.

Fallow ground precedes a rich harvest. I need the Holy Spirit to show me the thorns and then proceed to rip them out.

Jeremiah 4-6

Will you say, "We are delivered!" only to go on doing all these abominations? (Jeremiah 7:10).

It is comforting to have the temple of God in Jerusalem. The enemies will fear the powerful God who lives there. But much more important, the temple is good protection against the wrath of God. The Lord can hardly do anything against His own temple! The temple is a shield against pending danger. In addition, there is an altar in the temple. Sins are atoned there; in the temple, there is deliverance from sin. Surely the Lord cannot act against His own delivered children, His redeemed. As long as they can keep up the temple, they are safe.

This sense of security is blasted away by Jeremiah. Israel can chant all day, "This is the temple of the Lord, the temple of the Lord, the temple of the Lord." But God is not made inactive by a building. The temple means that God lives among His people, and deliverance means that they are not slaves to sin anymore. How is it possible that they confess God's presence and forgiveness and still commit abominable sins? Abominations can hardly be gilded over by pious words about deliverance.

The problem still exists today. The church, despite its proclamation of the gospel, does so little to show what it means to be delivered. What is the influence of Jesus' blood on my life? Can I just sing of forgiveness and wend my way to heaven? Or should I realize that I have to go through this world doing all that I can toward the coming of God's kingdom? Why have Christians had so little to say and to do about terrible political and social sins? So much more than "souls" needs to be delivered from the power of satan. If there is no Christian action, songs of deliverance are worthless lullabies.

"Jesus saves." Yes! But what for?

Jeremiah 7-9

Let us destroy the tree with its fruit (Jeremiah 11:19).

Jesus said, "A prophet is not without honor except in his own country and in his own house." That is what has happened to Jeremiah. In Anathoth, Jeremiah's birthplace, the people are not very proud of their native son. Sure, he is one of those bright boys who at fifteen is serving the Lord. He does get a hearing, though not a friendly one. But even in his home town, no one defends him. Instead, a plot is hatched to kill him. No one wants to hear his prophecies; in fact, people are willing to kill him in order to put an end to them. When they destroy the tree, the fruits of his words will be cut off too.

Why is it that people become so angry in their opposition to the Word of God? People dislike the knife cutting out their evil deeds; that kind of surgery hurts.

Religious leaders should question their message when tremendous crowds enjoy their meetings. When Jesus preaches, the crowds slowly but surely turn away from Him. Paul gets into plenty of trouble. Peter was probably crucified for his preaching of the Word. And Jesus said that if I follow Him, I, too, will suffer persecution and tribulation.

My faith is bound to meet with resistance and even hatred. I am on the right track when I am persecuted for Jesus' sake. Of course, persecution does not include the times when things go badly for me because of my own sin. But when I try to speak and live the Word of Jesus, I will know conflicts. The world will be offended when I proclaim Christ and denounce anti-Christian spirits. There is, however, no reason to be sad about conflict. No reaction too often means there is no action. People's reactions show that God is still working. And when He works, He is going to win.

Jeremiah 10-12

We acknowledge our wickedness, O Lord, and the iniquity of our fathers (Jeremiah 14:20).

This is not just a nice rhetorical technique, this speaking of "our" wickedness. Jeremiah would be fully entitled to say "your," and often he does. But "your" changes to "our" when he talks about rebellion against the Lord. He is one with the sinful people around him, even though he does not participate actively in their crimes. As is often done in Bible times, he assumes the guilt of their fathers as his own. But in these days, surely I carry no responsibility for what my fathers have done. Yes, I do. Human beings are one in their guilt.

The prophet has two positions. On the one hand, he speaks on behalf of God to rebuke the people sharply. But he also is a human being who feels at one with the people around him.

This dual role is most clearly demonstrated in our Savior. He is the one sent by the Father to bring His Word. But at the same time, He is the Son of Man and as such shares in our guilt and carries it.

Jeremiah identifies himself with the nation of sinners so that he might reach them, even though they may not listen. They must not turn away because of a haughty approach. They must hear in his words the voice of the Good Shepherd calling His lambs to come home.

Perhaps that is why I sometimes cannot reach the people around me when I talk about the Lord. If I isolate myself from them, they will reject me as a stranger. They will dislike my holier-than-thou attitude so much that they will reject the message. It is easy to say that people are stubborn and turn away from me because they turn away from God, but maybe the problem is my own approach. On my knees, I must realize that, in spite of all the grace of God, I am still a sinner. Then, along with all my brothers and sisters, I can speak of *our* Father who is in heaven.

Jeremiah 13-15

You shall not take a wife (Jeremiah 16:1).

Today, many men prefer to stay single. But in Jeremiah's time, bachelorhood is a very unusual status and a real hardship. Not only is it difficult to get by on one's own—there are no modern conveniences, no restaurants, no fully serviced apartments —but in Israel it is completely out of line to remain single. Men had a tremendous incentive to have a family: God's kingdom had to come through His people.

Yet, God demands that His servant Jeremiah make this sacrifice. The message of the coming exile is so real that already now Jeremiah has to accept the consequences. In those days of tribulation, it will be irresponsible to have a wife and children. Aware of a troubled future, Jeremiah knows that he has no right to get married.

If I believe the Word of God, I have to act according to it. If I speak one way and act another, I lose my credibility. People don't want to listen to thundering voices calling to repentance and advocating a sober lifestyle unless they see the preachers heeding those words themselves. It is silly to talk with tears in my eyes about the starving of the world while I continue to stuff myself and my children with all the goodies I can buy.

Jeremiah is told not to go feasting and sitting with people. Being a messenger of God requires personal sacrifice. Jeremiah can convey his deep concern about the whole sad situation in Judah by staying away from the joys of life.

Being in the service of my Father may demand a lot from me. But what if I gained the whole world and would lose my place in His kingdom?

Jeremiah 16-18

Perhaps the Lord will deal with us according to all his wonderful deeds (Jeremiah 21:2).

The prophet Jeremiah gets a call from the royal palace to give advice in political matters. Now Jeremiah is not respected at all, his own town folk tried to kill him, he has been thrown into prison, and nobody likes his sermons. Now finally he gets some recognition! But Jeremiah sees through this request for help, courageously he refuses to give a friendly response to King Zedekiah's humble plea for help.

Zedekiah's appeal sounds good. The king refers to the great actions of the Lord in the past; he seems to respect the wonderful deeds of the God of the covenant. But under his pious and humble words, lurk hypocrisy and deceit. Zedekiah says the king of Babylon is preparing to make war against him, but he does not admit the trouble exists because he himself rebelled against that king, breaking his solemn oath of obedience. Zedekiah acts as if he wants to hear the Lord's opinion. However, Zedekiah knows that the Lord has said constantly that the only way to salvation is to submit first to Babylon and then, through the exile, make a new start. But the king is determined to fight the armies of Babylon no matter what the Lord says. Maybe he can trick Jeremiah and get his support. Jeremiah's endorsement would convince everybody in Judah that the king's position was strong.

But it soon becomes clear that no king on earth can mock the Lord or fool Him. God sees right through his trickery. Zedekiah will be defeated by the king of Babylon, and his eyes will be put out after he sees his own sons slain.

It is good to inquire the will of the Lord, it is good to study His Word, but not with a deceiving heart. If I just want to hear approval for my own ideas and plans, then I am on the wrong track. God can save those who come to Him. But He will not save those who only act as if they come.

Jeremiah 19-21

Like these good figs, so I will regard as good the exiles from Judah (Jeremiah 24:5).

Jeremiah sees in a vision two baskets of figs, the one extremely bad, the other one very good. The Lord tells him that the basket of good figs symbolizes the children of Judah who have been deported into exile some years ago; the other basket symbolizes the group that remained at Jerusalem to take care of the temple and the service of the Lord.

It would seem obvious to me what the bad figs represent. In Babylon, idols surround God's people. It is extremely hard to keep the Sabbath when no one around knows about it. It is next to impossible to get the foods prescribed in the law of God. The feasts cannot be celebrated at the right times because they are not legal holidays. In short, the exiles can hardly be the faithful people of God.

That means that the good figs must represent those in Jerusalem. They have every opportunity to do the right things. They stick meticulously to the laws of God and pride themselves in it.

Now, through Jeremiah, the Lord gives this group a devastating blow. Bad, inedible figs—that is what they are. The people in exile are not good either, but they are regarded as such by the Lord. In the hardship of the Babylonian surroundings, they will have their faith purified and hardened as steel in the smelting pot. In the relatively comfortable life in Jerusalem there is no hope for the people; however, in the exile, the Lord will make Judah again what they should be, God's chosen people, ready, willing, and able to serve Him.

This vision of Jeremiah teaches me not to judge the church of God too quickly. I may look down on small, young churches or mission churches. Their lifestyle may be different from mine; their worship may be less traditional. But their faith could be stronger and more active than mine.

More than that, this passage forces me to examine myself and to answer the question, "Am *I* a living church member?"

Jeremiah 22-24

I made all the nations to whom the Lord sent me drink it (Jeremiah 25:17).

I sometimes dull the sharp sword of God's Word with my conventionality. But the Lord certainly isn't bound by convention.

The Lord tells Jeremiah to put on a play, probably near the temple. His faithful co-workers are to take various parts. All the nations and tribes between Egypt and Babylon are played by different people. Now Jeremiah gives each player a cup of wine. They each have to drink till they get drunk, vomit, stagger and fall. It is quite a spectacle: in the end they are all lying around in their own dirt, too drunk to get up anymore.

Now the Lord reveals through His servant the meaning of this play. All the nations who have rebelled against the Lord will have to drink the cup of God's wrath until they can no longer stand on their feet. Jerusalem is no exception; God treats them just as the other nations. The end result, that no one will stand before the Lord, is made graphic by a drunken group of people. Some of the people had refused to drink the cup, but God said that they had to drink. The will of God cannot be resisted. There is no escape.

I can imagine the impact this repulsive and shocking play had on its audience. When the message of the Lord becomes visual, becomes real, people are shaken and sobered.

Today, no one would teach God's truth in such a way. God's people would find it offensive. But perhaps that only shows that we are not willing to accept the reality which is grimmer and tougher than such a play. The Lord wants to open my eyes and ears. I had better look and listen.

Jeremiah 25-27

Seek the welfare of the city where I have sent you into exile (Jeremiah 29:7).

The people from Judah who have been deported to Babylon have problems discerning their proper relation to the world around them. Suddenly life is so different from their former well-protected existence in Judah. Their natural instincts tell them to resist their new government, to show their resentment against the deportation, to take revenge as often as they can. Also, they hope that they will spend only a very short time in Babylon. Surely, the Lord will soon lead them back to the promised land.

But this is not the way the Lord wants His people to live. Now that the danger and misery of the deportation are over, Jeremiah calls on the people to marry, to have children, and to find a job. The exile will not be short. It will take a long time of waiting to purge the children of Israel from their sinful ways.

As Paul pointed out to the Thessalonians, while we are waiting for the Lord's coming, we may not abandon our responsibilities. We have to work in this world as full-fledged citizens. This is God's world. Even Babylon belongs to Him. Our lives and work and relationships count. An attitude of resentment is negative and wrong. Pray for the city. Seek its welfare.

It is dangerous, admittedly. Some people start to like life in Babylon so much that they lose themselves in the world around them and never return to Jerusalem.

Still, I have to know that I am a child of the God who owns the world. Isolation is comfortable, but not the right answer. I should keep my identity as a Christian and then be a blessing in the name of Him who sent me here.

Jeremiah 28-30

I bought the field at Anathoth (Jeremiah 32:9).

Jerusalem is under siege, Anathoth is in the hands of the enemies, and Hanamel tries to sell his Anathoth property to Jeremiah. Of course, this is utterly ridiculous; the field is not worth a nickel anymore. Moreover, Jeremiah would seem to be the last person to try to sell it to, for he preaches that there is no hope of the enemy losing the battle, that, in fact, a long exile is inevitable. Nevertheless, Jeremiah buys the land, paying the full amount that would have been paid if there had not been a war. He wants the deed in duplicate, well kept in some kind of a safe. This must prove that preachers are not very clever businessmen.

Not really. The Lord has told Jeremiah to buy this land. Indeed there is no hope for immediate use of the field. But Jeremiah must tell the people by this transaction that after the exile there will surely be a return. And he wants a share in that coming kingdom of God.

It is good to spend my money on the "lost" causes in the world. There must always be plenty of money for Christian education, because children ensure the future God promises. Church and missions will need money that I could well use for many other things, but never for anything more important than the victory of God's kingdom in this world. When I use my possessions to help care for the helpless and oppressed, people will call me stupid. But Jesus tells me that I will have a treasure in heaven where it will never devalue. To spend for the kingdom is wise in the eyes of the Lord.

Jeremiah will never occupy the newly-acquired field. After his death, the deed will pass to some relative of his. But this purchase serves to comfort himself and others.

As a Christian, I have God's promise in my hands. And my share in it.

Jeremiah 31-33

The king would cut them off with a penknife and throw them into the fire (Jeremiah 36:23).

Baruch, Jeremiah's secretary, has written all the prophecies of the past years on a scroll, a tremendous achievement in itself. When he reads the words of the book to all the people who come to the temple to seek the face of the Lord in a fast, the response is tremendous. Suddenly the Word of God is respected. The forgotten and maltreated prophet finds new influence. His work is not in vain.

Soon the leaders of Judah become aware of the goings-on. They take the scroll to the royal palace; eventually King Jehoiakim is willing to sit and listen to his servant Jehudi read the scroll. It is more than Jeremiah could have hoped or prayed for.

But the king listens without any emotion. And as soon as a piece of the scroll is read, he cuts it off and tosses it into the fireplace. The invaluable work of weeks and months is destroyed by the whim of the king. Manuscripts of any type are so rare that they generally are respected, whether one agrees with or is interested in what the scroll has to say. But even worse than the king's disrespect for the manuscript is his disrespect for the Lord. His brazen, defiant gestures show that he could not care less for the Lord God of Israel and Judah. The scribes around the king urge him at least to show the scroll some common decency. But his hostility destroys anything.

I hear jokes about the Bible; people poke fun at Christian doctrines and Biblical truths. They use the name of God in vain so much that it gives me shivers. They become more openly derisive of the laws established by God. Is this the point at which the king and so many others slam the door on the Lord? They are, in effect, casting out the Holy Spirit and, with Him, the chance to repentance.

Now God does not send a stroke of lightning to consume this contemptible king. In His calm majesty, He tells Jeremiah to have another copy made. God's Word is never conquered. Who is the loser?

Jeremiah 34-36

*Then they drew Jeremiah up with ropes and lifted him out of the
cistern (Jeremiah 38:13).*

Jeremiah is surrounded by weaklings. The princes of Judah
hate Jeremiah's message, and they ask the king for permission to
kill him. The wishy-washy king does not know what to do, but
reluctantly he grants permission. However, the spineless princes
don't have the nerve to kill this man of God directly, so they throw
him down a well where he will die eventually.

But Ebed-melech has deep respect for Jeremiah, and he requests the king to allow him to save the prophet. And again the in-
decisive king changes his mind and grants Ebed-melech his request.
Later the king even honors the prophet by asking him what the will
of the Lord is. When Jeremiah advises he surrender to the Chal-
deans, King Zedekiah has to admit he is afraid to take any action at
all.

Among such a weak-kneed troup, Ebed-melech stands out as
the only one who knows what is right and who acts according to
conscience. He is an Ethiopian, a black man. The Israelites felt that
a curse had been cast upon the Negroid race in Noah's days and
that that curse still held. Ebed-melech had been made a eunuch and
was forced to serve in the courts doing tasks nobody else wanted.
But, though it seems unlikely, this man trusts in the Lord (Jeremiah
39:18), and it is the fear of the God of Judah that brings him to this
action.

He is not going to save Jeremiah's life in a sneaky way. He
openly goes to the king, taking other men along. He stands strong
when all the respected people waver.

This is not a story to glorify black men. We all are sinful, black
and white. But here is a good Samaritan, a person sent by God to
put the king and his princes to shame. He reflects the love of Jesus
who showed mercy and healing.

In a cruel world, the Lord leaves no servant of His alone.

Jeremiah 37-39

Ishmael the son of Nethaniah and the men with him slew them (Jeremiah 41:7).

The life of Judah is snuffed out completely. The whole population is carted off to Babylon, and all hope dies.

However, a few people are left behind to manage what remains of the promised land. They are able to appoint competent leadership, organize themselves, and get help from army groups that had hid themselves in the woods. Slowly but surely, something is growing again. Could this be the first flicker of a rising Judah? Might there soon be a fire blazing in Jerusalem again?

But the king of the Ammonites is threatened by this possible new beginning, and so he engages a man of Judah's royal family to kill Gedaliah, the leader of Judah appointed by the Babylonian king. Then the whole new beginning starts to disintegrate. Indeed, Gedaliah is murdered with all his men. No one is left to take political command. Then Judah's religious leadership is extinguished. Eighty devoted men who come to Jerusalem to bring offerings to the Lord are killed treacherously. Ten bargain to save their lives, but afterward they have no place in the service of God.

The last flickering embers of hope are now extinguished, and it is cold and dark in Judah.

That is exactly the way the Lord wants it. Seventy years from now the glorious return of the exiles to Jerusalem will attest to the mercies of God. Then, and only then will the temple be rebuilt and Israel become a nation again.

No cheap shortcuts fit into God's plan. When satan offers Jesus a shortcut to kingship over the world, He refuses. When at the Mount of Transfiguration Peter suggests that Jesus rest on His laurels, Jesus chooses instead to go to the cross.

When I am dead in myself and totally without hope, then I will be made alive. God saves completely.

Jeremiah 40-42

What I have built I am breaking down (Jeremiah 45:4).

This passage contains a complaint from Baruch, Jeremiah's closest co-worker and secretary. He feels that the Lord should give more attention to his efforts and toil for His kingdom. Baruch has tried to build up and it seems that God is breaking his work down again; he is tired and discouraged.

The Lord tells Baruch that his analysis of the situation is not quite right. It is not true that I do the building and the Lord breaks down. God Himself is the one who both builds and breaks down. It is essential for the future of God's people that they go through the ordeal of total breakdown before they can serve Him again. Now this is not easy for the Lord either. He rejoiced when that beautiful temple was built, when Israel was His own glorious land. It is not easy to pluck out and break up. But it is the only way to renewal.

One springtime, I saw that fields of beautiful nursery rhododendrons were ready to bloom. But the next day I saw that the owners had nipped all the buds. The nursery owner explained that by pruning out the flowers, the roots grow stronger and the plants can eventually be transplanted in people's gardens to bloom for their enjoyment.

This is God's way of working in my life too. Sometimes I cannot see much spiritual growth blossoming. But that does not mean that the Lord is not working. Growth can also be underground, where the root system develops and gets ready both for harder days and for richer blessings.

Baruch was told that he would find his life. So do I in Him.

Jeremiah 43-45

Was not Israel a derision to you? (Jeremiah 48:27).

A few loose ends have to be tied up before Jeremiah's prophecy can be finished. One is the impression that the exile of God's people makes on the surrounding nations. They watch with broad grins on their faces while Judah is being punished.

Secular people have their own ideas about God, the church, and personal happiness. They turn away convinced that it does not mean anything to be a church member, a believer. Those who believe experience just as much misery as non-believers, perhaps more.

The Lord will not tolerate this. When a father is punishing his son, he will be angry at those who poke fun at the situation. The Lord wants to make it clear that His dealings with His church are nobody's business but His. All the nations who are rejoicing in Judah's defeat are told that if God does this to His own people whom He loves, then those who reject Him can expect an even heavier judgment.

I should not despair when God, in love, goes to the roots of my problems to heal and to cure. I should not hang my head when people around me start wondering. And when satan and my old self tell me that apparently God cannot help, that God is not a God of love, God Himself comes to say that He will wipe the smirks off sceptics' faces.

As an indignant father, God protects His children even while He deals harshly with them. When people deride Jesus on Golgotha, the earth quakes, the rocks split, and the sun disappears. The Antichrist will laugh at the end of time, but that grin will disappear very quickly. He will find out that my Father cares.

Jeremiah 46-48

When you finish reading this book, bind a stone to it, and cast it into the midst of the Euphrates (Jeremiah 51:63).

Jeremiah never went along with his people to Babylon. He stayed for a while in Jerusalem and then was taken along with a small group going to Egypt. There he died, having no contact with the exiles in their new country.

Or almost no contact.

Some time before the exile, a delegation had gone to Babylon, probably to pay respect and tribute to the king there. On this humiliating trip, a man Jeremiah knew took along a book in which Jeremiah had written all the prophecies against Babylon. Seraiah was told to read this book aloud at the Euphrates river and then to bind a stone to it and cast it in the river.

It was a strange symbolic gesture. Nobody from Judah was as yet in Babylon. Still, when told to the people back home, this was a powerful story. When the exiles eventually arrived in Babylon, they would find out that God was already there with His Word, waiting for them. Jesus assures me that when I get into the deepest misery, when I experience the most difficult tribulations, He has been there, and He *is* there waiting for me. God does not lead me down dead-end streets, no matter how forbidding the path looks.

But the symbolic meaning of the book in the river is richer still. Eventually Babylon herself will fall to one of the strongest nations in the history of the world. The new conquerers will believe that they have everything under their control. But no: a time bomb waits in the Euphrates river. It may take seventy years, but eventually the Word of God spoken so many days before will be fulfilled. At God's appointed time, it will be clear that no power on earth can stop Him. Jeremiah will have died and the people who heard the story will have passed it on to their children. But God's Word lives. That is my comfort.

After all the harsh words of Jeremiah, the book ends with hope. God never fails.

Jeremiah 49-52

His mercies never come to an end; they are new every morning; great is thy faithfulness (Lamentations 3:22, 23).

It is perfectly acceptable for a Christian to lament. The sins and shortcomings of the church, the sad state of affairs in the world, personal transgressions, dishonor to God—all such things need to be lamented. The book of Lamentations, however, gives me some guidance in my sorrowing; its form shows structure and order. The five chapters are each arranged according to the twenty-two letters of the Hebrew alphabet; each has twenty-two or sixty-six verses. This is not a wild cry to the Almighty. Of course the Lord doesn't mind unorganized and rambling prayers. A scared child does not have to politely call his parents; a wild cry will be answered. But it should not always be so.

Lamentations also leads me through lament to the real cause of my problems. *I* have transgressed and rebelled. I have to realize that before I can hope for help and a better future.

Lamentations goes a step further. It seems that since I have departed from Him, He has given up on me. That sounds logical; however, in the covenant of God, it just is not true. His mercies never come to an end. They are new every morning. That is the miracle of God's love. The covenant means that God hangs on to me for reasons I will never understand, and He remains true to His goodness and love.

But the most important thing I am taught here, is that I have to discover this truth every morning anew. It must not become stale; I should never get used to it. When I wake up, I look my God in the eyes and I know what kind of day it is going to be. In sadness or in joy, His mercies never come to an end.

Great is Thy faithfulness, O Lord!

Lamentations 1-3

The hands of compassionate women have boiled their own children (Lamentations 4:10).

It is not pleasant to look at misery. I would rather look the other way. God's children for too long have turned away from the agony of the real world. They have closed their eyes to the suffering of the starving nations, to the plight of slaves, to the destruction of native cultures, to the true face of wars and the fate of their victims, to the cry of innocents who are caught between powerful forces.

The book of Lamentations is uncomfortably graphic about these things. While the men make war and the nation's leadership stubbornly sins on, some of God's people suffer immeasurably. While Jerusalem is under siege, hunger and starvation is atrocious. Mothers—not cruel and harsh, but compassionate—have been racked by a despair so deep that they have attacked their own children.

I impatiently reply, "How can a woman do a thing like that?" My reasoning and judgment shows that I have closed my eyes, that I have no insight into human despair and agony.

For one stark moment, I stare at the terror of sin and its consequences, at the innocent people who have to pay. Then I have to ask myself, "What suffering results from my actions?" I have to question my own share in determining how others have to live and die. And even if I have not contributed to the agonies of this world, I must ask if I have done anything to alleviate them.

It was for the sins of the prophets and the iniquities of the priests that those things happened (verse 13). I see the great Priest and Prophet, healing and not condemning. If I loved Him more sincerely, I would know more empathy and compassion.

Lamentations 4-5

Such was the appearance of the likeness of the glory of the Lord (Ezekiel 1:28).

Ezekiel has a three-fold task to perform. He has to prophesy to the group that is already in exile, he has to predict hard times to those who soon will follow them into exile, and he has to address himself to the few who will remain in Judah to take care of the fields and houses during the exile. To one group he has to give comfort and hope; to another group, sharp rebuke and tales of woe.

In addition to having a very difficult job to do, Ezekiel shares the frustration of many of God's prophets: hardly anybody listens to him, let alone believes him.

Despite all such opposition to the Word of God, one great comfort sees Ezekiel through his ministry. Ezekiel has a vision of glory, so great that he finds it almost impossible to describe. He struggles to give expression to what he has seen. (People nowadays have even interpreted his words as a description of flying objects from outer space.)

Ezekiel appears to have a vision of angels standing ready to serve God. That in itself is comforting. I am not alone in my service to God, I am supported by powers beyond me. Though I don't exactly understand what these angels do, I can and must know that God's messengers and servants are legions around me.

But then Ezekiel sees the center of it all, the heart of the matter, and that is the glory of God. Because he is a man of his time, he describes this glory in Babylonian terms. He uses his contemporary conventions to describe an age-old truth—God is here and the victory is His.

This theme returns again and again. Whenever Ezekiel is frustrated, he sees the glory of God. His only comfort is to see the One who revealed His glory in Jesus. At the beginning and the end, the alpha and the omega, my eyes see the glory of the Lord.

Ezekiel 1-3

Thus shall the people of Israel eat their bread unclean (Ezekiel 4:13).

Ezekiel sets up a brick model of Jerusalem which he places under a siege of wooden soldiers, battering rams, and camps. An iron shield between Ezekiel and the city symbolizes that there will be no help coming from God.

For three hundred and ninety days the prophet has to lie on his left side, bound with ropes, to indicate the punishment days of Israel. Then he has to lie forty days on his right side as a warning against Judah. So far it must look ridiculous to the bystanders.

But the "game" continues. Ezekiel has to eat bread made of grains and beans. Now this was an abomination in Israel, for the Lord has commanded them never to do this. Even then, Ezekiel has to measure out the tiny amount of bread and water he can consume each day. The bread is to be baked on a fire fueled by dried human dung. It was not uncommon to use cow dung for this purpose, but what the Lord tells him to do now is so terrible that Ezekiel pleads with the Lord to change His command, a change God makes. Still, it remains an extremely strange sight to see God's servant in this awkward position.

This charade depicts dramatically the fate of God's children if they do not repent. They will not be able to eat much during the siege (vs. 16) and frightening days lie ahead of them. In Babylon, they will not be able to observe the strict laws of God anymore. For many years they will lie there, bound by the ropes of God's wrath.

I must be shown what I can expect if I choose to live without my Savior: the gospel confronts me with the stark reality of a dirty, rotten life without God.

Ezekiel was allowed to diminish his repugnant plight somewhat, but for Jesus there was no respite from hellish agony. Such would be my own fate, but Jesus assures me that there is hope—in Him.

Ezekiel 4-6

There were about twenty-five men, with their backs to the temple of the Lord . . . worshiping the sun toward the east (Ezekiel 8:16).

The Lord lets Ezekiel see what is going on inside the temple buildings in Jerusalem. Occult practices, witchcraft, secret meetings in honor of foreign gods—a host of abominations are being perpetrated in the house of the God of Israel. It is not bad enough that the people are serving false gods; they are doing so in the temple. They have tried to synthesize the true religion with false religions to get an all-purpose mixture. God will be pleased with His share in it; the idols will be satisfied that they are not forgotten.

But the Lord will not tolerate such an arrangement. He has shown His glory to His people, and no one can ever mix that with the darkness of idolatry.

The Lord makes plain to His prophet what really is going on. Twenty-five men who worship the sun visit the inner court of the temple of the Lord. Sun-worship was a common practice in ancient religions, for the sun was considered the supreme power in the world. As they bow down to the rising sun in the east, the sun worshipers—perhaps unintentionally—turn their back to the temple.

This depicts something deeply true. I cannot combine anything idolatrous with the worship of my God. If I do so, I turn my back on my Savior, even if I may not mean to do so. When I bow down to the idol of money or work or any other god, I am forced to turn from my God.

I have to make up my mind. I cannot serve two masters.

And why should I?

Ezekiel 7-9

I have been a sanctuary to them for a while (Ezekiel 11:16).

In Ezekiel's "parish" are the people who occupy the deserted lands which used to be the promised lands flowing with milk and honey. They carve out a living for themselves and their families, though life is difficult in the now-desolate country. But at least they have a place to call their own. Since they were likely the poorest segment of the population, they probably never owned property before. They are proud that they possess this land.

Now, carefully and tactfully, the prophet has to take their pride from them. They may live here and enjoy their temporary good fortune. But one day the children of God will come back from the foreign lands where the Lord had brought them because of their sins. With a song of joy, they will reoccupy their fields and houses.

Nothing is final as long as the mercies of God endure. Though all seems hopeless for the nation of God, in Babylon the Lord has become their sanctuary. There is no temple there, no place for worship, but God Himself gives them a sanctuary where they can find Him. When they faithfully turn to Him, worshiping Him in spirit and truth, the Lord will eventually return to them an earthly sanctuary as well. Then the lands and fields will have to be returned to their legal owners.

Ezekiel's prophecy is a prophecy of hope. The children of the present owners, though they lose their properties, will find refuge in the new temple and will enjoy the glory of God's temple.

As long as the Lord lives, there is hope. I may not assume that I will remain as I am. God, through His Spirit, can do unbelievable things in my life. In the church, awkward divisions and fights and schisms are never final in the eyes of God. The turning away from God in the world and the turning to injustice and cruelty is not an irreversible process. When God says it is only for a while, He means it.

Ezekiel 10-12

The wall is no more, nor those who daubed it (Ezekiel 13:15).

The church's image must be improved, and so it concentrates on getting more comfortable pews, a new, more exciting order of worship, more participation by members, more special music, better advertising, more interesting topics, more guest speakers, and more . . . and better. Now these elements make worship more meaningful. But if they represent the sum total of an effort to keep the church alive, they are useless and senseless.

Ezekiel calls this process whitewashing or daubing. He sees that the people should be rebuilding the walls, and yet the prophets of Israel are encouraging them merely to patch up and whitewash the walls.

The prophets in those days were predicting pleasant things, the priests were continuing worship in the temple, and the kings were speaking of hope and trust. Meanwhile, the people of God continued down the road to deep misery because there was no real repentance and change of heart.

So much energy is wasted on worthless busyness. But it looks nice, and looks seem to be what counts.

But God says, No. Your visions, your prophecies of peace are delusions. They are lies. There will not be peace as long as My people do not see the need for a complete change of heart. It is no good to patch up the wall with nice looking whitewash. The wall must be brought down to its very foundations and then be rebuilt entirely.

I know how convenient it is to whitewash at times. I try to keep up good appearances with the world, my neighbors, and my family, concealing the actual state of my heart and life. But this is a waste of time. God knows that the only way to improve cracked and delapidated walls is to rebuild them. Though my whitewashed walls may look good, when the enemy comes they will tumble.

It is about time that I face sin and do something about it.

Ezekiel 13-15

How lovesick is your heart, says the Lord God (Ezekiel 16:30).

God tells a story about the origin of the people of Israel, their exodus to the promised land, their growth into an awesome nation. It is a love story. God saw a little baby girl abandoned by everyone, and tenderly and lovingly He took care of her. When she grew up, He exulted in her beauty and bought her precious gifts and prepared her to be His bride. But then she started to use these things, not for her great Lover, but for anybody who came her way and lusted after her. She played the harlot, ignoring a life-long relationship of tenderness and love. She left God standing there, forsaken and miserable.

If I were treated that way, I surely would not wait around. But the Lord patiently keeps on loving Israel and calling her back to Him.

God says that the fault of His people is not lack of love, but an overabundance of love. How lovesick is your heart, says the Lord God. But your love is misdirected. Because you find so much to love in the world, there is no time to love your Bridegroom.

My problem is not that I start to hate God. But my attention is drawn away from Him by a world that looks more important to me. Satan opens the world to me and shows me many challenging, exciting pursuits. He doesn't tell me that they can never mean anything to me, that they will leave me out in the cold and the dark.

The heart of my God is lovesick for me. And His love endures forever.

Ezekiel 16-18

When you offer your gifts and sacrifice your sons by fire, you defile yourselves (Ezekiel 20:31).

Ezekiel mentions quite often a terrible ritual that occurred commonly in Israel. A fire was lit beneath the gaping bronze mouth of an idol. When the flames came leaping out of the god's mouth, a young child was thrown into the mouth to die in the flames. Behind this practice was the superstition that in order to have happiness and prosperity, one had to sacrifice something, even a child. Imagine the grief of the parents whose turn it was to give up their child for the good of the community.

Many people, though disgusted by the thought of child sacrifices, still think, for example, "I am so happy that it cannot last." One wishes someone luck by telling him to break a leg—the lesser evil may prevent a greater catastrophe. Heathen religions still demand tremendous sacrifices in order to fend off misery and death. All this stems from the idea that the insurance of happiness is in my own hands. The child sacrifices in Israel show how far humans go if they are scared enough.

Not surprisingly, God is very upset by this practice. Those babies are His. He has given them the token of His covenant. Their life is a precious work of His divine art.

But the deepest insult is that the Lord is replaced by an idol that demands instead of gives. God has given His Son unto death for me. How would He ever want me to give my son for Him?

Now I had better be honest. Am I sacrificing my wife, my husband, or my children to an idol, or even to an ideal? I must commit my future to the God who gives life.

Ezekiel 19-21

Sigh, but not aloud; make no mourning for the dead (Ezekiel 24:17).

The life of a Christian is a total commitment. There is no moment in life when the Lord does not demand I serve Him. His commitment to me is also total. I never call upon Him in vain.

Ezekiel feels this call to obedience intensely when the Lord tells him that his wife will die. All of a sudden she will be taken from him. And then he may not mourn. He may not tear his clothes or sprinkle ashes on his head as everyone else in Israel would do. The Lord tells him that he may sigh, and grieve, but not in public. That must have been hard; he calls his wife the delight of his eyes and the desire of his soul.

In this moment of grief, the Lord has called on Ezekiel to prophesy. Soon Jerusalem, the delight of Israel's eyes and the desire of their souls, will die and the sword will slay their sons and daughters. But then there should be no mourning: they asked for it. Their sins forced the Lord to punish them; therefore, they should accept that punishment when it comes.

This is the last prophecy Israel will hear from Ezekiel's lips until Jerusalem falls. His lips are sealed and his tongue is struck dumb. Nothing beyond this last, powerful message can be said. The Lord uses Ezekiel's personal loss and grief to speak powerfully to His people.

Am I willing to let my entire life be a proclamation of the gospel? Do I witness in my grief and sorrow as well as in my joy? Do I radiate God's good news, even in bad times? Do I sigh, then, to God, but not aloud? If so, I may mean something for the coming of God's kingdom.

Ezekiel 22-24

O Tyre, you have said, "I am perfect in beauty" (Ezekiel 27:3).

Ezekiel uses three chapters to tell Tyre that it is doomed. How could that have meant anything to the people of Israel, let alone to the church of God today? Perhaps I should omit these chapters from my Bible reading, discard them as pretty useless material. What did the Holy Spirit have in mind when He used the prophet to speak and later to write these words in a book?

The end is near for God's people, at least for the time being. And when they are carried into exile, Tyre will look on smugly. Tyre has always had to pay to use Israel's facilities for her trade and business. After the exile, no customs or duties will have to be paid anymore. But Tyre is smug for a more fundamental reason: it seems that the world in all its beauty survives and the people of God perish. Tyre is not an enemy of Israel or God. It is merely proud that it does not need any help from the Lord.

The world tries to convince me that I am a fool for trusting the Lord. Make your own life, trust in yourself, be confident and active. Don't rely upon anything but your own powers and qualities. I have heard this so many times that sometimes I begin to wonder. Results seem to show that people don't need God at all.

But God tells His people that this is just not true. Tyre may be a beautiful ship, but it will be shipwrecked soon. And Jerusalem, which seems defeated, in God's own time will be inhabited again, the temple will be built, and there will be a new future.

All beauty and power on earth passes away. But in Christ Jesus, the kingdom of God is secure. I may trust my future to Him, knowing that He is much more dependable than I or anything else in this world could ever be.

Ezekiel 25-27

When they leaned upon you, you broke (Ezekiel 29:7).

Egypt played a very special role in the development of Israel. It served as an incubator for the fledgling nation. Later, it pushed the small group out of the nest so that it would fly into a freedom and identity of its own. But since then, there has not been much of a relationship between the two. So it is surprising to hear Ezekiel's prophecies against Egypt. Is it any of his business what happens to Egypt? And could it be of any comfort to the children of God?

When I read how God deals with other nations, I see clearly that the Lord rules the world. These prophecies show that what goes on between the nations of the world is in God's hands.

There is, however, a special reason that Egypt is mentioned. When the power of Babylon loomed dark over Israel, the prophets told the people to submit to a temporary punishment of the Lord. Their path would lead through the dark to a new dawn. But Egypt told them that they should never give up, and that they would help Israel. Because of this encouragement, many Israelites kept on resisting Babylon—with disastrous results. Egypt actually wanted Israel to serve as a buffer between itself and Babylon. So when Israel fell, Egypt did not help. They were a staff for Israel to lean upon, but a staff made of reed, and Israel fell on its face.

Now the Lord is angry with Egypt and tells them that they will never again be a super-power among the nations. Of course, Israel should never have trusted Egypt. But Egypt's deception hurts the Lord.

Even when I am sinning, God cares deeply for me. He gets angry when people hurt me. What a Father!

Ezekiel 28-30

I have no pleasure in the death of the wicked, but that the wicked turn from his way and live (Ezekiel 33:11).

To Israel as a nation, the Lord speaks harsh words. The sword will come upon them, the exile is near, perhaps already in progress. But the picture of a grim God who loves to punish His people is totally wrong. To the individual people of Israel, the Lord speaks pleadingly. Return to Me. Why would you die? God cannot change His Word concerning the future of Israel. But each person could yet know hope and goodness and joy, if only each would return to the Lord.

The great truth Ezekiel teaches me is that with the Lord, there is never a closed door unless I slam that door myself. If the wicked one turns away from his sins, he will find forgiveness and hope. I cannot say that since I am bad anyway, I may as well continue in my evil ways. That is what Israel felt in verse 10. But God tells me that I can turn around anytime and face Him again. That also means, of course, that I cannot rest in the righteousness of the past. Each day I must turn to the Lord in righteousness.

Modern psychology may say that I am a product of heredity and environment. But God says that I am not cast forever in a certain mould. He calls me to be what He wants me to be, and then He sends the Holy Spirit to work change within me. The situation in my family, at work, among friends, in the church, does not have to remain static.

God tells me that He has no pleasure in the death of the wicked. The Father is keeping watch for His straying children throughout the night, coaxing them home.

What does it mean that the wicked shall live if he turns back? The exile and the chastisement of God will still fall upon Israel. I cannot count on exemptions from the results of sin. But in the darkness around me, I can walk in the light. I can live!

Ezekiel 31-33

I myself will be the shepherd of my sheep (Ezekiel 34:15).

The Lord is very honest in His dealings with His people. They have sinned and strayed away from Him, but He tells them that it is not all their fault. The leaders of Israel were supposed to lead them as good shepherds, but they have neglected their task. In their concern for their personal well-being, they hurt the sheep and rob them of the joy of life. It is no wonder that people lose their way when those who should lead them deceive them and forsake them instead.

The Lord knows that many people are not serving Him because other people do not show them the way. Those who should be living examples of God's grace are not.

I too pollute God's message. When I seek money or honor or acceptance, I obscure what the Lord really wants to say through me. That makes me partly responsible for the turning-away of crowds from the Lord.

On the other hand, this does not excuse those who turn away. Can I ever blame others for my sins? Not really. Where did *I* go wrong? That is the first question for parents and church leaders and governments and marriage partners. Before I condemn others, I must recognize my share in the general breakdown.

It is a great comfort to me that God is so just. Even in paradise God admits that satan is co-responsible for the first sin. I can trust Him to judge rightly.

God says, "I Myself will be the Shepherd of My sheep." Jesus came to be the Good Shepherd. And I will be held accountable for my attitude to the Shepherd, no matter how other people influence me. The whole truth is that the Shepherd is calling me. There is no excuse for saying no to Him.

Ezekiel 34-36

I will put my Spirit within you, and you shall live (Ezekiel 37:14).

Ezekiel sees a whole valley full of bones—a symbol of Israel's condition while in exile. Never before has any nation survived such a crucial blow. But now the Lord promises to bring those skeletons together, to cover them with flesh, and thus to restore the wholeness of Israel. How thrilling for Ezekiel to see this happen in his vision and to know he could bring this message of hope to his people.

However, even though the bodies come together completely, a deadly silence remains. Nothing moves. Whole bodies are a prettier sight than dry bones spread all over the valley, but death still reigns. Death reigns until the Spirit of God breathes upon the bones. That makes all the difference. Now the dead stand up and live.

This passage helps me to see how important it is that I take care of social structures and organizations. The efforts of people are tools in the hands of an almighty Father in heaven. But without the Spirit of God, these organizations are just dry bones. They cannot function. The Holy Spirit must give them the pulse of life.

The importance of the indwelling of the Holy Spirit cannot be overemphasized, and yet its importance is so often overlooked. Israel will return to Jerusalem and life under the law of God. Yet in time it will deteriorate to the lifeless condition which Jesus knew during His days among the scribes and Pharisees.

So I have to ask myself: Does my Christian life really live? Is my church or any other organization that I am associated with really a living body of Jesus Christ?

Ezekiel sees a glorious future for Israel. A king greater than David will reign; the laws will be obeyed; the temple will be rebuilt. But above all, God's people will know real life.

Spirit of God, enter my heart.

Ezekiel 37-39

This is the table which is before the Lord (Ezekiel 41:22).

Some people go on a long vacation to distant places without so much as consulting a roadmap or train and bus schedule. Others start planning long before, studying various routes, cutting out information on daily trips, reserving good trailer parks or motels, counting the miles, figuring the exact cost, all in eager anticipation. One of these people is Ezekiel.

Ezekiel sees the future national and spiritual restoration of Israel. He will never be able to share in it, but it is as if he is living already in that day when the temple will be rebuilt and the people will come to worship the Lord in Jerusalem. Such is the joy of visionary men. Pity the church that has no visions. Sometimes, I feel I have to assume a "wait and see" attitude. But why wait, when I can see the coming victory now in the Word of God?

The Lord reveals to Ezekiel the structure of the new temple in detail. And Ezekiel is so happy that he enthusiastically passes on all the dimensions, structures, and activities. I smile and share his joy. I know very little about the new Jerusalem. But it is great joy to live in the assurance that it will come and to read all the details that God chooses to reveal at this time.

Only visions? Yes, of course. I never claim to have an accurate description of the new heaven and the new earth. But it is enough to see that great liberation coming and to rejoice in it. At last I will be free to serve the Lord whole-heartedly. The new heaven and earth will be a busy, productive place.

In the temple proper, Ezekiel sees only one piece of furniture: the table on which the showbread was put. The children of God will come to His house to dedicate themselves and all that they have received into the service of their Father. Finally God will be honored and praised. I will finally say, "Take my life and let it be consecrated, Lord, to Thee." That means glory and happiness.

Ezekiel 40-42

*The Lord, the God of Israel, has entered by it; therefore it shall re-
main shut. Only the prince may sit in it to eat (Ezekiel 44:3).*

In the new temple which Ezekiel sees in his vision, most of the
gates are wide open for all God's children to enter. They may sit
there and eat the food given them by the priest as a share in the offerings.

However, remarkably, the East gate remains shut. Perhaps
this gate is so close to the precipitous side of the mountain that people stepping out of it might fall down the cliff. But this is not the
reason the Lord gives Ezekiel for keeping the East gate closed.

When the temple was opened, the cloud of fire, symbolizing
the presence of the glory of God, had entered through this gate. At
the gate of the rising sun, the Sun of Righteousness had walked into
His own house to take possession of it.

Now in holy remembrance of this solemn moment, nobody
should enter into this gate. The closed East gate reminded all God's
people of His glorious entry.

Still, a closed gate makes the temple imperfect. Which it is.

The prince was to be allowed to sit at the gate and eat, though
he too had to use a different entrance. The name prince is used instead of king, because the kings have sinned so badly in the past.
This new name is used for a new concept of king. The prince in the
line of David will sit there and eat the bread of God.

Here Scripture points to the One who will eventually come to
open this gate. In the Revelation of John, I read about four gates,
all wide open. Once more the Lord will enter through the gate in
His final coming as the Prince of Peace. Till then, the situation is
not perfect.

This only makes me yearn for that greatest day when God will
be all in all.

Ezekiel 43-45

And behold, water was issuing from below the threshold of the temple (Ezekiel 47:1).

The temple is not an end unto itself. Ezekiel sees that a stream of living water is flowing from the temple. It springs from beneath the altar, for along with forgiveness through the atoning sacrifice there comes new life. But that life does not stay in the temple. It flows into the world. There the water brings an abundance of trees, plants and flowers. Rushing through the Dead Sea, it turns that place of death into a place of abundant life. Fishermen stand along its shores and fill their nets with fish. Water for irrigation transforms the desert into a paradise. A few marshes are left because salt is important for human life, but otherwise there is no trace of the doom of death. As the wilderness through which it passes becomes drier, the river becomes deeper. The more it is needed, the more it will supply. Miraculously, every month the trees will bear fruits and the leaves will be used for healing.

This description of the new Jerusalem is strikingly similar to the description found in the Revelation of John. However, this passage puts the blooming wilderness not at the end of time, but at Pentecost.

Now the church, the temple of the living God, too often has found its purpose in itself. It has hoped the Lord would be pleased by a sound and obedient church. But this church should not be collecting water for itself. It must send it out, for God has His eyes on the dry wilderness of the world.

Jesus told me that when I believe in Him, streams of living water will flow out of me. It will flow into me too, of course, through the Holy Spirit. But when I send blessings into the world, the Spirit will amply supply all that I need. The stream will deepen when I go further into this world.

The beauty of Christian life doesn't arise from what goes into it, but from what streams out of it into a desperate world.

Ezekiel 46-48

But if not, be it known to you, O king, that we will not serve your gods (Daniel 3:18).

The book of Daniel does not mean to glorify the courage of people but to glorify a God who keeps His covenant.

Israel and Judah are in exile. The temple treasures are in a Babylonian temple to honor false gods. In this seemingly hopeless situation, God demonstrates that nobody can steal His covenant children.

When the Babylonians try to force young Daniel into a pagan way of life in the courts of King Nebuchadnezzar, they find out that not only Daniel's courage but also his upbringing in the covenant and the ways of the Lord protect him. Later, Daniel knows both the king's bad dream and its interpretation. The whole nation of Israel is disobedient to God, but a young boy shows that God can use anybody to glorify His name.

In this passage, the Lord once again shows that He lives in His children. When the music sounds, everybody has to fall down and worship the golden image Nebuchadnezzar put up on the plain of Dura. Only the three friends of Daniel remain standing.

The great miracle in this story is perhaps not that these three companions come out of the fiery furnace. The great miracle is that they went in. It is hard to remain standing when everybody falls down. Many times I cannot muster the courage to be different. These men do.

Not only do these men stand up for what they know is right, they explain their position to the king. They tell King Nebuchadnezzar that God will protect them in the fiery furnace. But even if He doesn't, they will not change their position. They are not depending on a miracle. They would just rather obey God than anybody else.

Miraculously, a fourth person appears in the furnace. The Son of God is there when I follow my God. First I must walk in His ways, and then I will find His nearness and power.

Daniel 1-3

He got down upon his knees three times a day and prayed (Daniel 6:10).

When everything else fails, satan tries to hinder God's work by cutting off Daniel's prayer. He knows better than I often do that prayer is the lifeline between God and me. When God and I do not talk together, the covenant has become an empty shell.

The two presidents and the hundred-and-twenty satraps of Babylon are jealous of Daniel, and with good reason. King Darius has set this foreigner over all of them. After considerable deliberation, they realize that the only grounds for any complaint against Daniel will have to be in connection with the law of his God. Their scheming results in a document signed by King Darius saying that no one will petition any god or man except himself for thirty days.

Now this tactic of satan's is vicious precisely because it would be so easy to get around it. Daniel could close his windows and nobody would be the wiser. He could pray only during the dark night hours. He could also assume that the Lord would understand if he stopped praying for awhile. It must have been tempting for Daniel to dodge the perils, to escape the lion's den.

Daniel knows he just cannot give in on something as sacred as his communication with God. So he goes on doing exactly what he has done in the past. Knowing that he may end up in the lion's den does not make any difference.

This story teaches me that God keeps communication open with His people. In my own strength, I would not often commune with my God. But His Spirit leads me to the windows through which I can look toward Jerusalem. He also makes me aware of satan's efforts to cut my link to my Father.

It is not surprising to read that, as in the fiery furnace, there is an extra person in the lion's den. The angel of the Lord, the Son of God, protects Daniel. If I trust in God, and even if I don't, He will protect me. How reassuring that my salvation does not depend on my courage or perseverance but on God's grace.

Daniel 4-6

We have not obeyed his voice (Daniel 9:14).

The return of the exiles to Jerusalem must wait until they have acknowledged that the Lord was righteous in His doings and that they deserved these years of hardship. But there is no indication that God's children did repent. The people have adapted to life in another country. Because generations have passed, they no longer feel very guilty for what their fathers have done. All this makes it difficult to see any possibility of a return. Where God's people do not admit their wrongdoings or acknowledge God's righteousness, there is no hope.

Or is there? If God had to wait until I recognized my sins and shortcomings, if He could not help me because I did not confess my guilt, I would never be saved.

God provides an intercessor for Israel. In exile with Israel is a man who is not only courageous, wise, and prophetic but who above all is a mediator, who prayerfully intercedes for his people. Daniel makes a confession on Israel's behalf.

Daniel's approach to the Lord is beautiful. He gives honor to God, recognizing that He is not to blame for any of the problems and miseries that befell His children. And Daniel makes himself one with the evildoers, now and in the past.

In this chapter of confession, I see Christ who stands in my place, interceding for me. The future of God's people never depends on their own doing, not even on their own repentance. God delivers me because Christ intervened for me. But Christ had to do more than just say words of confession. To pay for my sins He had to drink the cup of the wrath of God.

Now I can try to follow Him. Deliverance does follow confession. But first of all I follow my Savior, who is the One who delivers me.

Daniel 7-9

The words are shut up and sealed until the time of the end (Daniel 12:9).

The second part of the book of Daniel is hard to understand. The meaning of those strange visions of the future escapes even Daniel. When he asks for an explanation, he is told it is not possible to make all these things clear now.

What is clear is that these visions speak of a wonderful, exciting future. Daniel receives a clear picture of Messiah in the midst of His oppressed people. But he sees further developments that defy description. The Revelation of John uses many of these same apocalyptic details to prophesy the new Jerusalem. For me, it is comfort enough to know that there is such glory waiting for me. I can relinquish trying to understand every detail of the prophecy.

If Daniel himself or if I myself had written these books of the Bible, we would have done it differently. We would have described these events lucidly and simply. But then it would have been the word of humans; now it is God's Word to me.

Why should the Lord describe the new world in mysterious terms? Because it will be so different from what I am experiencing now that it escapes my limited comprehension. My lack of full understanding is due to my limitations, not God's.

At the end of time, as the Lord points out, the meaning of these words will be clear to those who need to understand. Some passages in the Bible had immediate significance. But there are also words whose meaning will only be clear for the generations who will live in this old world in its final stages. A road map speaks as I drive, not when I sit at home. I have to wait until I get that far, but I know that then God's guide will be ready for me, ready to point the way.

Daniel 10-12

I will answer the heavens and they shall answer the earth (Hosea 2:21).

What actually is idolatry? How do I know when something has turned into an idol? Scripture pays so much attention to the problem of false gods that it must be more of a problem than I realize.

In verse 21 and 22, Hosea describes a long chain of related events. When I eat bread, I see the flour and the grain, the farmer, the seeding and the fertilizing, the rain and the sunshine. When I drink wine, I visualize the grapes and the man who prunes and dresses them. Hundreds of people are involved in this chain.

But do I see God my Father at the end of the line, beyond the sun and the rainclouds? Maybe not. I may see nothing more than human ingenuity and hard work, nature, or fate. Then those are the idols, taking God's rightful place away from Him. When I do not see God behind my children, my wife or husband, my work, my achievements, my money, or whatever I have, I know where my idols are. But if I know that they are all gifts from my heavenly Father, I can honor Him in my prayers. Then, too, I will know what I must do with these gifts. I have to bring them back to God with love and gratitude woven into them; I must present them to Him as a living sacrifice.

If that is not happening, God warns that I may have put something in His place or beside Him. He is jealous of my love.

Hosea sees this chain properly. Israel had lost sight of God. Since a human being always holds something dear, somebody else or something else had taken His place to fill the vacuum.

I must ask, "Who gave all this to me? To whom shall I bring it all?" Then I will hear the voice of God speaking in the bread and the wine and the oil. He says, "You are My people." And I say, "You are my God."

Idolatry locks me into my little world. Faith opens my world wide—to God.

Hosea 1-3

Let us know, let us press on to know the Lord (Hosea 6:3).

Throughout his prophecies, Hosea insists upon a better knowledge of God. Now this might be heard as an appeal for better religious instruction for both children and adults. But that is not exactly what Hosea has in mind. The problem is not that I don't know *about* God, but that I don't *know* Him. To *know* is the word that the Bible often uses to describe the most intimate relation between a woman and a man. Adam knew his wife and she bore a son. To know somebody (in the Biblical sense) does not depend on knowing details of weight and height, age, or occupation. And so it is with God. My knowing God does not depend on being able to list His attributes as they are revealed in the Bible. Rather, to know God means that I must embrace Him with my whole being, submit to Him, and make His goals my goals.

The vital question remains: Do I really *know* my heavenly Father? Am I willing to see God as revealed to me or do I prefer to conjure up my own ideas of what God is like? Do I imagine a God who is lenient and easy-going, one who can be taken for granted? Or do I perhaps think of God as cruel and demanding, impossible to please?

Hosea warns the people to take a good look at their God. The second commandment warns me not to cling to my imaginations of the Lord. He presents a clear image of Himself in His Son Jesus Christ and in His Word.

There is one more thing. Lasting love requires commitment. God sees the love of Ephraim and Judah for what it is: a morning cloud, the dew that evaporates early. God rejects such love.

To know God means to abandon my fantasies, to see Him as He is, and to give myself steadfastly to Him. That is not easy. But it is worth it to know God, to press on to know Him. He is my all, and utmost.

Hosea 4-6

In the morning it blazes like a flaming fire (Hosea 7:6).

Things are quiet in the baker's shop at night. Between the barrel and the oven, nothing stirs. The only sound is the snoring of the baker in the next room. But Hosea says, Don't be mistaken. Before he went to sleep, the baker stirred the yeast into the flour, and now the dough is rising. He kindled a fire in the oven and the flames are spreading. It becomes clear in the morning that a lot was happening during the quiet night.

The Bible often compares sin to yeast: sin can spread its corruption throughout my entire life without drawing any attention to itself. Before I know it, the dough will creep out of the barrel.

Sin can also be seen as a spark that kindles a fire. In the morning, when the oven is opened, the heat hits you in the face.

It simply is not true that a peaceful life is always a good life. For the baker, the quiet of rising yeast and burning wood are good. For the child of God, peace may be disastrous. If I realize that sin is working, that the fire is burning on, I might check it in time. But I am often lulled into deep and pleasant sleep.

That is the dangerous situation Hosea detects. He cannot put his finger on great transgressions Israel has committed against the Lord and His messengers. Something is wrong, but it is so hard to say exactly what. Yet Hosea knows that the spark of sin is steadily but inconspicuously growing. When the doors of the oven are opened, the heat will be there.

Hosea calls for a deeper awareness of what is going on in my life, and in the church. Disturbing the peace is unpleasant. But the Lord calls me to act before it is too late, for He is concerned about me.

Hosea 7-9

I led them with cords of compassion (Hosea 11:4).

Hosea describes how God feels about His wayward and stubborn people. He is their Father.

With affection, He remembers the young child Israel, called out of Egypt.

He taught His son to walk. Through the desert, the strong hands of a loving Father guided the toddler's stumbling feet. The Father used cords of compassion and bands of love. Rather than restrict and confine, they allowed the young nation the freedom to choose its way, even though ultimately God still guided His child.

God took Ephraim up in His arms, and cuddled him. When he was sick, his Father healed him with pleasant medicine. Ephraim never realized that it was God who healed him.

God nourished His child with manna from heaven, and gave him His Law to guide and guard his way. God stooped low and worked hard to make the child strong and happy.

God could not have done more than He did; He sent His only begotten Son to me.

But, unbelievably, the Lord must complain that His child runs away from Him. "The more I called to them, the more they went from Me." When their children turn away, earthly parents may ask themselves, "What did I do wrong?" But God has done nothing wrong. He can only ask, "What did you have against Me?"

At first, the harsh reality of rebellion angers God. He seems to throw up His hands, saying, "If My people are so bent on living without Me, they will have to suffer the consequences."

But soon, His heart recoils within Him and His compassion again grows warm and tender. How can God treat His children as if they were strangers or enemies?

God's love is everlasting. How can I respond but to love?

Hosea 10-12

O Death, where are your plagues? O Sheol, where is your destruction? (Hosea 13:14).

These well-known words are Paul's triumphant shout of joy that by His resurrection Jesus has destroyed the power of death. In the first epistle to the Corinthians, these words express the tremendous love of God who defeats my most frightening enemies.

However, when Paul quotes these words from Hosea, he changes their meaning completely. In Hosea, the words spell doom instead of triumph. The Lord is calling on the powers of death and grave to come forward; they help God punish His disobedient people. God has just stated that He is not going to redeem them from Death; He will not ransom them from the power of Sheol.

Was Paul's quotation a sloppy use of Old Testament Scripture? Perhaps because copies of the Bible were not as readily available then as nowadays, the words were vague in Paul's mind. Perhaps he was so enthusiastic about the gospel of Jesus' resurrection that he did not take the time to check whether the quotation was correct.

I do not have to make excuses for Paul or for the Spirit who inspired him. Hosea hears the Lord calling His servants, Death and Sheol, to punish His people. The time for compassion is past. But through the death and resurrection of Jesus, that has changed. The power of death and hellish agony have been vented on my Savior. God let the rage and tempest of these forces spend their powers on Him. Now in triumph God calls to them again. But this time He asks, "Where are you now? What evil can you do?"

What seems to be a mistaken quotation is actually the great fulfillment of the prophecy.

Hosea 13-14

I will pour out my Spirit on all flesh (Joel 2:28).

The prophet Joel is a lucky man. Other prophets, burdened by a message of gloom and disaster, had to face the rebellion and hostility of their audiences. But Joel's words are much more optimistic. True, just now a plague of grasshoppers is devouring everything in the fields and ruining the harvest. Joel reminds the people that the root of that disaster is their own disobedience to the Word of God. He has to call His people to repentance.

But Joel can go on to announce that better and brighter days are ahead. Beyond the present darkness, he can see the faraway light; he may speak of the mercies of God and of His forgiving grace. God, full of pity for His people, will vindicate them. He will drive back their enemies into the sea.

Then Joel describes how good life is going to be. The wilderness will again be pasture, the trees and vines will again be laden with fruit. An abundant harvest will compensate for the years the grasshoppers and locusts have eaten the crops.

But then Joel makes a daring statement. He proclaims that the highest joy in life is not to eat and drink and be merry. What God's people need most is to know the riches of God's presence. Therefore God will come and live in His people and pour out His spiritual gifts. And these gifts will not be restricted to a "spiritual elite." All of God's people must experience His presence. Son and daughters will prophesy, old men shall dream dreams. Even the often neglected servants will receive God's gifts.

If I do not have a living relationship with the Lord, all else becomes meaningless. Material blessings are just tokens of God's goodness. Only spiritual happiness makes life rich and meaningful.

Yet Joel does not promise the people merely joyful hearts. They will go out and actively prophesy. Spiritual riches compel me to work in God's kingdom.

Joel 1-3

But you made the Nazarites drink wine, and commanded the pro-
phets, saying, "You shall not prophesy" (Amos 2:12).

The fledgling nation, nurtured and protected by God, has
grown into a decadent vulture. The poor and afflicted have become
the prey in Israel; they are trampled into the dust, or turned
heartlessly away. Israel has also become morally perverse. It seems
to be common practice for a man and his father to go in to the same
woman. Such disregard of the strict law on this matter profanes the
holy name of God. The very worship of God has been desecrated.

How can a nation whose very life-blood is its relationship with
God come to this point? God has done so much for these people.
He has destroyed their enemies, including the powerful Amorites.
He has led them out of the bondage of Egypt. Most recently, He
has often sent His prophets to warn them; He raised Nazarites to
proclaim to Israel the error of their way of life. But the prophets
speak of things that Israel doesn't want to hear. And the Nazarites
lead a life so pure and holy that it embarrasses Israel.

However, rather than listening to the prophets and trying to
imitate the virtuous lifestyle of the Nazarites, Israel insists that the
prophets shut their mouths and tries to lure the Nazarites into
breaking their vows.

Amos exposes the futility of this desire. What do I profit when
someone else falls into sin? Will I be cleaner because others are getting dirty? Misery loves company, but so does sin. Can I hide in the
mass of sinners, hoping that the eyes of the community will not
detect me?

The Lord recognizes my efforts for what they are. He is ready
to strike down those who scorn His efforts to make them worthy to
be called His people.

I must step out of the crowd and into His marvelous light.
There I meet Jesus.

Amos 1-3

Here this word, you cows of Bashan (Amos 4:1).

No one can accuse Amos of being too delicate in his speech. Amos is a farmer, a country man not used to sophisticated city life. It would be natural for Amos to be suspicious and perhaps even envious of the sumptuous living of the city folk, especially when compared with the austere life of farmers in the desert. But Amos is not ashamed or embarrassed by his lack of social grace. He knows that he brings the Word of God to the people.

In this passage, Amos addresses the ladies of Samaria, calling them "Cows of Bashan." Now Bashan was a region east of the Sea of Galilee noted for its rich pasturage; this title is a reference to the sleek, well fed cattle of that area. What did these women do to deserve this label?

Apparently, this group of women had become preoccupied with the accumulation of wealth and social position. To achieve their goals, they were quick to oppress the poor and crush the needy. They were downright mean in their dealings in the marketplace, and they paid servants disgustingly low wages. Even the partnership between husband and wife became subservient to their insatiable desire for more things.

Amos spells out their coming doom in brutal terms. When the city is captured, they will lie stripped of their finery and dead in the streets. Scavengers will drag their corpses away to the refuse pile—a fitting end for dead cows.

This passage warns all those who pursue wealth and luxury at the expense of the poor and oppressed. I had better make sure my lifestyle does not contribute to that kind of sin. Also, when I believe that my own power makes me independent of God, then I have forgotten that all power belongs to Him.

Such a bitingly sarcastic term may sound harsh, but God is calling all His children to repentance and real piety and faith. Sometimes I need harsh language to make me listen.

Amos 4-6

I am no prophet, nor a prophet's son; but I am a herdsman . . . and the Lord took me (Amos 7:14).

The priest of Bethel warns Amos that he should not prophesy as he does. Amaziah says that a prophet should stay out of politics —as if the Lord's Word could possibly have no bearing on political or social or scientific issues! He commands Amos to leave Bethel and go to Judah; there he can say whatever he wants. Amaziah also lets Amos know that no donations will be coming his way if he keeps on prophesying.

Amos is not scared by the threat of the loss of his wages. He is not applying for the official, government-supported position of prophet. He is just a farmer who has been called by the Lord to pass on a message; all he knows is the calling of the Lord.

I don't have to be a minister or elder or deacon to work in the church and kingdom of God. Those official positions have value and serve a purpose, but they can become a trap. Far too much emphasis has been put on official installations and special positions. The service of God can be hampered by a strict observance of accepted procedures, behaviors, and formalities associated with ecclesiastical titles and positions.

Amos is happy to be just a rancher and sycamore tree dresser, knowing that the Lord has called him. When "official Christians" claim to be the special servants of God, they may exclude from service others who are willing to serve. I don't have to be a prophet's son or have an official position to serve my God. The Lord can use me as I am.

Amos 7-9

But in Mount Zion there shall be those that escape (Obadiah :17).

Throughout the ages, there has been a struggle between Jacob and his brother Esau. Esau can do without the covenant with God if that will be a more profitable way to live. He wants to prove that he can achieve his own happiness. Jacob, despite all his sins and shortcomings, believes that a relationship with God was important. He demonstrates that even a liar and cheater has to rely on the mercies of the Lord. My sympathies go to the straightforward, strong Esau, but I have to acknowledge that Jacob receives the blessings and is taken up in the line of the coming Messiah.

The conflict between Jacob and Esau has continued down through the ages. At first, when Israel is a successful nation, it looks as if Jacob has won. But in Obadiah's days, when the children of Jacob are deported into exile, the children of Esau stand and watch them with grins on their faces. They even kick Jacob when he is down; they help in the deportation, killing those that try to escape exile.

Case closed? Not yet. Obadiah sees that many years from now the sons of Jacob will return to their land where they will rule over Edom, Esau's offspring.

However, this prophecy seems undercut, for when the Romans conquer Israel, they place a son of Esau, Herod the Edomite, as ruler over them. So finally Esau wins.

Or does he? Jesus escapes Herod's murderous attack on Bethlehem's children. In the end Esau and Edom will have disappeared, but the Messiah, Jacob's greatest Son, will rule forever.

Obadiah's task is to tell God's children that in spite of their present misery, Jacob's children *will* triumph over Esau. The victory is on Mount Zion. And those who want to escape judgment and flee from Esau's mount to Mount Zion will find mercy. Salvation is in Jesus Christ.

Obadiah

It displeased Jonah exceedingly, and he was angry (Jonah 4:1).

I can understand why a man would be afraid to prophesy. But I can't understand a prophet who gets angry when his mission is successful. So many prophets have hoped and prayed for fruits of their labor to no avail. Here is a man who converts an entire city, but then he is angry at the Lord.

Jonah is a symbol of Israel. They relish the position of God's elect and chosen people, and don't want to share that status with anybody else. Even though throughout the Old Testament the Lord God hardly ever instructs them to be missionaries, when He does, they show that they don't think much of the idea of letting other nations share in God's mercy. If Nineveh will perish, so what? They deserve it, dirty sinners that they are.

Like Jonah, many of God's people today are delighted with God's grace but are unwilling to open up our arms and call others out of darkness into light.

This is behind Jonah's original reluctance to call Nineveh to repentance. He finally obeys, all the while believing that it won't work anyway. When his preaching does lead to total conversion and commitment of the pagan city to the Lord, Jonah feels angry and disgusted. He has spent his life in God's service, while the people in Nineveh are simply responding frantically to a prediction of destruction. What chance that their lives will change? They are just scared, not really God's children!

God's mercy contrasts sharply with Jonah's attitude. The Lord assures him that He has compassion on the children and even on the cattle of that great city.

Now, after Pentecost, I can be sure that my Father's arms are open wide. If I am jealous when my brothers and sisters respond to God's commands, then I can't love my Father very much.

Jonah 1-4

Jerusalem shall become a heap of ruins (Micah 3:12).

At first reading, there seems to be nothing unusual about Micah's prophecy. The prophets have predicted the doom of the unfaithful city of Jerusalem so many times that one hardly pays attention to such words anymore.

But there *is* something different about this Word of God through Micah. After this prophecy, the armies from the North do come and lay siege to the city. Micah holds his breath, for now the Lord will show that His servant spoke the truth when he predicted Jerusalem's fall. But then the king of Israel bribes the enemy with treasures and money, and the troops break up the attack and go home. So it just is not true that Jerusalem became a heap of ruins. Life goes on normally. The prophet can wait expectantly until he dies, but nothing will happen to the city. His prophecy failed miserably.

How does Micah square this with the certain knowledge that the Lord had spoken to him?

I, too, have problems with the Word of God. Often it seems unreliable. I have no ready explanation when people question me about certain claims of Scripture.

Micah's predicament is not solved during his lifetime. But a century later, Jeremiah remembers the words of Micah. Jerusalem is still standing, but now it is finally God's time to do what Micah predicted. Jeremiah 26:18 shows me that God's Word never fails. He is the ruler of the nations and ages.

There is, however, a second comfort. Though Micah would never know it, his prophecy produced results. Jeremiah reports in verse 19 that Hezekiah feared the Lord; he listened to Micah and repented. He prayed that the destruction of Jerusalem be averted and the Lord answered His prayers.

It does not matter whether I can understand every word of the Bible; but the effect that it has, the fruit that it bears, both now and in the future, is important.

Micah 1-3

*But you, O Bethlehem Ephrathah . . . from you shall come forth
for me one who is to be ruler in Israel (Micah 5:2).*

Micah would never have imagined that many centuries later,
scribes and priests would look at his prophecies and then tell wise
men from the east exactly where they could find the Messiah, born
in Bethlehem. Micah knew that Bethlehem was David's city and
that from the house of David the Messiah would come to rule over
His people. But the description of the coming Savior is so accurate
that it transcends Micah's ability to discern the future. The Spirit of
God is enlightening his visions, enabling Micah to show me the
road to Bethlehem.

However, the amazing thing is that when, many years later,
the scribes pass on this information to the wisemen, nothing happens—or at least nothing good. Herod uses this passage to find the
place where he can murder the hope of God's people. Jerusalem
does not react positively. Why?

Micah's prophecy, like the rest of Scripture, is not just information. The revelation of God is always a call to obedience and
faith. Jesus' challenge disturbed the people in Jerusalem and
brought Jesus to the cross.

Jesus is not just a good man, or even a savior of souls. He is
the ruler of the earth, the king to whom everybody should bow
down.

Satan doesn't mind if I respect the Bible. He does not mind if I
agree with Biblical data. Since archeologists confirm that the facts
are reported well and historians admit that things may actually
have happened as the Bible says, I don't deny that the Bible is true.
But satan does not want me to find out that it is the Truth, the
faithful message of God's love to me. Jesus did not come to tell me
true stories. He is the Truth, and He demands a response to Him.

Micah 4-7

Hearts faint and knees tremble, anguish is on all loins, all faces grow pale (Nahum 2:10).

Nineveh's power will be broken for good. That is the message that Nahum may bring to God's people. The Hebrew people, both the North Kingdom and the South Kingdom, have suffered more from the harsh and relentless Assyrians than from any other oppressor. For two and a half centuries Assyria has harassed them, driving the North Kingdom into cruel captivity and virtually demolishing Judah while forcing her kings into rigorously enforced subservience. Now at last, Assyria's end is near. Nahum calls Judah to start celebrating already.

God punishes the wicked and helps His people defeat their enemies throughout the Old Testament. But no prophet describes war so vividly as Nahum does. He sees soldiers in their scarlet uniforms, flashing chariots, the progress of the battle and the final victory.

But Nahum paints a dirty picture. Heaps of corpses, men and women who should have enjoyed long, rich lives; fainting hearts and trembling knees, pale faces staring in agony at approaching death and destruction. There is nothing glorious about war. The price of God's deliverance is heavy.

The earth is drenched in blood. People created in God's own image are ripped apart and trampled under galloping horses. War brings out the worst in man. Plunder and rape are cruel ways of celebrating victory. For years there will be the dark aftermath of these days of war.

I must not pray casually for the deliverance of the Lord. In this sin-filled world, the price of deliverance is always too high. My salvation was very expensive. Only through tremendous suffering can this world be clean and joyful. And I may expect to suffer with Christ.

Nahum 1-3

Yet *I will rejoice in the Lord (Habakkuk 3:18).*

One of the greatest words in the Bible is that very small one *yet*. It means that there is a road where nobody sees it. Though it looks like a dead-end street, it is the highway of my King. I am poor, yet I am rich. I am a sinner, yet I am righteous through the blood of Jesus Christ. "Yet" expresses the miracle of salvation.

Habakkuk lives in dark days. The place of Israel in world politics makes Habakkuk tremble and his lips quiver. He waits for even darker days and sees even more trouble in the future. He foresees no blossom on the fig tree, no fruit on the vines, no olives to be harvested, no food in the field, and no herd in the stalls. He foresees the total bankruptcy of his existence.

Yet he will rejoice in the Lord.

Habakkuk is not clinging to some cheap comfort. It would be easier to say that things are not as bad as they look. Rather, Habakkuk sees the Lord walking through the ages. In the past, He has demonstrated that He knew where He was going; Habakkuk trusts He knows now as well.

It is true that when God makes a path for Himself and for His kingdom, those things that stand in His way must be cleared out. I may be required to contribute, to let the Lord take away something that obstructs His path.

But Habakkuk is not bewailing the sacrifices that are required. His eyes are glued to the coming of the Lord.

Habakkuk tells me that I should never forget that God holds reality in His hands. I see only one part of the puzzle; yet, there are other parts that only God knows.

I am sad, yet I am happy. It sounds strange, but God's children know it is true in Christ Jesus.

Habakkuk 1-3

Yea, at that time I will change the speech of the peoples to a pure speech (Zephaniah 3:9).

It is remarkable how the image of Christ and the Holy Spirit become clearer the closer I get to the New Testament. Throughout the minor prophets, the sense of getting there intensifies. The fulfillment of God's promises is almost within the grasp of His children, and the Spirit of God can hardly wait until it will all be fulfilled.

The voice of prophecy changes. The closer Jesus' coming, the more I see the signs of the times. The call of the Bridegroom to be united with His bride is getting louder and clearer.

Zephaniah is bothered by a problem that previously seemed unimportant. He has discovered how hard it is to communicate with the strangers around him. There are so many languages and dialects. In the final years before the exile, Israel admits that their language is that of a small, insignificant country; hardly anybody understands it.

Now the Lord has promised that Israel will again become a power in the world. But how will they reach those nations where Hebrew is not understood?

I encounter the same problem when I try to communicate the message of Jesus Christ. The barriers to communication are deeper than language. How can I reach those who live in such a different world? Evangelism is often frustrated until the message has been translated into my neighbor's terms.

In the face of this problem, the Lord promises that He will change the speech of the peoples. Once at Babel He confused the language so that there could not be a unified attack on the church. Now He will reverse Himself. On Pentecost I see the Spirit reach all people: everyone hears the good news in his own language.

If I speak through the Spirit, doors will open and hearts will understand.

Zephaniah 1-3

The latter splendor of this house shall be greater than the former (Haggai 2:9).

After the return from the exile, God's people hesitantly set out to construct a new temple for the Lord. The people anticipate a small, unattractive house of God, nothing spectacular, certainly nothing to be proud of. No foreign nations will come to marvel at it as in the days of Solomon. They are hardly enthusiastic about the rebuilding process.

Haggai wants to change this. He talks about the splendor of the new temple, a splendor even greater than that of the former temple. The nations will bring their treasures again, and the silver and gold will blind their eyes.

Let us be honest: what Haggai promises never happens. And it is dangerous, even deceptive to set goals that will never be reached. Such tactics may boost moral momentarily, but then it will fall to new lows.

Was Haggai deceiving God's children? Certainly not. He knows of the coming splendor but the only words he can find to describe it are words of the past. Similarly, I talk about the new heaven and the new earth in terms of this world and life. I know that it is not an accurate description, but what else can I do? It certainly is not a lie, not even an exaggeration. In fact, it is less than the splendid truth.

In this temple that the people now build, the Son of God will appear as a child, inspiring Simeon to praise God. Here Jesus will speak and suffer under the sins of His people. Here the curtain will be ripped apart, opening God's sanctuary to everyone. Here the Spirit of God will come with the sound of wind and the glow of a fire.

Haggai cannot verbalize this glory; yet he tells his people to proceed and build, their labor will not be in vain.

I am a temple of the Holy Spirit. May His splendor fill my life.

Haggai 1-2

The Lord said to Satan, "The Lord rebuke you, O Satan"
(Zechariah 3:2).

Zechariah speaks in glowing terms about the future; the Branch shall build the temple and bring the full glory of God's kingdom. However, two obstacles still hinder entrance into the golden age. The first one is satan.

As Israel rebuilds after the exile, they struggle not against flesh and blood, but against the spiritual powers of darkness. Satan can't stand seeing his evil plan destroyed by the coming of Christ. So he tries to stop the coming of the glory of the Lord through the sins of God's people.

The second problem is that satan does have a certain right. Through my sins, I have allied myself with him and denied the sovereignty of my God. So satan points this out to the Lord.

Zechariah sees the high priest Joshua standing in dirty clothes. The highest and purest man in Israel, even he is defiled through his transgressions. Triumphantly satan makes it clear that there is little the Lord can do now.

But then the angel of God commands that the dirty clothes be removed and Joshua be dressed in splendid robes of state and a clean turban. God finds a way in which Joshua can be cleansed of his iniquity and again prepared to serve in God's kingdom. And in doing so, He deals satan a death blow. Satan is rebuked; all his malicious efforts count for nothing.

Zechariah does not explain how this cleansing could be done. The Lord only speaks of His choosing, His divine election. The angel of the Lord, the Son of God, was standing nearby, but He had not yet appeared in human flesh.

If God can break through the barrier of my sins, He can do everything. All I need is faith. Then as His kingdom proceeds, I can be part of it.

Zechariah 1-3

Not by might, nor by power, but by my Spirit, says the Lord of hosts (Zechariah 4:6).

Several texts in the Bible are used as proverbs or maxims by those who have no respect for the Word of God, and who therefore rip the text out of its context.

Even in the church, Scripture can be misunderstood or contorted. Whenever there is action to be taken and we are straining at the bit, some wise people remind us that we should not be so active. "Leave it to the Spirit!" they say, quoting this Zechariah passage. They warn us not to usurp God's task. "Wait and see what the Lord will do!"

But in this text, Zechariah is not telling the people to take it easy. On the contrary: the temple has to be built, and society has to be reorganized; everyone's help is urgently needed. Power and might are essential for the future of the national, cultural, and religious survival of God's covenant people. Zechariah wants to emphasize, however, that all their zeal and working and building will not bring victory. Behind and through the might and power of God's people is the Holy Spirit who uses them as His tools. The honor is never due to my efforts but to the operation and faithfulness of the Spirit of God.

Why stress this element? The Lord wants to save me headaches. Knowing that there is so much work to do, so many problems to solve, and so little prospect of success, I can get frenzied or paralyzed. When I get nowhere, I give up. Now the Lord says that I am just in His service, and His Spirit will accomplish what my power and might can never achieve.

Instead of taking it easy, this verse calls me to renew my actions, but it guarantees my success in Him.

Zechariah 4-6

Lo, your king comes to you; triumphant and victorious is he, humble and riding on an ass (Zechariah 9:9).

After the exile there are good leaders in Jerusalem, as there must be for the renewal of Israel. But it would be exciting to have some pomp and splendor as well as ordinary, down-to-earth leadership. Royalty and pageantry have always captured the imaginations and dreams of people. But Jerusalem is too busy for things like that. And now the times are too demanding for unnecessary expense.

Then Zechariah announces the coming of the King. He sees Him coming in His triumph and victory. The people must prepare a place for Him. The glory of royalty is not only a thing of the past; it is also in the future.

But Israel has bitter memories of vain-glorious kings who cruelly oppressed their subjects. They wanted to be served instead of to serve. So Zechariah with joy announces that the coming King will be humble; He will come riding a lowly donkey.

Now frankly, that picture is not full of splendor. God does not cater to my frivolous need for showiness. When Jesus enters Jerusalem, the crowds remember this text and anticipate the start of a glorious episode in Israel's history. They become frustrated when it becomes clear that Jesus will not satisfy their demand for cheap royalty, but will rule His people from a cross where He will be the King of the Jews that they really need.

I must look beneath appearances to discover the glory of Jesus' kingship. The whole world cries for power; my King brings justice. I instinctively feel that a king should rule; Jesus chooses to serve. Yet I also know, based on John's Revelation, that my King is triumphant and victorious and will eventually be surrounded with splendor.

Zechariah 7-9

They weighed out as my wages thirty shekels of silver (Zechariah 11:12).

Some Bible passages defy logical explanation, but likely no passage is more evasive than this one. A variety of interpretations exist, but no consensus has been reached. To complicate matters, some words can be translated in different ways, for example, the word *treasury* can also mean *potter's house.* The crowning touch comes in Matthew 27:9 where Matthew misquotes this passage and then identifies it as being from Jeremiah rather than from Zechariah.

It is likely that this passage is neither messianic nor eschatological but an allegorical description of some historical situation that occurred long before the exile and is now unknown to us. But basically these verses are a reminder that there are two parties to a covenant. If one party violates his part of the bargain, then the other is released from his. God officially breaks off relations with Israel after the people have defaulted on them. Then two things happen: God withdraws His grace, and strife and struggle take the place of community. The people are given over to external enemies and internal strife.

Perhaps Matthew did not understand the nuances of this story. But it strikes him that Judas' betrayal of Jesus is basically what the people of God have done throughout the ages. In Zechariah's story, the bad shepherds want to terminate the work of the Good Shepherd, and so they give him the pay-off of thirty shekels. The low amount, merely the price of a slave, expresses their spite for God's value. And yet they are willing to pay good money to get rid of Him.

At times I squirm under the guidance and leadership of God. But to forsake God's covenant with me is to invite emptiness and disunity.

Jesus paid the price of His blood to remain my Shepherd. Now it is up to me to choose.

Zechariah 10-12

Every pot in Jerusalem and Judah shall be sacred to the Lord of hosts (Zechariah 14:21).

This passage is eschatological; that is, it describes the final days. The end of Zechariah's prophecy is an exultation in the future glory of God's kingdom, and it describes what can be expected when God comes to His people to live among them, just as John describes the apocalypse in Revelation.

Throughout his prophecy, Zechariah has stressed the need for performing ceremonial duties in the house of the Lord. The danger of Pharisaism seems to lurk around the corner; Zechariah's ideal of holiness seems somewhat formalistic and superficial. But now it becomes obvious that Zechariah considers the temple rite not an end in itself but a means to a more glorious life with God.

Zechariah sees that in the future the vessels in the temple will not be of any special holiness anymore. At last Israel will be a kingdom of priests. The sacramental bread will be broken in every home; the family hearth will be the dwelling place of God. Ceremonial sacrifices will be unnecessary. All of life will serve God, and the church will no longer be buildings and ceremonies, but will be seen in people, the Body of Christ. Work in God's kingdom will not imply missions and worship services; daily life will be worship. God will be praised just as much in factories and in kitchens as through the formal rites of worship.

This is the era of the Christian church. Pentecost has marked the end of the temple. Now all God's children are temples of the Holy Spirit. Even the bells of the horses, freed from constant battling to protect God's people, now ring to the glory of God's holiness.

This can be somewhat intimidating—*every* pot must be made sacred to the Lord. But then God will have full glory. If I trust in the Lord and His Spirit, this can come true in my life.

Zechariah 13-14

The Lord was witness to the covenant between you and the wife of
your youth (Malachi 2:14).

The last book of the Old Testament urges the people to
prepare themselves for the coming of the Messiah. Malachi
describes it as a great and terrible day of the Lord. He does not
mean that the coming of God is not to be desired. He is saying only
that there is so much to be done to prepare for Him. What is not
right will have to be burned. But there is also a word to the
believers: the sun of righteousness is coming to heal, and there will
be joy like the leaping of calves from the stall in the springtime.

This passage in Malachi tells how several men in Judah decide
that their marriage is a dull affair and that it would be nice to start
all over again with another woman. So they casually send their life
partners away and take the "daughters of an alien god" or
idolatresses as their new wives.

Now those deserted wives have been coming to God; their tears
have been falling on His altar. Later, the husbands come to the
altar, while the tears of their ex-wives are still upon it. The Lord
says, How can you start crying on My altar because I refuse to accept your offering? You know what you have done and I know it. I
was a witness at your wedding, and I have seen what you did in
your cruel selfishness. Where is your love? How can you love Me
when you don't love the wife of your youth?

I sometimes complain that the Lord is not answering prayers,
that He is hiding Himself. But is the fault mine? When I ban the
Holy Spirit from my life, how can I expect Him to fill me with
peace and happiness? When I break the laws of God's love, how
can I ask the Lord to bless me?

But God calls me back. He asks me to lay my life at His altar
so that we can live in love once again.

Malachi 1-3

They fell down and worshiped him (Matthew 2:11).

Matthew writes to convince the Jews that Jesus is the Messiah. Therefore, he often quotes Old Testament passages which he sees fulfilled by the coming of the Savior.

With the story of the wise men, Matthew shows how simple and beautiful knowing the Christ can be. A star in the skies is enough to lead these sages to Bethlehem. They naturally take along precious gifts for the newborn King.

They could have given up in Jerusalem. The scribes and priests know that Bethlehem is the birthplace for the Messiah, but nobody but Herod shows any interest. And he wants the information so that he can kill the child. When the three travelers finally arrive in Bethlehem, they find nothing impressive: just a baby; no people to worship and adore Him. What are the chances that they accept this baby as the King of Israel? But miraculously, they bow down and greet the Savior of the world, presenting unto Him gifts.

This story puts Israel to shame. Israel has all the answers, but they ask no questions. The wise men have no answers, but they ask the great question, "What can we do to share in this tremendous event?"

This story makes me uncomfortable. Seeing only a star, the wise men go, but where am I after all my Bible study? They persist in spite of the indifference of the official church, and the hatred of the world. They discover the Savior and worship in faith without seeing any splendor. What am I waiting for? Why do I often lack that childlike faith?

I pray for the wisdom that knows to bow down and worship, and to bring the gift of my life.

You are the light of the world (Matthew 5:14).

Often I think of the Sermon on the Mount as a new and better version of the Ten Commandments, or at least an improvement over the law of God as explained by the scribes and Pharisees. Jesus calls His disciples to obey a new set of rules. He tells His followers they should be the salt of the earth, to preserve life and make it pleasant. They have to be like a bright city on a hill that preaches without words.

But as I think about it, I discover that the Sermon on the Mount does not tell me what I hoped it would. If Jesus had said, "*Try* to be the light of the world," I would have had some good excuses. "Jesus, You are the Light and I am only a small wavering candle; don't count on me too much. I will do my best, but the darkness is immense." I could bring my good intentions to Jesus.

But Jesus does not ask me to be the light of the world; He states that I am. He tells me what I am in Him.

That is not an intimidating task. If I live as Jesus' disciple, the light *will* shine. When I live in Jesus, He lives in me. That is why He can call me the light of the world with no hesitation. Jesus does not push me; He simply tells me of the glorious position which I have in Him. The only thing Jesus asks me to do is to let the light shine. Then I can point the world to Him who made me a light in His service.

I hear admonition as well as reassurance. For I have tried to obscure my riches; I have kept my salvation for myself. I have limited the light to one day a week. But Jesus calls me the light. Let it shine!

New wine is put into fresh wineskins, and so both are preserved (Matthew 9:17).

Sometimes I get stuck in a rut. This inertia, this lack of movement, can also afflict the church. Some people call that inertia "preserving the old traditions," but others see it as conservatism.

Jesus does not choose between progressive and conservative. Change just for the sake of change is futile in His eyes. But stubborn resistance to every change can also be bad. Jesus points to an alternative not on the progressive/conservative spectrum.

When Jesus' disciples point out that John the Baptist's disciples have a different lifestyle than theirs, Jesus tells them that that is naturally so. The new wine, alive and fermenting, needs new wineskins. The kingdom of God is moving on. The days of preparation by John are over now that the fulfillment in Jesus is here.

Every period in the development of God's work brings a new harvest. New forms have to be found to fit new situations. The church must not insist on the old customs and habits, not because new ideas are so interesting, but because the old forms are bursting at the seams.

Am I so full of the life of the Spirit that I need new forms of expression, or could I easily stick to my old form of life? Is the gospel and its influence on our world and times so powerful that I have to do something about it. Or has something died in me and my church?

Jesus assumes that I have the new and sparkling wine of His Spirit. Now, shall I merely patch up my old life? No, the wineskins may burst, wasting the new wine. I have to ask myself what form and style of life will fit the power that is in me. That is not an easy question, but it is one that I cannot avoid.

It is like children sitting in the market places (Matthew 11:16).

One of the most subtle ways to escape the call of the gospel is to play games. God Himself blessed life with playful humor. Often I have to find respite from the harsh reality of life in game-playing. But game-playing is dangerous when it is used to avoid confrontation with the real issues in life.

Matthew senses that his efforts to convince the Jews that Jesus is the promised Messiah have met with little success. Jesus explains it for him. When John came and called people to repentance in austerity and urgent warnings, the Jews complained that he took things far too seriously. When Jesus comes and brings the joy of the gospel in healing and mercy, they accuse Him of being light-hearted. In other words, there is always something to complain about when God does not play things the way I want Him to.

Perhaps my frivolous dabbling with God's call to obedience is only for fun. Perhaps it has little to do with the serious world where decisions have to be made and where acts are final. However, the Lord expects me to be child-like, not childish.

The Jews were playing games with the temple and the law. They spent hours debating Biblical word puzzles and trying to find deeper meanings behind Biblical expressions. Unfortunately, they never understood the power and urgency of the Word of God.

I can debate matters of God's kingdom, only to realize later that it was just for the sake of argument. Debates about religious topics and discussions of moral values can be exercises in polemics, games played with a smile.

How much of my life is adult business and how much is child's play? I pray God that I may grow up even while I remain a child.

He sent and had John beheaded in the prison (Matthew 14:10).

The man who prepared the way for Jesus is put in prison and, as a reward for a good dance act, his life is taken. It seems so senseless. Why did John meddle in the affairs of a non-Israelite, Herod the Edomite? Was he sure that Herod's marriage to his sister-in-law was against the will of God? Couldn't John have escaped this cruel death?

John the Baptist was convinced of the power of God's Word and he was not going to tone down its demands. He knew that God is ruler of every one of His creatures. God's message was too important to dilute just to save his own skin. So he did not beg for mercy.

Yet, couldn't God have protected His servant? Herodias's cruel demand which silenced the voice of her accuser; the king's drunkenness—wasn't all this too shallow to be a fitting end of this great prophet's life? Where was God?

God does not always further His kingdom the way I would. Later Herod seems haunted by what has happened; when he hears about Jesus' activities, he assumes that John has been raised from the dead. The Word of God cannot be silenced. John's death pursues Herod to make his life miserable. His pleasures are spoiled; his conscience is burdened. God keeps on speaking.

Even more important in this story is what John's death means to Jesus. When John's disciples tell Him what has happened, Jesus knows that now the real struggle for the salvation of His people starts. The fore-runner is dead; the preparations have been finished. A stranger has killed John; His own people will kill Him.

Now my sympathy for John disappears, and my eyes are drawn to Him who will go to His death for me.

I do not say to you seven times, but seventy times seven (Matthew 18:22).

Jesus had been talking about the tender care His followers should have for each other and how much should be done to bring a sinner back to God and to the congregation. Wanting to show that he has understood the message, and full of his usual enthusiasm, Peter asks Jesus to agree that he should forgive a brother who sins against him seven times in a row.

This seems hard. When somebody hurts me deeply, how much effort it takes to tell him that it is all over, that the matter is forgiven and forgotten. If the same thing happens again a few days later, I can still reason that that is the old nature of the sinner acting up, and in that light, make room for another word of pardon. But when this repeats itself seven times, forgiveness cannot be the answer. Such repentance cannot be real. It would be better to teach the sinner a lesson; my love and understanding seem to encourage his further sinning. Perhaps he is purposely taking advantage of me—a gullible fool.

All the modern educational and psychological theories contradict Peter's approach. But Peter wants to show that he desires to strive for the ultimate in Christian love.

Then Jesus tells Peter that seventy times seven is a better number. Now this is sheer madness; it is humanly impossible. And therein lies the message. Peter is talking about his own power to forgive. However, God's love and pardon are the only sufficient source of love towards my fellow men. I ask for pardon every day; I can always go to Him who gave me His love so endlessly.

The Lord gave me so much in Jesus Christ. Now I must try to follow in His footsteps. The mercy I receive from the Lord I must pass on to my neighbor.

Take what belongs to you, and go (Matthew 20:14).

In the parable of the laborers in the vineyard, Jesus describes two groups of people. The first group of workers are the scribes and priests who have toiled all their lives in the service of their God, doing what they believed was His will. They receive their wages, just as they expected.

But these people are shocked when Jesus gives the same wages to those who have not been working in the vineyard all day. Some worked a half-day, some hardly at all.

The latter group represents the tax collectors and the harlots. When they come late in life to Jesus, they receive His mercy. Now the Pharisees and scribes are angry because they have done so much for God and yet have gotten paid just the same as those "sinners."

The Pharisees and scribes have received a just wage; the others received joy and happiness because they were surprised to receive the same reward as the faithful workers. Jesus loves to see the joy of those who experience mercy and grace, who don't understand it, but accept it in deep gratitude.

So it is with me. If I think that all my work for God entitles me to wages, I should take them and go home. But then I really have very little. If, like the harlots and tax collectors, I can see what grace is all about, then I experience deep happiness.

Jesus gets angry when the first workers interfere with the joy of those who received grace. When they claim that it is unfair, He sends them away.

The murderer on the cross received the same reward as Paul who spends his life in God's service. Or does he? Isn't it better to be called to serve God all my life?

Thank You, God, for enabling me to serve You. May I also continually savor the joy of being saved by Your grace.

And call no man your father on earth, for you have one Father who is in heaven (Matthew 23:9).

Jesus' warnings against the Pharisees seem to refer only to His days. There are, of course, some Pharisaic people around me, but generally I am so scared of hypocrisy that it seems unnecessary for Jesus to keep warning *me*.

Jesus, however, also talked about how I avoid close contact with the living God by building kingdoms on earth where I can dwell without looking up to heaven. In Jesus' days, the Jewish leaders were rabbis and fathers whose laws, rules, doctrines, customs and rites were overwhelming. Ironically, nobody recognized God when He stood before them in the person of Jesus Christ. There was no place for the Son of God in their earthly kingdom.

Jesus literally forbade anyone to call a spiritual leader "father." The organization of church life can be a screen between God's children and God Himself. The Bible can be replaced by small, simple "how-to" manuals. Human authorities, office-bearers and spiritual leaders, may claim to speak the Word of God although they do not. And I may respond by dodging rules, correcting them, or fighting about them. Then I look spiritually active even though I am actually avoiding the real confrontation between God and His people.

I would love to feel the approval of all those dignitaries who by solemn customs, clothing, and titles convey a false sense of importance. But I must not let my thoughts and my love stray in wrong directions.

Jesus realized that this hypocrisy would lead to His death. But if I would exchange my Father for an earthly "father," I too will die. That is why Jesus used such strong language to cut through this web of avoiding God. He came to bring me back to my Father.

But Jesus was silent (Matthew 26:63).

Jesus must be sorely tempted to speak. Standing in the courts of the high priest, He is accused by liars. It would be easy to lash out at this terrible perversion of justice. Jesus could perhaps talk Himself out of the spot He is in. But in majestic silence, He begs for no mercy, accepting death for His people.

However, Jesus is active even though He does not speak. Fulfilling His own Word about turning the other cheek, He accentuates the sin in the authorities' display of human cruelty. Besides, to argue would ascribe some importance to the false accusations. So Jesus only stares straight into their eyes.

At the same time, Jesus forces the high priest to abandon his hypocritical schemes and to get to the real issue at stake. Everybody knows that the big question is whether Jesus is to be accepted or rejected as the Savior. Is God standing here in His Son? Are they willing to bow down before Him?

The high priest has to find out that he cannot play games with God. Jesus' silence forces the man to come to grips with what is the only important issue. Caiaphas gets furious, as people do when God exposes their games.

Jesus is willing to die for His people, but only on the open admission that the Son of the living God dies to take away the sins of the world.

There is, however, yet another reason for Jesus' silence. He could have spoken about the sins of the council, about the cowardice of the disciples who left Him, about me and all my sins and shortcomings. But He kept silence before God and men. He did not come to condemn but to save. Because His mouth remained shut, my mouth can be opened to praise Him who never says a bad word about me to His Father.

My son, your sins are forgiven (Mark 2:5).

These words seem misdirected. A man who desperately wants to find a full and normal life comes to Jesus. Being a paralytic keeps him from employment, social activities, marriage, and most of all, the dignity of taking care of his own life. Four friends rip open the roof of the building in order to get him close enough to Jesus to be healed. Now Jesus can with one word dispel all the dark shadows from this man's life and restore to him the fullness of life.

What frustration when Jesus tells him that his sins are forgiven! What a disappointing statement, the right thing to say, but at the wrong time. True, we all need spiritual health, but is that the real problem Jesus faces in this man? Jesus' comment has led people to conjecture that the man was suffering from a guilty conscience, or that his paralysis was the result of a sinful way of life, or that his disease was psychosomatic, just a physical reaction to an inner struggle. But surely the Bible doesn't support this.

Why do I feel that Jesus' word about forgiveness is disappointing? Am I so far from God and His values that the forgiveness of sins seems less important than physical health?

Then Jesus asks the questioning scribes, "Which is easier, to say to the paralytic, 'Your sins are forgiven,' or to say, 'Rise'?" Jesus hints at the tremendous burden He carries. He will pay for the sins of the whole world. It would have been much easier and certainly more spectacular to heal and to give in to the people's desires for power and glory on earth.

Too often I am blasé about the forgiveness of my sins. But if Jesus would have given some merely external blessings leaving my sins alone, I still would have had no future. That would have been much easier, but Jesus takes the hard way. Even when I am uninterested in my spiritual health, He pays attention to the real essentials of my existence.

They began to beg Jesus to depart from their neighborhood (Mark 5:17).

Satan sends his legion of evil spirits into a man, making him a danger to those around him. He breaks the fetters with which his neighbors try to restrain him. But he also hurts himself: he bruises his own body, and he lives in the tombs.

That is the stark reality of a demon-filled world. Demons and their father, satan, encourage us to hurt each other, to cause agony around us, and even to ruin our own lives by doing things that can only cause misery. But the Word of the Son of God, who came to destroy the realm of satan, can break the bondage and free this man—and us—to go back to society as a blessing instead of a curse.

In this world of senseless suffering and misery, the Savior stands with authority. Already in Paradise we invited satan in, but Jesus sends him out. We gave the demons the power to destroy; Jesus comes with the power to heal.

The man sitting at Jesus' feet, well clothed and in his right mind, is evidence that the gospel can radically heal the misery of this world. When Jesus, through me, goes into this life, restoration must follow.

The cost of this healing is pretty high: about two thousand swine are lost. So in effect, the whole community has to pay for the well-being of this demoniac. It appears that they are unwilling to do so. Before anything of the kind can happen again, they beg Jesus to go away. Money and prosperity are more valuable to them than the healing of a demon-possessed world. They don't realize that there will never be true prosperity while satan rules.

Am I ready to stop the work of satan, even though it may demand sacrifices? When I look at Jesus, who was willing to pay the highest price to break the power of satan, I know what my answer must be.

I believe; help my unbelief (Mark 9:24).

A man has brought his son to the disciples, hoping that they can drive out an evil spirit that made the boy suffer. But they are not able to cure him. When Jesus and the three disciples who have been on the Mount of Transfiguration arrive, the father of the child appeals to Jesus to heal his child, if He can. Jesus' response is an incredulous, "If *I* can? That is not the problem. *Your* faith must be strong; *you* must believe and trust that My healing strength can be supplied."

Now the man has to respond to Jesus. Everything dear to him is at stake. The source of healing is there, the suffering boy is waiting; now his faith should make the connection between them. The man may be tempted to fake it, just mumbling a few words not absolutely true.

I have lied under less pressure than this father feels. To keep up appearances with my fellow Christians, I may have acted as if I were the greatest of all believers.

Now this man gives an answer that is extremely risky. On the one hand, he confesses his trust in Jesus, but he also has to admit to a measure of doubt in his heart. The fight between light and darkness rages inside him.

When the man confesses his struggle to Jesus, he cannot be sure that his child will be healed. But he just cannot lie. He is not proud of his doubts either, as some are. He knows his faith should be stronger, but still he appeals for help.

Then Jesus does not condemn, does not even look disappointed. He offers a smile of grace, a word of deliverance, and an outstretched hand to the seemingly dead boy.

Is it possible that I exhibit the most faith and trust in Jesus when I am honest with Him?

Many rebuked him, telling him to be silent (Mark 10:48).

It happens too often in the Bible—people put up barricades which block someone's way to Jesus. Now, a blind man wants badly to get to Him. The crowd hears his plaintive cries; since he cannot approach Jesus himself, he must call Jesus to him. But the crowd sharply rebukes the man, telling him to be silent.

Why?

Perhaps it bothers them to hear those cries. There is something repulsive about watching other people suffer. Guilt would rather remain undisturbed.

A second reason may be that they have seen enough miracles. Perhaps their curiosity has been satisfied.

Or perhaps they know that Jesus is on His way to Jerusalem. Because a confrontation with the priests seems inevitable, tension hangs heavy in the air. The possible clash between this holy man and the leaders of Israel makes for exciting speculation. How will that turn out? The development of those events is much more important than an individual case of suffering.

Yes, I say. All the confrontations in life are so urgent and stimulating that personal needs just have to wait or be put aside. the blind man is not as significant as the struggles between the authorities. The individual at times must be sacrificed for the mass.

Jesus disagrees emphatically. He calls the man, asks him what he wants, and heals him.

Only one reason for the crowd rebuking the blind man still seems justifiable. Perhaps they feel that Jesus is too good to be bothered. Perhaps this thinking also led the disciples to turn back the mothers and their children.

At times I may feel that I shouldn't pray, that I shouldn't bother God with my demands. But Jesus would rather hear me calling and expecting His help. That is what He came for.

They compelled a passerby, Simon of Cyrene, the father of Alexander and Rufus, to carry his cross (Mark 15:21).

Understandably, certain elements have been included in the story of Jesus' passion and death that are actually unfounded. Painters, poets, and storytellers have added sentimental or imaginative details that are not the stark reality as reported in the Scriptures.

On the way to Golgotha, the Roman soldiers seize and compel a stranger from Cyrene to carry the cross for Jesus. Why? No reason is given. Perhaps Jesus was too weak to bear the cross Himself, but there is no evidence to support this theory. Though it is good to recognize how violently Jesus suffered under the wrath of God, it is dangerous to add details not found in the Bible. Embellishment may cause me to miss the real message.

It is irrelevant whether the soldiers were trying to hurry up the whole crucifixion, were poking fun at the stranger returning home to Jerusalem, or were simply following a standard procedure. The fact is that even the dignity of Jesus' bearing His own cross was taken away from Him. The gospel of John emphasizes the glory of Christ's crucifixion; however, the other gospel writers stress the shame of the cross.

The world considers it desirable to handle one's own problems. Older people lose their dignity when they are required to accept aid. Children are offended when parents or teachers push them aside, to do things for them. Underdeveloped countries resent the clumsy patronage of richer countries. There springs that eternal hope in me that I can manage my own affairs.

Jesus had to suffer for me. He tells me that I should accept His help and salvation, because He has accepted the burden for me and taken it away. The shame was for Him, the glory of the cross for me.

And she gave birth to her first-born son (Luke 2:7).

Throughout the ages, people have given romanticized explanations of what was so very special about the birth of Jesus. Jesus must have been very poor—didn't Mary use swaddling clothes? The fact is, every mother in Israel at that time did that. There was no place in the inn for the poor, weary travelers, one of them a mother likely in labor: how cruel the inhabitants of Bethlehem were! But the fact is that this city was inundated by citizens registering for the census. When there is no room, there is no room. The fact that the newborn was laid in a manger has led to many charming poems, songs, and paintings, all portraying Jesus amidst clean, docile, almost worshipful farm animals.

When I strip the nativity scene of all its quaint trimmings, there is not much left over. God very simply describes the coming of His Son into the world. Mary gave birth to her first child, a son.

Nothing should be allowed to obscure the simple truth about the greatest of all moments in the history of the world. God Almighty comes to earth in His Son.

The Son of God enters this world of mine almost unnoticed. He quietly takes over my unspectacular life. Before I realize it, my life, my sins, my past and my future are taken from my own shoulders and put on His.

Just as my life can be so common and uninteresting, just as there is little to tell about me, so there is little to tell about the Son of God who stands in my place. The spectacular is not in what I see, but in what I know through the revelation of the Lord.

When I accept Jesus as God's revelation of Himself, then suddenly songs break forth. Glory to God in the highest, and on earth, peace among men with whom He is pleased.

He rebuked them and would not allow them to speak (Luke 4:41).

Several people who are demon-possessed shout aloud that Jesus is the Son of God. Now if ever there is an unbiased testimony about Him, this is it. These demons cannot profit from their profession, since they will be tormented when Jesus casts them out. But they have to say it anyway. They cannot keep silent in the face of Jesus' divine authority. The crowd is interested only in miraculous healings and bread, and the scribes, Pharisees, and priests deny His authority and slander Him. Jesus must have welcomed a proclamation about His being the Son of the living God.

But Jesus does not accept their proclamation of His greatness. He tells the demons to keep their mouth shut.

The words of demons cannot praise Jesus. His enemies have no intention of promoting His kingdom. The demons want to destroy God's work upon earth, no matter what they say.

Not every method of spreading the gospel is legitimate. Organizations using the gospel as a means to make money, slick evangelism campaigns, and million dollar churches may shout to the world that Jesus is the Son of God, but in many cases, God is not glorified.

When people accept Jesus as the Christ, they must do so out of faith and personal dedication. The shouts of demons reveal nothing about Jesus' love and mercy. Demons fear Him and want no part in His salvation.

Jesus calls me to tell the world that He is the Christ. The good news should be obvious in my life; I must reflect the love of my Savior. Love makes the message genuine.

Jesus said, "Who was it that touched me?" (Luke 8:45).

Jesus is on His way to heal a dying twelve year old girl. Every second counts, but still Jesus stops to ask who touched Him. It seems a silly question: a whole crowd is surrounding Him, pressing upon Him. When Jesus has finished His discussion with the woman who was healed of her disease, the message comes that He is too late—the child has died. This woman has suffered for twelve years; she could have waited. Why the delay?

First of all, Jesus is not satisfied when people are healed merely from their physical diseases. Jesus' miracles have no meaning in themselves. Today's emphasis on faith-healings and miracles may obscure the fact that without Jesus' love and mercy nothing really changes; death is not really conquered. This woman may not go home without hearing the word of salvation.

What if I gain the whole world but my life is not in Christ?

There is another reason for Jesus' delay. The father of the child is asking for immediate help, and the messenger announces that it is too late. People are putting limits on Jesus' power. But time and conditions do not affect Him.

I cannot tell Jesus what can be done or what should be done. When I assume that something is beyond hope, He tells me that I am wrong. The times of my life and the world are in His hands; nobody is going to make a time-table for Him. In Him, even the power of death is broken. I have only to live out of His victory.

How much more will the heavenly Father give the Holy Spirit to those who ask him! (Luke 11:13).

This passage does not say what it seems to say. It encourages me to pray for all I want, but seems to add that what I will get is the Holy Spirit. It seems that all my concrete demands are too small for the Lord. Besides, I should not care too much about them anyway, for I have to live a spiritual life.

This explanation of this text is terribly mistaken. Jesus tells His disciples just the opposite. I may ask for all the small things in life. I must go in trust to my heavenly Father, confident that He is listening.

God does add a qualifier. I may even ask for things that He cannot give me because to do so would hurt me or the coming of His kingdom. In those cases, God promises me He will replace the good I request with something even better. I may have to look at what I receive from God and say, "This is not a fish, but it is not a serpent either. It is not an egg, but it is definitely not a scorpion." God sometimes must answer my prayers by giving me a substitute for the things I ask for.

Unfortunately, sometimes I accuse God of not responding to my prayers even while He points at His gifts and calls them good. Then I shortchange myself.

Jesus wants to open my eyes so that I can see what the Holy Spirit has given me. He makes me blush about my accusations.

I am so rich, but He teaches me to see it.

*What man of you . . . does not leave the ninety-nine in the
wilderness, and go after the one which is lost? (Luke 15:4).*

When a shepherd misses one of a hundred sheep, he should accept his loss. One percent is not bad. And if he goes after the one
lost sheep, the whole flock could be harmed. Wisdom should
prevail over feelings. The lady in the next story loses one coin. That
is a heavier loss: ten percent. She turns the whole house upside-
down until she finds the lost coin. Then, strangely, she throws a
party for the neighborhood that probably costs her far more than
the value of the coin. Then there is the father who loses one of his
two sons: fifty percent. When the son finally returns home, the
father organizes a celebration as if something extremely significant
has occurred. I would agree with the older brother that it just does
not make sense.

Until now, the Pharisees and scribes have been very upset with
all that Jesus does, particularly with how He associates and eats
with the less desirable elements of society. They disagree
wholeheartedly with His emotional approach.

Now Jesus tells them stories which confront them with the
mysterious love of God. Yes, He wants to save tax collectors and
sinners, and only His love explains that.

These stories cite approximate human parallels for God's love.
What man of you would not leave the ninety-nine, and what
woman would not invite the neighborhood for a celebration of the
coin that was found, and certainly what father would not receive
his son back home without one harsh word? Understanding and
sympathizing with these instances helps me to begin to fathom the
unfathomable love of my heavenly Father, a love that is beyond my
comprehension. There is no real parallel in human love.

God wishes that none of these sinners will get lost. I don't have
to understand God's love—just so long as I share in it.

If some one goes to them from the dead, they will repent (Luke 16:30).

People have assumed that in this parable Jesus gives an accurate description of life eternal and death eternal. But one may not assume that all the details of a parable are meant to be revelatory. The details of an allegory have specific meanings and some parables, such as The Sower, do operate as allegories. But most parables turn upon only a point of comparison. In this case, Jesus assumes the view of heaven and hell prevalent in those days in order to make His own point.

The first lesson of this parable is that the rich cannot buy their future happiness, nor are the poor shut out from the love of God. In eternity, matters will not be arranged according to the patterns of this world.

But then Jesus comes to the real message. It appears that the leaders of Israel have rejected the teachings of Moses and the prophets. The Word of God has no real influence anymore. God's revelations about His will, about rich and poor, and sin and salvation have been cleverly dulled. It is possible to talk so long about the Bible that the Bible itself is no longer heard.

The man in the parable knows this. He should have listened, but he did not like what he heard. He lived his own affluent life only to find out that without the Lord and His Word he was doomed.

Now he wants to warn his five brothers by sending Lazarus back to earth to witness to them. But Jesus says that even if a dead person would rise and warn them, they would not accept his words.

It is not that we do not know, but that we don't want to listen. People *have* been raised from the dead. Miracles *have* happened. Jesus rose from the grave and preached. My heart is what has to change.

Zacchaeus, make haste and come down (Luke 19:5).

Zacchaeus, the hated chief tax collector, takes a risk by climbing the sycamore tree. But he *does* want to see Jesus, and so he takes his chances.

Why is Zacchaeus so anxious to see Jesus? There have been several theories. Was he repentant? Did he hope to start a new life? If so, that would fit into my theory that if I see my sins and confess them, then I can receive mercy. But the Bible says Zacchaeus is curious, nothing more. Jesus calls him because of His own divine love. The call of my Savior is the only ground for my salvation; nothing that I feel or do can save me.

Then Jesus invites Himself to dinner with this sinful man. I would have expected a strong lecture, a sermon about sin and salvation, a harsh rebuke and an admonition. But nothing of the kind happens. In Israel, the most sacred communion was to share a meal, and now Jesus sits at Zacchaeus' table where they break bread together.

My deliverance does not depend on words. Rather, the Son of God comes into my life, accepts me just as I am, and assures me that He is with me.

Words and preaching may not convince me. But when Jesus holds my hand and others share with me in His name, I know love that melts the ice in my heart.

Now Zacchaeus shows what Jesus' love has meant to him. His promises are outrageous: he wants to give away half of his goods, and then repay fourfold what he has defrauded. This is probably not financially possible. But did Jesus ask him to be more realistic? Of course not. Here is new life, here is a new son of Abraham, here is faith and love. And that is what counts. Enthusiastic love for my Lord can only please Him.

He interpreted to them in all the scriptures the things concerning himself (Luke 24:27).

If only I could have walked with Jesus from Jerusalem to Emmaus, hearing His explanation of the Old Testament as it relates to the Christ in His coming, His suffering, and His resurrection. But even more, I would love to have been so close to Him. He can seem so abstract and far away; it is not easy to love somebody I have never met personally. I would have loved to see His hands breaking the bread, an action which was the sign of His suffering and, at the same time, of the glory of His resurrection.

But the real message of this story is that Jesus' bodily presence is not essential for faith and joy. When Jesus walks and talks with the two men, He does not want them to know who He is. The joy of His salvation must come to their lives through the power of the Word of God alone. Their hearts burn, not because they recognize Him, but because their eyes of faith are opened to the treasures of His revelation. As soon as they really see with their own eyes who He is, He disappears. He does not engage in a discussion after He has made Himself known to them. Now they have to go to the other disciples and share the power of the message itself.

Now this story comforts me. If my salvation depended on a personal encounter with Jesus, I would be out in the cold. But Jesus wants to make it clear to future generations that I am not less privileged than the apostles. His Word is with me. The New Testament gives Jesus' interpretation of the Old Testament. The Holy Spirit has come to lead me in all truth. Mysterious encounters with Jesus are not needed. Rather, I have to take His Word and study it and believe. As I do so, I can walk and talk with Jesus.

Making a whip of cords, he drove them all, with the sheep and oxen, out of the temple (John 2:15).

The temple was flooded with cattle sellers and money changers who were dishonest, loud, and irreverent. When somebody wanted to sacrifice to God, they could not just bring their own ox. Such animals had to be inspected by a priest and the rules were so stringent that it was nearly impossible to get one's sacrifice approved. So the cattle sellers made money. And the money changers made a profit because ordinary money had to be exchanged for special coins before it was acceptable for the temple's treasury.

Such rules had made worship a cold, formal ritual. The priests stood between God and His children. They acted as if there was real sacrifice and worship going on, while they went through only the motions.

Jesus drives all hindrance to true worship out of the temple. People must go to the Lord of the temple.

I hope that I can see the angry face of my Savior when my worship becomes a routine, an empty habit. He loves me too much to say only that I ought not to do that. He takes a whip, not to throw me out, but to scourge from my life all that is meaningless.

Amazingly, nobody stands up to Jesus. The temple guards do nothing; the sellers offer no resistance. Jesus acts with such authority that they all understand what is happening, and they all know that it is right.

Then when it seems that this whole action is negative, Jesus explains to the Jews that He is the temple of God who will build up a new and living temple. As Jesus tells me what not to do, He leads me into the fullness and beauty of a living temple in Him.

I pray that I can be just as upset as Jesus about things which trouble communion with God.

It is no longer because of your words that we believe (John 4:42).

In her discussion with Jesus, the woman from Samaria introduces topics such as the position of women in society, the discrimination of Samaritans by Jews, the common ancestry of both Jews and Samaritans from their father Jacob, the matter of worship in Samaria or Jerusalem, and finally, even the coming of the Messiah. It all makes for interesting discussion, but the woman is avoiding the real problem in her life. Jesus cuts through all her evasion with the simple command, "Call your husband and come here."

Jesus realizes that I often try to hide from reality in a web of words and thoughts. The real problem in my life is sin, and Jesus wants to bring into my broken, barren life the living water of His Word and grace. First the woman tries to squirm out of a direct confrontation with Jesus. But when she surrenders at last, she can accept Jesus as the Messiah. I can meet the real Jesus only in the forgiveness of sins.

Now that the woman believes that her sins are forgiven, she talks to her neighbors about her former sordid way of life. After I have faced God with my trespasses, I can face others also. Hesitance to confess sins betrays a lack of faith in God's forgiving grace.

Another problem arises, however. The woman becomes the focus of a spiritual revival in the city. That is dangerous. Sordid sins can become glamorous. Talking about them can turn into an addictive, fascinating, and even profitable business. I hesitate when I hear the woman talk so openly about her past. Does she glory in it? I have heard too many sordid and shallow testimonies.

Jesus has a solution for this too. He goes to the city and preaches Himself. Then the people tell the woman that they do not believe in the Messiah because of her words, but because they have heard Him with their own ears.

I love to tell the story of Jesus, not the story of my sin. Thank God that I may be an instrument to His glory.

Go, and do not sin again (John 8:11).

This story is hard to find in some Bible translations. Some manuscripts omit this passage from the gospel, some add it in John or even in Luke. Uncertainty about this part of Scripture is understandable. Those who copied the early texts of the Bible had difficulty with the story about this adulterous woman. I can see righteous defenders of moral values in life shake their heads about Jesus' attitude and erase this passage from the manuscripts.

When the Gospel offends me, I may choose not to listen. Then I miss the most beautiful truths of the Bible.

This story exposes the hypocrisy of the scribes and Pharisees, who use this case of adultery as a test for Jesus' orthodoxy. They are not really concerned about what the woman did. They want to trap Jesus, and in their machinations the woman has a function, not a personality. When Jesus hears their accusations thrown at this woman, He ignores them by writing in the sand. Some people have said that He wrote the names of the Pharisees' mistresses in the sand; every time Jesus looked a man in the eyes, the accuser became the accused and stole away. That sounds good, even if nobody can prove it.

Actually, Jesus makes personal the problems of this woman. There are no "cases," just sinners who need grace and mercy. Jesus cuts through a jungle of rules and regulations to find a trembling woman.

I am not just a case; I am a sheep that has strayed, and the Good Shepherd is after me. He chases the wolves away, and takes me in His arms.

On the one hand, Jesus dismisses the accusations as false and hypocritical. But at the same time, He does not ignore the woman's sins the way the Pharisees did. He speaks to the woman of forgiveness. He calls sin sin, and tells her to stop sinning. He did not win the case. He won the sinner.

I am the resurrection and the life (John 11:25).

It is all so confusing. Jesus deliberately postpones going to Bethany, but He is so sad that He cries when it appears that He has come too late. Confusion multiplies when He starts talking about the resurrection of His friend. Martha believes that her brother will rise again; at the end of time, all the dead, including Lazarus will rise. But right now Martha sees no hope of restoring the family.

Martha knows that somewhere, somehow, something will comfort her, but that comfort seems vague and hard to feel here and now.

That is often my problem. I see the light at the end of the dark tunnel, but it is difficult to make God's promising assurances real in my everyday life. So many questions arise which I cannot explain with the Bible in my hand.

Jesus now takes a general and therefore meaningless idea and turns it into a very practical and therefore comforting reality. He is not going to raise all the dead now. That would draw attention away from the real comfort Jesus wants to give. He does not claim that He will bring resurrection or that He can give instructions how to get it. He says that He *is* the resurrection. He *is* the life.

Many people have wondered what it is like to die and receive the new life in eternity. It is one of those concerns that hardly anybody talks about but everybody wonders about. These questions cannot be answered right now. Besides, it is not important what form our new life will assume.

Instead of giving information, Jesus asks me to look upon Him. He raises Lazarus to indicate that His promise is neither vague nor empty. He uses this one case to teach me that His promises are not a dream, but reality. Because Jesus is the life, He will give me life.

He immediately went out; and it was night (John 13:30).

Judas' betrayal of Jesus is a frightening story. I share in the disciples' question of Jesus, "Am I the one?" It could be me! In the famous painting of the Last Supper, none of the disciples looks like a traitor; it is extremely hard to pinpoint Judas. I have come so close to trading in my Savior for thirty pieces of silver. If God did not hang on to me, I would be no better than Jesus' betrayer. In fact, I am no different from him except by God's grace and mercy.

In a word, John explains what it is like to betray the Master. When Judas steps out of the light of Jesus' communion, there is nowhere to go except the night of satan.

Now it becomes obvious that Judas is not the main player in this drama, satan is. Satan wants to make things dark for Jesus. He flaunts the fact that it apparently is possible to share Jesus' goodness for three years and still sell Him out. He demonstrates the terrible weakness of Jesus' followers. Soon satan will laugh as Israel crucifies its King.

Jesus suffers, for He knows that He may not keep this man from going into utter darkness. His loving heart goes out to Judas, but He has to let him go. The beautiful whole number of twelve will be reduced to the ugly scar of eleven. The kiss of friendship will become a sign of disloyalty. Judas will turn his face away from Jesus so that their eyes will never again meet.

Peter denied his Lord, too, but he experienced bitter tears of repentance. For Judas there is only the night of suicide.

There also is glory in this frightening matter. As one man goes into the night, satan loses his grip on eleven others. But most importantly this betrayal opens the road to the victory of the cross. Even this treasonous act fits into God's great plan of salvation.

Nobody and nothing in the world can stop my Savior. He is victorious, and I may share in that victory.

Then Simon Peter, having a sword, drew it and struck the high priest's slave (John 18:10).

It is easy to identify with Peter. What he did was not right, but at least he cared enough to do something. He did not accept the footwashing, he wanted to keep the heavenly glory on the mountain, he followed Jesus into the high priest's court. It all came out wrong, but at least he cared. I wish I could be more like him; less passive and silent. Only Jesus has the right to put Peter in his place.

Peter's problem is not his enthusiasm, but the fact that he does not accept that he himself has to be saved, helped, and protected, before he can get things done for Jesus. Jesus has to go through the trial by the Sanhedrin and the bitter sacrifice symbolized by the footwashing and preached by Moses and Elijah on the Mount. The results of impatience are obvious. If I run ahead of Jesus, everything goes wrong.

So it is in the garden of Gethsemane. When Peter attempts to help Jesus, he does the opposite of what Jesus wanted to do in the world. He inflicts pain and misery on a slave. Nothing is gained by such action; violence has never produced a better world. The Son of God did not come to hurt, but to be hurt for others. Worst of all, Peter's action shames Jesus.

I wonder: for all that I mean well, do I really promote God's kingdom, or do I break it down?

Jesus restores wholeness at once by healing the slave. Jesus has to restore and repair what I ruin. But again, that is what He came for.

Jesus also protects Peter. The other gospels do not mention Peter's name. Now John, many years after Peter's death, may say who did it.

His hand is stretched over me to protect me too.

That disciple whom Jesus loved said to Peter, "It is the Lord!"
(John 21:7).

The long days of waiting are getting to be too much for Peter.
He decides to go back to his old job. The other disciples join him.

Now there is nothing wrong with fishing. I can serve and
glorify God in my daily work; there is nothing more sacred about
one job than another. It is not a matter of what I am doing but of
how I do it. Evangelist or fisherman, I must do my work to the
glory of God.

The problem is that Jesus told them He was sending them on a
mission. He rose from the dead and now He is waiting until He can
pour out His Holy Spirit and make their mission successful. If
Jesus can wait fifty days, so should Peter.

But Peter is not the waiting type. So Jesus gently leads the
disciples back to their real calling. He reminds them of the day He
miraculously gave them an abundant catch and so called them to
their special task to be fishers of men (Luke 5:1-11). As the story
repeats itself, Jesus proves that He is risen indeed and still the same
Master in their midst.

However, nobody recognizes Jesus in the dim light of
daybreak. Neither do they recognize His voice. Though they have
been with Jesus every day for three years, they now have trouble
identifying Him when He stands on the seashore.

But the miracle of the overwhelming catch with its echoes of
the first calling speak to John. John is like an eagle who sees more
than others. He saw the glory of the Son of God in His humiliation.
Now he recognizes the Lamb of God in His exaltation.

Only a heart that has loved and listened to the Lord can see
Him. In all the activity and bustle of daily life, the church needs
people who hear the Word and see the living Christ.

At once John shares his discovery with the others in the boat.
When I see and hear my Lord, I too must share it with others.

*One of these men must become with us a witness to his resurrection
(Acts 1:22).*

Not many people approve of the apostles' appointing someone
to take Judas' place. The fact that Peter initiates it is enough reason
to cast some doubts on the action. But apart from that, it simply
seems unwise at this stage, while waiting for the Holy Spirit to
come, to make such major decisions. I always hear that I should
wait for the Lord and not take action unless He tells me to do so.

That good advice does not apply in this case. Peter sensed a
flaw in the congregation. Instead of the twelve, there are only
eleven disciples. He does not hesitate to mention the sin which
caused this flaw. Peter is convinced that the Holy Spirit can come
only to people who acknowledge the power of sin and the need for
repentance.

Peter knows what power satan has. When he hears satan laugh
at their broken ranks, he decides to repair the breach.

Peter is also looking forward. To witness of the risen Lord is a
tremendous task, and the disciples will need all the help they can
get, especially from people who were witnesses to Christ's life on
earth.

So the congregation attempts to put together what has fallen
apart. They are only the channels through which the Holy Spirit
will send His streams of fire and power, but to be even that requires
diligent preparation.

Perhaps something in my life is obstructing the pouring out of
the Holy Spirit. It is time then for me to call sin sin and to do
something about it. Blocked channels, clogged ducts—perhaps
such obstructions to the Spirit cause many of the explosions in the
church.

I may not simply wait till something spectacular happens. In
all obedience, I have to prepare for the waiting Spirit.

Why has Satan filled your heart to lie to the Holy Spirit? (Acts 5:3).

Peter uses strong language. A man who himself has denied the Lord perhaps should be more careful when judging others. What Ananias did was wrong, of course, but did it deserve the death penalty? What exactly was Ananias' sin? Was it stealing from the Lord? Or lying? Did he wish to gain respect in the congregation while being unwilling to give himself wholeheartedly? More important than asking all these questions is listening.

The fledgling church of which Ananias and Sapphira are members is in tremendous danger. Peter, with the help of the Holy Spirit, discovers satan behind the actions of this couple. Though defeated, the devil would still love to destroy the fruit of Jesus' work. Satan wants people to have little respect for the Holy Spirit. He suggests that now that the Spirit's love dictates their actions, it no longer matters what they do or do not do.

At stake here is the question: "Does God rule when the Holy Spirit enters?" When Jesus was on earth, people did not recognize the Almighty God in Him. Now the same thing could happen to the Spirit.

Before anyone gets the wrong idea, the Lord uses Peter to show how holy and strong and real His presence in the church is. The sins of Ananias and Sapphira were not the greatest in the world. But they cannot fool the Lord. Once and for all, I should know who it is who has filled my heart and life.

When Jesus returns, real shalom will come to this world. Until then, I must be on the lookout for the snares of the devil.

The judgment upon this couple is strong warning to all those in the service of the Holy Spirit. The loss of their lives may protect many lives in God's church.

And Saul was consenting to his death (Acts 8:1).

There are striking similarities between Jesus' and Stephen's experience. Both Stephen and Jesus are falsely accused about their attitude concerning the law and the temple; both see the heavens open; both pray for forgiveness for their killer; both commend their souls into God's hands.

But there the similarities end. Jesus' death is an agonizing event, while Stephen's death is somehow peaceful, even triumphant. No wonder, for Stephen has only to follow in the footsteps of his Master. The trail has been broken.

Still, there are only twelve apostles to bring the message of Jesus Christ to the world. And from the seven helpers, Stephen is taken away. How can the gospel fill the world if the resistance is so great and the workers are so few?

Stephen's death answers this question. His ordeal makes it clear that the good news cannot be stopped. As the people stone him in hatred and fear, Stephen proclaims the living Jesus. They can kill the messenger but not the message. Stephen does not beg for his life; he has his life in Jesus. Jesus is standing before him, watching over His servant. It is hard to feel sorry for a man who experiences death as this kind of victory. Rather, I feel sorry for those people who plug their ears, who hate and kill, and yet who know deep down that they have already lost the fight.

There is, however, reason to smile at this story. When the enemy takes one of God's servants, the Lord claims one of their men for His service. Saul is a power in the enemy camp. In fact, in this passage, Saul oversees the execution of Stephen. Some time later, he will deeply regret his role in killing God's children, and then he will commit his life to the spreading of the gospel.

Why do I ever doubt God's victory? There is no stopping God. I am on the winning team.

They said to her, "You are mad" (Acts 12:15).

This story brings a smile to my face! Herod tries to please the Jews by killing Jesus' disciples and arresting their great leader Peter. Peter is guarded by a host of soldiers; he is chained and locked behind iron bars and heavy doors. They will take no chances after what happened with Jesus.

The key to opening all these locked doors is prayer. The whole congregation prays earnestly in the house of Mary, the mother of John Mark.

Their prayers are answered. An angel releases Peter from prison and sends him on his way. Peter first assumes he is dreaming, but soon reality dawns on him. Yes, God's kingdom is like a dreamland, and yet it is all real. There is no limit to what the Lord can do for His church.

Now the story becomes humorous. When Peter knocks on the well-locked door where the praying congregation huddles to find safety, the maid Rhoda recognizes Peter's voice. In her excitement, she forgets to open the door and runs to tell the others. Peter is left standing in the street, with no protection but his God.

But the strangest thing happens inside the house. The people do not believe their prayers are answered. They declare Rhoda crazy, and when she insists that Peter is at the door, they say that it must be his angel, whatever that means.

Is it possible that I pray and pray but refuse to accept the answers to my prayer? I sometimes do not really believe that my requests are heard. How many times have I stared in disbelief when God answers a prayer? I have to learn to open my hands and stretch out my arms to receive all the blessings God gives. Otherwise, my prayer is not an expression of faith and trust.

Remarkably, while nobody apparently expected a quick answer to prayer, still God gave them what they were asking Him for. He freed Peter. I cannot stop the Lord with my lack of trust. Thank God that the future of His work does not depend on my prayers.

There arose a sharp contention (Acts 15:39).

The picture of the church in the Acts of the Apostles is sharp and clear. We see miracles and the overflowing goodness of the Lord. We see great acts of faith done by those early Christians, but also their sin, their lapses into unbelief. We even see contention within the ranks of the leaders of the church. Perhaps the book should have had a different name. This book is not really about the acts of the apostles but about the completion of Jesus' promise to claim the world for Himself.

In the fight between Paul and Barnabas, it is hard to determine who is right and who is wrong. Barnabas wants to take John Mark along on the mission tour. True, the young man had once failed, deserting his missionary work because he became scared. But in God's kingdom, everyone is entitled to a second chance. Paul is very much opposed to including John Mark. Paul realizes that it is all-important to get the message delivered as soon as possible. He feels he cannot take chances with unreliable servants.

I can agree with both men. I know that in the battle, I must be able to depend on the officers, and that God is not served by fainthearted messengers. But I agree with Barnabas that without love, there is no gospel and no victory. Both sides possess elements of truth.

The church often faces issues that have no clear-cut answers. Nevertheless, decisions have to be made. And only God knows the right course of action.

Unfortunately, Paul and Barnabas start to fight about their problem. They do not listen to each other; they do not pray to ask the Lord's answer. Each holds tenaciously to the validity of his own view. And that is where satan sneaks in. When I do not admit that I am limited and that others may be right too, satan gets a chance to wreak havoc.

The Bible tells me that later Paul and Barnabas become friends again. John Mark becomes a useful servant once more. God knows the path where I do not see it.

Come over to Macedonia and help us (Acts 16:9).

This text is familiar to every pastor who has received a call to another congregation. Men from Macedonia abound. The problem is deciding whether to accept the call or not.

But that is not a difficult matter for Paul. The Holy Spirit gives Paul specific directions throughout his missionary travels. When Paul sees a beautiful chance, the Spirit says no. When he decides to go somewhere, divine intervention makes it impossible.

Paul finally gets to the harbor city of Troas. Surely opportunities to spread the gospel abound in this port city. But in a vision the Holy Spirit again shows who is boss in the church, and Paul is called to Macedonia, Greece.

It is comforting to know that I need not make all the decisions. Through prayer, I can maintain contact with the Lord of the church.

But it is not always easy to accept the calling. To go into Europe is difficult. How will Paul make a Jewish gospel relevant to a world full of different ideas? Paul will find out in Athens that the Greek mind is not ready for a message of resurrection and final judgment. The language is not the problem, the message is.

Paul must have had some second thoughts when he saw the first results. A business lady and a slave girl come to Jesus. Paul faces stiff opposition everywhere and finally is cast into prison. Was his decision right?

If I am convinced that I am following the Lord's instructions, then I may not look back. Even when I doubt whether I chose the right path, I may know that the Lord uses me.

Through Paul, the gospel enters Europe and from there the whole world eventually will be reached. As Christ's disciple, I should have more visions! No population is beyond the power of Jesus. I am blessed when I hear the call to help!

Jesus I know, and Paul I know; but who are you? (Acts 19:15).

It is not enough to use the name of Jesus. If I do not belong to Him and work and speak in His service, I will have no power at all. And it is frightfully dangerous to get caught in the middle of the intense battle between Jesus and satan.

The seven sons of Sceva attempt to gain status by casting out demons. When these itinerant exorcists see how successful Paul is, they copy his methods. But then they discover that only Jesus can conquer evil spirits and the realm of darkness, because that is His rightful jurisdiction and dominion.

Why is the church often so unsuccessful? Why is there so little power in my life? Am I only using the name of Jesus without really belonging to Him?

The seven sons of Sceva suffer disaster. The evil spirits attack them and they flee, leaving their clothes at the scene—to loud guffaws, no doubt. When I try to manipulate the power of God, I receive shame instead of honor.

Now the crowd realizes that the battle against demons does not depend on human ingenuity. Only Jesus can master the evil powers, and so they turn to Him.

Now they do more than use the name of Jesus. They repent of their sins; they stop depending on superstition and sorcery; they even burn their books of magic, books valued at fifty thousand pieces of silver. They will never return to their old practices.

This is what Christianity is all about: a complete turnabout to total commitment to Jesus Christ.

The evil spirits ask, "Jesus I know, Paul I know, but who are you?" I need to answer that question.

Take courage, for as you have testified about me at Jerusalem, so you must bear witness also at Rome (Acts 23:11).

Frankly, Paul's attitude in this passage is simply disrespectful. As he confronts the high priest, he uses language that is not fit for the apostle of Christ. And does Paul really not know the high priest Ananias or was he being less than completely honest? Then he plays on the dissent between the Sadducees and Pharisees by mentioning a heavily debated topic. Isn't that just being tricky? He cleverly uses his Roman citizenship when he is falsely arrested. He speaks of all his experiences so boldly that I sometimes wonder where his humility is. I become suspicious when he praises the Roman rulers who have to judge his case.

The Bible does not ask me to approve of the actions of a man like Paul; his life is not a pattern for mine. Only Jesus' life is that.

Later that day, Jesus has a word with Paul. The Savior knows that Paul is scared and needs a word of encouragement. Jesus tells him that there are many more tribulations waiting for him. He will even have to go to Rome. But he need not be afraid, for God is with him.

Harsh words and tricky actions often may cover lack of confidence. Apparent conceit may be a shield to hide fear. And I am sly when I fear being forthright.

I need not condemn myself or others when this is the case. Frankly, I often regret the way I react. Paul, too, may have had a sleepless night. But Jesus comes to both of us and, with His love, He covers whatever went wrong. It becomes more and more apparent that the gospel moves on not because of human courage but only because of Jesus' constant presence.

*Preaching the kingdom of God and teaching about the Lord Jesus
Christ quite openly and unhindered (Acts 28:31).*

How strangely the book of Acts ends! Paul is going to appear
in Caesar's courts, and I am anxious to know the result. Probably
he is released from custody, but then arrested later, and finally
after more imprisonment, executed. But I do not know for sure,
and that is a shame.

But the Lord never intended to give us a thriller or a happy
ending or even a biography of Paul. Jesus promised before He
ascended into heaven that He would bring the gospel from
Jerusalem to Judea and Samaria and then to the end of the earth.
Through the operation of the Holy Spirit, Jesus would march on in
His apostles. So the end of this book is the only possible ending.
Jesus kept His promises; finally, a witness to the Savior speaks
openly, boldly and unhindered in Rome, the center of the whole
empire. It is a long journey from Bethlehem to Rome. From here,
roads lead to the whole earth.

Many things prepare the road for Jesus' army: the Jews'
hatred, the strictness of the Roman system of justice, roaring seas
and shipwreck. God employed the Roman system of justice to
bring His apostle to Rome, which will become the center of the
Christian empire.

Now I realize there could never have been a more beautiful
ending. The last word of Acts is "unhindered." Nobody can get in
the Lord's way. To know exactly what happened to Paul and how
his life ended would have been of much less value. Then I would
have seen human tragedy instead of glorious victory. I see the
crucified Lord in the greatest city of the world. From there nobody
can stop Him.

Now the righteousness of God has been manifested (Romans 3:21).

It is quite a step from the gospels and the acts of the apostles into the book of Romans. The stories about Jesus are simple enough for a child to understand. But Romans includes heavy doctrine and complicated explanations. The move is like stepping out of kindergarten into high school. However, the gospel of Jesus Christ is a complex message. The gospel is free, but it is not cheap.

I enjoy looking at a beautiful painting, just drinking in the colors and design. But when someone begins to explain the details and the complexities of the painting, I have to admit that a whole new world opens up for me; for the first time I really see a work of art.

So it is when Paul tells me about the righteousness of God. The glory of the gospel is that I have been saved justly. I have made this world and my own life crooked. But God cannot forgive and forget as sinners have to do. He is just and may not sacrifice His righteousness to save me. God cannot deny or overlook the fact of sin and the condemnation of the law. When Jesus dies in my place, He maintains the righteousness of God.

God fulfills His Word exactly as He takes a straight way out of the mess that I made. It is good to know that. If God could overlook things, if He could falsify His Word a bit, I would have lost my God. He will never resort to my tricky devises.

Romans proclaims God as the One who never breaks His Word, who is faithful to what He once said. He is a God who would rather let His Son die at the hand of murderers than to let sin go unpunished, a God who gives full salvation, so full that I may look Him straight in the eyes because my sins have been wiped out completely. If I think this is not so important, I lack insight into the straight ways of my Father.

We were buried therefore with him by baptism into death (Romans 6:4).

The simple symbolism of baptism has sometimes been lost in ritual and ceremony. Many elements of baptism should remain peripheral to its central meaning. It is true that by baptism I become a church member, experiencing an outpouring of the Holy Spirit, cleansing of sins, renewing of life, and a sign of the covenant. But in all this, I may lose track of the central significance of baptism.

Quite simply, when I go into the water, I am drowning. Symbolically, I am dead and buried in my grave. And I deserve that, for I am a sinner who has broken the law of God. God is fulfilling His warning that whoever sins will die.

But then a hand lifts my head up out of the water. I rise from the grave, eager to go into life again to do God's work with new zeal and fervor. I died and I arose.

This does not happen only at the end of my life. Already now I pass through judgment and find salvation. I need not wait for death anymore, for death is now behind me.

Little children are promised new life even before they start their journey in this world, for baptism is not a confirmation of my faith but of the faithfulness of God. My decision does not count, for the Lord has decided for me. The emphasis of baptism is on what God is doing in me and through me. I have to accept the fact that I deserve death, and that I escape that death through Christ.

Verse six states that I am buried "with Him." When I go into the watery grave, I am not alone. Christ was once buried into death, but then, on Easter morning, the Father's hand lifted Him up out of the grave. Now every time someone is buried in the water of God's judgment, Christ is there, making clear the possibility of new life. When I realize that His death gave me that life, I am determined to live in Him.

I do not understand my own actions (Romans 7:15).

The mark of true greatness is humble honesty. Paul writes this epistle to the Romans to introduce himself as one of the leaders of the church. But he writes the opposite of what every politician would say. He tells the people in Rome who he really is in the eyes of God. He admits that he is a sinner.

Paul goes on to explain that sin never makes sense. It ruins things instead of improving them; it hurts other people and makes Paul himself very unhappy. And still he does it.

A crucial step for me as a Christian is to step off my pedestal and tell people who I really am. Yet I have trouble letting my children know how sinful I am, not wanting to undermine my position of authority. Political leaders think cover-ups are essential to staying in power. Being frank and honest is dangerous! But to establish himself as a leader of the church, Paul exposes himself. If the Romans do not accept him as he is, they are not a Christian community. A church whose members do not confess sin to one another is not a church of the gospel.

Now amazingly, Paul goes one step further. Paul does not glory in a statement of his sinfulness or his total depravity. Rather, Paul says that he sins, but does not like it, for he yearns to do what is right. It is not true that he is totally depraved. By nature he is, but God's grace has changed that. He admits to the work of the Holy Spirit who gave him a new heart and a new will. He is not living in sin as if he enjoyed it. That is all over now.

Paul describes a baffling situation in which he loves God but still sins. His own sin torments him. There is no aura of holiness around Paul.

Who will deliver me from this confounding conflict in my heart? I thank God through Jesus Christ my Lord.

For the gifts and the call of God are irrevocable (Romans 11:29).

Paul cares deeply about the Jewish people who do not accept Jesus Christ as their Messiah. If he lived today, he would feel more frustration and grief. After they rejected Christ, the Jews have been persecuted and killed, hated and chased all over the earth. Even the church of Christ has done little to help them, and sometimes has participated in the persecution. Lamentably, the church often based its loveless attitude on such slogans as "They have killed Jesus," and "That is what happens when you do not accept God's grace."

The Jews have received many and varied gifts from God: their good sense for business, the spirit of community which unites them, their ability to come out of terrible suffering with new ideals and new courage.

The gifts and the call of God are still there. But if this nation does not live in the new covenant with God in Jesus Christ, their gifts are worse than useless. They provide only jealousy. Electrical wiring and appliances are useless in a house without electricity. Similarly, without the power of the Holy Spirit, any God-given gift is wasted.

My call to be a Christian may bring with it tremendous treasures, but if I do not obey the call, all those gifts can only make life miserable for me. The same Christian church that has persecuted the Jews has overlooked the fact that having gifts without pledging obedience to the call is also their fundamental flaw.

When I receive the gifts of God which He continues faithfully to give, I had better examine my dedication to Him and His world.

Greet one another with a holy kiss (Romans 16:16).

This is another apostolic command that the church no longer follows literally. That is the case with many Biblical directives: clap your hands, shout to the praise of the Lord, fall prostrate before God's face. I sometimes wonder how true to the Bible we really are.

However, I am happy that we do not greet each other with a holy kiss. When I look around in church, I see many I would rather not kiss. Actually there are only a few who are close enough to me to share a kiss of communion. To kiss others might be inappropriate, for the arousal of sexual feelings would make it less than a holy kiss.

I try to laugh off this exhortation. But am I ready to overcome both my aversion and my unholy desires so that that holy kiss would be possible and appropriate?

As Jesus knew, the kiss was a token of close friendship. That's why Judas' kiss represented the greatest possible betrayal. Today, the embrace is still a sign that two people have no major difficulties between them, that they belong together.

Does the church really experience such harmony? Loneliness is rampant in the church, in families, even in marriages. The kisses that are exchanged are often either formalities or expressions of lust.

When Paul exhorts me to live as a Christian, he means first of all that I should give myself to others who need me. Mutual love is a first fruit of the gospel. When God stooped to me, as close to me as a bridegroom to his bride, He pointed me to those around me. To love God is to find Him in my unfriendly brother and ugly sister. To embrace hostile people and to care for thankless persons is to follow the divine example. I should be ready to give that holy kiss.

But we preach Christ crucified (I Corinthians 1:23).

Paul is faced with a dilemma: his message actually does not fit the requirements for religion set by the people he seeks to convert. The Jews want to see signs; they want a religion that yields profitable results. The Greeks' ideal is wisdom; they are interested in philosophical systems that solve theoretical problems. Paul realizes that he cannot satisfy either group. Neither does he want to. If Paul could alter the Christian message, there might well be more followers. But to do so would mean the people would accept something that is worthless. Human inventions are swept away by the stream of time while the Christian message remains victorious.

I feel this temptation every day. People desire a theology which eliminates their responsibility for the underprivileged and oppressed in the world, a comforting and undemanding church life that is not continually jolted by the demand to sacrifice. It is tempting to bend the Christian message, but to do so would eliminate knowing the Holy Spirit, the love of God for the poor, the real fruit of the transforming power of God in lives. Good feelings and ethereal expectations must not be allowed to replace the ugly cross of Christ.

But it is just as dangerous to proclaim that love for the oppressed is the whole message of the Bible. That would also be a way to avoid a confrontation, this time not with the suffering world, but with a suffering God. God calls me to communicate with Himself, to pray, to accept and study His message in the Bible, to worship and adore Him, to build the church to the glory of His name.

Paul feels the pressure to accommodate his hearers. Nevertheless, he brings the message as God has given it. Then the Holy Spirit does the miracle. Greek and Jews do not like the message, but they accept it. It pleases God through the folly of what Paul preaches to save those who believe. For the foolishness of God is wiser than men and the weakness of God is stronger than men.

You are to deliver this man to Satan (I Corinthians 5:5).

The congregation of Corinth is convinced that Paul is over-reacting. At first I tend to agree. Apparently a man's father died, and now the man takes his father's wife as his own. It is unusual, but is it wrong? No incest is involved; the woman is not his mother. Paul does not mention any Jewish or Roman law that was broken. He just appeals to the fact that even pagans would not do a thing like this.

The congregation in Corinth is not convinced that the situation is so bad. But Paul demands, "How can you be so proud of yourselves? You should be in mourning. A man who does a thing like that ought to have been expelled from the community." Paul deplores their failure to exercise discipline and instructs them to have a congregational meeting to deliver this man to satan for the destruction of the flesh. The hope is then that eventually, in the day of Jesus' coming, his spirit may be saved.

The Corinthians believed in Christ's redemption and still they lacked the fervor of dedication to God. Paul accuses them of being puffed up, of thinking they know better, of being convinced that they are always right.

Paul reminds the Corinthians and me that we need not judge those outside the Christian community or to disassociate with all those leading immoral lives. That would mean withdrawing from the world altogether. But he does call us to task in the judging and disciplining of our brothers and sisters in Christ. My avoidance of that task may stem from an indifference for the glory of Christ and the well-being of the church. The church should shine with holiness; the flesh can be hurt to save the spirit.

Where is my flame of love for Jesus, for fellow sinners and for the honor of God?

I want you to be free of anxieties (I Corinthians 7:32).

The Corinthian church had many questions about marriage, sexuality, and remaining single. Paul gives specific answers but does not lose sight of the main issue. Too often tensions and problems concerning marriage and sexuality can prevent our seeing the fullness of life in Christ.

God has enabled Paul to overcome the fears and obsessions which apparently plague the people in Corinth. For the sake of Christ, Paul has sacrificed marriage. He does not boast about his sacrifice; he simply gives his life to Christ who sacrificed so much for him.

Is it really necessary to discuss these matters continually? Are they so important in the context of the full Christian life? Paul does take time to address specific questions; he explains and guides gently. But his instructions point to the full message of the gospel: Jesus Christ must influence and direct my entire life. Individual problems cannot be solved piecemeal. Living my life in the light of Christ gives me a whole new perspective on life's problems.

In this context, Paul also talks about the coming tribulation which he foresees for the church. The impending distress already casts its shadows on the life of the congregation. Will it be possible to remain faithful to Jesus Christ or will people care more for their individual needs than for the coming of God's kingdom?

Paul knows that anxieties will persist; rather casually he speaks of all the hardships that befell him. But then he tells the congregation that they can forego many comforts and still be very happily dedicated to the Lord. Personal anxieties must not becloud the main issue.

Total deliverance of body and soul to Jesus Christ resolves much anxiety. In His freedom, problems shrink to their proper size. Instead of belittling people who are engulfed in their own problems, I should pass on this message of salvation to them through the Spirit of God.

If a woman has long hair, it is her pride (I Corinthians 11:15).

Why does the Bible have to concern itself with women's hair-dos? Most churches do not take this passage seriously. Women hardly ever cover their heads while praying because "any woman who prays with her head unveiled dishonors her head." But is it still improper for a woman to pray to God with her head uncovered? People who insist the church follow all Biblical commands literally might just as well admit that we choose which rules suit us and which do not. Why does Paul talk about women and their fashions, attitudes, and position in the church?

The gospel transforms the whole of life. The transformed women of Corinth believed there should be no difference between men and women. They cut their hair short, they spoke loudly in church, they tried to seize leadership and, after ages of male domination, they believed that they should now have the upper hand. This movement shook the whole city of Corinth.

Paul deplores the women's attitude, not because his male ego is hurt or because he cannot accept changes in society. He is opposed to this new approach for the sake of the women themselves. God had made male and female and both men and women should accept that, rejoice in it, and make something beautiful of it. Women should not try to imitate men (which would be admitting their so-called superiority), but as women should try to find their place and use the special talents given by the Lord. When women find the place of dominion God has given to them, they will be a tremendous blessing. He wants us to use to the utmost the talents He gives us.

He who prophesies is greater than he who speaks in tongues (I Corinthians 14:5).

This passage deals with a matter that has been relatively dormant in the church for many centuries: speaking in tongues. The Corinthians were proud that on several occasions in their church many people uttered unintelligible sounds which had to be explained by those who had the gift to interpret. Speaking in tongues was seen as a manifestation of the Holy Spirit who so possessed God's children that they could no longer control themselves. Since those days of the early church, this gift has nearly disappeared.

Lately certain groups claim that this gift has returned, but it serves for them as a mark of the true believer. If one does not speak in tongues, he must not be Spirit-filled. I try to ignore this thinking, but often I wonder, "Am I really a child of God? Is the Holy Spirit really filling my existence? If so, why do I not speak in tongues?" Many people are nervous about this.

Paul admits that tongue-speaking exists. He has received this gift also, so there is no reason for him to be jealous of the Corinthians or for the Corinthians to look down on him as an unspiritual person. But at the same time, Paul is not entranced by this gift. If it is the will of the Holy Spirit to give him that talent, that is His business. But Paul would rather prophesy, that is, be busy proclaiming the Word of God.

The Spirit of God can give many varied gifts and I humbly accept them when they come to me. But I prefer to hear a church speaking understandably and intelligibly about the joy of salvation in Jesus Christ. Far from being the mark of a true church, tongue-speaking is an additional gift that can be given to the church, just as other gifts that have a special purpose or meaning. Certainly some people have this gift, just as certainly as I can live without it.

At the root of this whole matter is the freedom of the Lord to do what He pleases with me. God deals with each of us personally and individually. I should never judge others by what I experience in my life of faith; neither should they judge me. The spokes of the wheel all point to the center. We are united in the Spirit.

Who comforts us in all our affliction, so that we may be able to comfort those who are in any affliction (II Corinthians 1:4).

Paul is speaking about one of the most agonizing periods in his life. He describes it as a time when he was so utterly, unbearably crushed that he despaired of life itself.

The first thing that strikes me is that Paul does not go into details. Nobody is ever really helped by hearing all the heart-rending things that happened to me or all the sordid particulars of my sins.

Paul wants to use that what happened to him as a tool to help others. So Paul does not complain about the doings of his heavenly Father. He knows that all that happens to him is for the coming of the kingdom and the glory of God. He believes that even the most successful apostle has to be prepared by God to do his job. The hurts in my life are instruments in my Father's hand to prepare me for my task.

Now Paul does not try to help other sufferers the way people usually do. When people find someone in a bad spot, they often say, "I know just how you feel." This is a lie; everyone reacts in a different way to misery. Then such people proceed to tell about similar things that happened to them. This is no help either, for it makes no one happier to know that others have also suffered.

Paul finds out what the tribulations in his life meant, how the Lord helped him through those agonies. He distills from them knowledge about the Lord and His dealings with His people. Then he can go to people with comfort.

Beneath my words of comfort to others must be a trusting acceptance of the hardships in my life and God's comfort to me.

He who raised the Lord Jesus will raise us also with Jesus and bring us with you into his presence (II Corinthians 4:14).

The church of Corinth is not the most friendly congregation. They are conceited, loveless, and critical of Paul. How does Paul treat them?

On the one hand, when Paul wants to save them, he uses very strong language and severe threats. He is well aware of the fact that he is an apostle of Jesus Christ with all the authority of his Sender.

But Paul never assumes a spiteful and revengeful attitude. He remembers that God in Christ is begging the Corinthians to be reconciled with Him. God is making an appeal, beseeching, sending ambassadors, entreating them to accept His grace. God, though almighty in His authority, can stoop down and beg me to be reconciled to Him.

Paul has to learn that neither the constant pressures of his busy life nor all the hardship and suffering on his missionary trips nor the constant fear of being killed and tortured may make him irritated or unfriendly. Rather he has to bear the image of his Sender.

I may never be spitefully angry or short-tempered. From time to time anger may indeed reflect God's attitude toward sin. But anger may never become an outlet for my frustrations.

Too often in the Christian church God's children have given up hope for each other and have split to go separate ways. But Paul is talking in this text about his future in the kingdom of Jesus, and he expresses confidence that he will share the presence of God with the Corinthians. Paul does not speculate about whether or not they will be saved. He knows that none of us will be included in God's kingdom because of our own merits. So in a real sense, it is all of us or none of us. Thank God, Christ's blood is sufficient to cover all of us.

So give proof, before the churches, of your love (II Corinthians 8:24).

The New Testament speaks often about the collection that is held for the poor churches in Jerusalem and the surrounding area. This may not surprise anybody; offerings seem to be a trademark of the church.

But this offering has nothing to do with the domestic needs of the Corinthian congregations. Their first love for Christ must have made their hearts generous enough to supply all their own needs. The problem is with their offering to help churches outside their locality; Paul finds it necessary to exhort the church of Corinth to do its part.

The believers in Jerusalem are in bad shape. The well-to-do Jews have rejected the gospel; the poor and destitute live in Christ. Constant hatred against Jesus makes it hard for believers to find employment, and constant threat of persecution keeps them in dire financial straits. The communal meals at the Lord's Supper supply immediate relief from hunger, but eventually nobody has anything to share anymore. So the richer churches are urged to support their sisters and brothers in Jerusalem.

This is not just an act of benevolence. No doubt the Corinthians could have helped many needy persons in their own neighborhoods; benevolence can be exercised anywhere. But this collection is to demonstrate the unity between the mother church and the daughter congregations.

The new churches in Europe are different from the Jewish church in Jerusalem. The laws of Moses, circumcision, and many other customs have been abandoned by the new Gentile Christians. Within the church, such difference may lead to suspicions. But this offering is a visible hand of love extended. It is the confirmation that only love unites.

My grace is sufficient for you, for My power is made perfect in weakness (II Corinthians 12:9).

We know very little about the bothersome problem facing Paul. He calls it a thorn in the flesh, a messenger of satan to harass him. Many suggestions have been made. Paul may be nearly blind. He does not write his own letters and several people state they would gladly give their eyes to Paul. Perhaps Paul has a speech impediment; apparently he believes himself stronger in his epistles than in his speaking. Perhaps some other deficiency in his body limits his activity. That bothers a man who is so completely absorbed by his will to serve Jesus.

But behind this deficiency, Paul hears satan jeer, "Where is your God?" So three times Paul begged the Lord to take the thorn away. But the thorn remains.

God tells him that the thorn will remain because it serves a purpose. If Paul was a man without deficiencies, he might not only become too independent, but people around him might look more at his gifts than at the grace of God working in him. A nearly blind man who travels the world to preach the gospel shows convincingly what the Lord can do. A preacher who stammers and stutters can hardly be appreciated for his finesse on the pulpit but rather for the message he brings.

If I have everything the way I like it, no one will wonder why I am happy. But through the weakness of His servants, God's power shines. Paul's successes cannot be attributed to his talents; the Lord uses a weak man for His powerful message.

If I really want the Lord to be praised, I will show in my life that His grace is sufficient for me. Then He will use me as His channel.

When Cephas came to Antioch I opposed him to his face (Galatians 2:11).

The Bible does not hesitate to mention confrontations between Christians, perhaps so that I realize that all the love of God does not erase self-love and pride. However, some confrontations are not sinful in themselves. When the truth of God is at stake, people must have the courage to stand up for it and rebuke others when they are not true to the gospel.

Paul has problems with the way some Christian Jews accept the grace of God. After the first joy of embracing the gospel, they return to the old works of the law. It cannot be true, they reason, that the grace of God is so free and undeserved. False teachers draw them away from the preaching of the full gospel by telling congregations that believers should somehow contribute to their salvation. This infuriates Paul, for it implies that Jesus did not do enough.

When even Peter is influenced by this and withdraws from Gentiles who turned to Christ, insisting on the old Jewish rites and works of the law, Paul explodes. This leader of the church may draw others away from trust of the total grace of God. Barnabas is hesitating already, and the Galatians can now quote an authority when they question the free gift of God in Jesus Christ. In such a situation Paul cannot keep up the facade of unity. The offending member must be attended to, though that may be painful.

Church history includes several conflicts for which I may thank God. Schisms and separations are not pleasant, but it may be better to risk a break in the church than to see the whole church lose the truth of God. There is never an excuse for remaining quiet when Jesus is offended and God's children are led astray.

Peter and Barnabas and the Galatians do turn back to the sound, strong gospel. The greatest love is not always manifested by superficial nicety. I should ask God to help me to speak up when it really matters, when much is at stake.

But the fruit of the Spirit is love (Galatians 5:22).

Nowadays there is a strong emphasis on the importance of the Holy Spirit. And rightly so. Too often His gentle and quiet work has been overlooked. The Holy Spirit is something like a mother in the family. She is often overlooked because she does not demand attention; when everything runs smoothly and nobody notices her, her efficiency and strength are proved. Though she is happy when others get attention, it should not be forgotten that she works faithfully to support them.

The Spirit certainly should be recognized and acknowledged. However, the Bible does not exhort me to talk about Him all day or to expect spectacular revelations about and through Him.

Many of God's children have been disturbed by the idea that one can only be called spiritual if he experiences astonishing and startling things: speaking in tongues, faith healings, prophesying, and other strange manifestations. For the Galatians, uncomfortable resting in the free salvation of Jesus Christ, proof of salvation was an attractive idea.

And some condemn me if I cannot come up with such proof. With no startling experience to reveal, I and my church are unspiritual, not born again, dead. People who once shared the community of faith with me leave to go their own ways.

At this point I hear the warnings of this passage: the fruit of the Spirit is love. If those people are actually in the Spirit, they should stay and try to convince me of the truth in love. They should not judge me so harshly. Why do all the small groups and sects condemn each other? Perhaps deep down, we all try to preserve the idea of our own worthiness, even through what we call fruits of the Spirit.

Paul tells me to stand fast and to not submit to a yoke of slavery again. The freedom of the Spirit should show in love!

Among these we all once lived in the passions of our flesh and so we were by nature children of wrath, like the rest of mankind (Ephesians 2:3).

Paul is reminding the people in Ephesus of the time when they were Gentiles in the flesh, separated from Christ, strangers to the covenant of promise, alienated from the commonwealth of Israel, having no hope and without God.

Now I would like to agree with Paul's statement, admitting that I also once lived in worldly passions, that I was dead through trespasses, following the prince of the power of the air. But I cannot do that in all honesty. Thanks to God's goodness, I was born in a Christian family, I received the token of His covenant, and I was brought up in the Word of Christ. Certainly I have sins aplenty and more unbelief than I care to admit. But I may not pretend I was born a heathen and later came to Christ.

When covenant children come to realize how rich they are and accept Christ for themselves, they have not been converted. Rather, finally God's work has broken through to their consciousness and wills.

So I may not take these words and apply them directly to myself. Paul shows that God is able to bring even Gentiles living far from the covenant into the glorious light of the gospel. So great is His power and love that He transforms an entire pagan culture into a Christian community. He conquers the power of satan; He raises the dead and makes them alive in Christ Jesus. Now if He is able to do that to the Ephesians, imagine what He can do in me, how He can transform my own life into glory! And yes, what gracious work the Lord has been doing throughout the generations of the church and covenant.

I cannot always equate a Biblical situation with my own situation. I am not Abraham, Jacob or David, Judas, Cain or Saul. Rather, God proclaims His greatness and His dealings with me in various ways; the gospel is demonstrated in many different people and communities. The question is always, "If Christ worked and conquered there, how is He working now in me?" Answering this question takes thought and study. God's gift of His Word deserves time and attention.

This is a great mystery, and I take it to mean Christ and the church (Ephesians 5:32).

Paul cannot speak about his own marriage, but the Lord has given him special insight. Marriage, he says, is a reflection of the relationship between Christ and the church.

In our confused and perplexed society with all its tensions and pressures, people do need help to keep their marriage going. But the main and principal solution for breakdowns is to look upon Christ. The knowledge of Christ Jesus should permeate marriage as well as all areas of life.

What are the guidelines given for a husband? In Christ, he sees leadership, comfort, respect for his marriage partner, self-denial, constant affection, forgiveness, togetherness. For every problem in his marital relationship, a husband can look to Jesus' example to see where he went wrong and what he is expected to do and say.

The Bible also gives directives to the wife. How does Christ expect His church to be? If a woman's husband would be Jesus, what would she do for Him? Though her husband does not even remotely resemble Jesus, her attitude is to be directed by her love to Jesus: accepting leadership, bringing sacrifices without pride, caring and loving. I can learn by imitating the position of the church in relationship to Christ.

Paul sees it all as a great mystery.

It is said that marriages are made in heaven; certainly they are maintained when we lift up our hearts to heaven. This is of course only the start; Christ goes on to tell us how to make our relationships God-glorifying. But the beginning of the remedy for broken relations is a rebirth through the Spirit.

My desire is to depart and be with Christ. But to remain in the flesh is more necessary on your account (Philippians 1:23, 24).

In the Christian community, speculations about heaven and the new earth have almost obscured the sober revelation of God's Word. Self-invented particulars may comfort some people, but in the long run they alienate people from the Christian faith. Most of my ideas about life hereafter are molded by how I would like it to be, and my wishes push the needs of the world and the future of the kingdom of God into the background. The promise of heavenly glory was never supposed to block our vision of our task for God's children and His world.

Paul is uncertain about his personal destination, but that does not seem to bother him at all. He knows that, just as in the departure of a ship on its way to its final destination, so also in the death of a Christian, there is glory and expectation. The trip is not aimless; the goal is Jesus Christ. The simple faith of Paul, marked by hope and longing, is inspiring. Indeed, Paul mentions having been in the heavens, having seen unbelievable things. But Paul does not want to talk about such things; they are immaterial and irrelevant and may even obstruct the vision of the Christian's task in the world.

I must admit that often I do not desire to depart. In fact, I even fear the unknown, for after I reject all the silly speculations about heavenly bliss, I experience a vacuum.

What I need is a personal relationship to Jesus Christ, a definite commitment to Him, an active prayer life, and open eyes for the misery of sin in this broken world. Paul experienced all of this, and he wanted to go to Christ. But he was also willing to remain in the flesh for the sake of the Philippians and others who needed him. I also should go forward joyfully, on to whatever God has planned for me.

You have come to fulness of life in him (Colossians 2:10).

Some people experience a peculiar joy when they voluntarily deprive themselves of many of life's good and pleasant things. An ascetic way of life supposedly pleases the Lord.

Paul disagrees. It just pleases self. The issue includes more than the strange way in which some people rejoice in self-inflicted hurt. Self-inflicted suffering reveals my desire to pay for everything in life. Since one gets nothing for nothing, I feel I must sacrifice something to earn salvation. Deeply embedded is my belief that what I get for nothing is not worth as much as what I have to pay for dearly. But, in effect, such unnecessary sacrifices are a rejection of the free gift of God in Jesus Christ.

Paul refers to people who have many regulations: "Do not handle. Do not taste. Do not touch." Other Christians see them as tremendously sincere and devoted children of God. But Paul warns them to stop playing this game.

I find it hard to accept the grace of God just like that. I desire to build my own life with good works. I don't want God to have to help me. But actually, then I am pushing Jesus Christ aside.

Paul tells the Colossians that Christ came to make their lives pleasant and full of joy. If I refuse to experience a full, happy life, I deny God's ability to make life rich and beautiful, a thing to be savored. Smiles, songs, and rejoicing are marks of life in Him.

God wants to be praised and thanked—no stern faces, sad hearts or empty lives. I may step into the world with confidence, knowing that the fullness of life is given to me in Jesus Christ.

Of course, I have to avoid dangerous indulgences. I may have to sacrifice certain things also, but only on God's command. And even these sacrifices serve as a contrast to the glory of the life that is waiting for God's children.

You accepted it not as the word of men but as what it really is, the word of God (I Thessalonians 2:13).

It is simplistic to assume that all sermons must be regarded as the Word of God. The listener needs to assume a critical attitude, not in order to tear down but to evaluate the material set forth as God's will.

Those who bring God's Word must be convinced that they are not called to share personal insights or favorite ideas. On the other hand, they must try to apply the gospel to everyday life experiences. Preachers must lead believers to a confrontation with God; from there each believer will have to find his own way with his Lord. Others' suggestions may be worthwhile, but they also may obscure one's view of Jesus Christ, the living leader of His church.

The listener or reader has to do some soul-searching. His critical evaluation of the sermon may reveal that the preacher is mistaken and does not bring the Biblical message. But he may also be denying and rejecting the message in order to escape indictment by the Word of God. A lot of criticism of sermons is actually the reaction of an unwilling heart which does not want to admit to being touched by the Word of God.

Another obstacle to hearing the Word of God may be the preacher's lack of talent. Paul realizes that he is not an impressive speaker and that even his writing is not always very enjoyable. But he is happy that the Thessalonians have detected the real Word of God in his message anyhow.

I should engage in continual effort to find the real Word of God in all the words spoken in His service. When I and others talk it over, building each other up, we should be trying to achieve something that is as close to the Word of God as possible.

Paul knows all this as well as I do. But boldly he calls what he brings the Word of God. In all my struggles I may know that God speaks through sinful people to sinful people. In spite of my errors, He still uses me.

You are not in darkness, brethren, for that day to surprise you like a thief (I Thessalonians 5:4).

I read in the gospels that Jesus will come back as a thief in the night. But a sneaky robber is hardly a good analogy of the King of glory. This comparison also makes me fearful and reluctant to look forward to the event.

This description also implies that Jesus could come back any minute. Strange ideas go through my head. I know a lot of occasions and places where I rather would not be when Jesus suddenly returns. Parents have said, when they did not want their children to go somewhere, "What if Jesus came back and found you there?"

Paul explains that I am apprehensive because I don't really understand what Jesus meant when He used this expression. He is only coming as a thief in the night for those who do not believe in Him, who laugh at the idea of His return. For them, it really will be a frightening surprise. But believers need not fear.

God lets us know what will precede His coming. The signs of the times are clear: the preaching of the gospel, persecutions, signs in nature, the appearing of the antichrist, the falling away of so-called Christians in the fiery test. God has given the book of Revelation as prophecy. When such events unfold, the children of God will recognize the signposts and lift up their heads expectantly to look for the final redemption. No, Jesus will not come back tonight, for the process is more majestic than that.

Will this notion make me less alert? Of course not. I have a little more time to preach the gospel and to get prepared for the final onslaught of the enemy. And watching the signs of the times, I experience mounting expectant joy.

The mystery of lawlessness is already at work (II Thessalonians 2:7).

I have learned to look upon the coming of the antichrist as a fearful thing. And it will be, at least for those who belong to Jesus Christ; others will enjoy his rule.

The antichrist is the person through whom satan will try to rule this world in the final battle against God. The devil knows that in order to rule, you first have to appeal to the people. So the antichrist will carefully choose his bait. He will tell people to disregard the law of God, to murder, steal, and commit adultery as much as they like. Of course, he will not say it so crudely. "Abortion on demand," "death with dignity," "smart business," "trial marriages"—those are his more acceptable terms.

In this way, the antichrist breaks the umbilical cord that has always attached God's creatures to Him. A God-less world will be established openly and frankly. It will seem pleasant to live in that state of freedom. However, in the long run it is not pleasant for a fish to be free from water. Such unnatural freedom means death.

Christians who still hang on to God will learn that they have to make a choice. If they do not follow satan, they will suffer under the great persecution which will make life unbearable. But in that moment, Jesus will come to take His followers unto Him in the great and final victory.

This all is predicted, but sometimes I wonder, "Why do I have to know it?" I have to know in order to prepare myself for it. The mystery of lawlessness is already at work. The first signs of an antichristian rule are already visible. The opposition to God's law, the secular miracles through which the antichrist promises me heaven on earth—it is all there in principle.

Will I be able to stand firm? Perhaps I should re-evaluate the depth of my commitment to Christ.

If anyone aspires to the office of bishop, he desires a noble task (I Timothy 3:1).

I realize that Paul spoke through the Holy Spirit in this passage, but my first impulse is to disagree with Paul's statement. Today, serving as an elder or deacon is often seen as a duty that one fulfills grudgingly rather than as a noble service of God and His church. True, some people occasionally want to become elders but they are the exceptions. Generally, when the church calls on its members to serve, they insist that they are not suitable, that they are too busy. Finally, under pressure and without enthusiasm, they accept.

If somebody really wants to have a position of leadership, is he conceited and proud? Have we made church functions so glamorous that people are complimented to be chosen and honored to be appointed? Or have we made the jobs so demanding that most members prefer to avoid being "saddled" with them?

Paul goes on to describe nearly impossible requirements for eldership. Often I have heard the sighs of present office-bearers when this part of Scripture is read. Congregations are critical when they compare their office-bearers with this ideal.

There is good reason to look into the whole matter of church offices. Throughout the ages, offices in the church have evolved until they barely resemble the descriptions given of the early Christian church. Apparently everybody pitched in then, using the talents that the Lord had given each. Offices were not as sharply defined as today. All men and women found channels for actively serving the risen Lord in the congregation.

I wish we could return to a simplicity of church life which would permit this text to be functional again. I must frankly ask, "Lord, may I help You? Show me how I can best serve You and Your church."

Let the elders who rule well be considered worthy of double honor (I Timothy 5:17).

Throughout the ages, church life has developed and changed so that now it is hard to conjecture about life in the early Christian church. The role of women, the variety of offices, the laying on of hands, the frank attacks on people who strayed away from the truth—all these no longer seem to fit our modern church situation.

To add to the confusion, in this passage I read that elders were paid a salary for their work. This verse is not referring to ministers; they are mentioned later as preachers and teachers. Elders were rewarded for the time and effort they invested in the congregation. The word *honor* is actually the word for honorarium, a payment for professional services for which custom or propriety forbids a price to be set. This made it easier to serve, especially for those who had to work day and night to make a living. Now more than the rich could serve as office-bearers.

But it seems even stranger that if the officer worked well he got double pay. No one hesitated to judge performance and to pay accordingly. Equal pay for the same function was apparently not a hard and fast rule. The New Testament Christians did not hesitate to say what we today do not dare mention: one person often does better than another. They not only said so, they acted on it. Diversified salaries based on quality of work required personal and continuous contact with the elders and their work.

The whole arrangement astonishes me at first, but then starts to appeal to me. Where is the openness and the frankness that should exist in the Christian church? It would be great if I could break through long-established barriers and rediscover values that have been buried under the dust of centuries. The Word of God calls for continuous reformation of the church. I may not be able to repeat a situation once found in the church, but at least I should confront the many questions it poses.

When you come, bring the cloak that I left with Carpus at Troas,
also the books, and above all the parchments (II Timothy 4:13).

This epistle, probably the last Paul wrote, is in some ways very
sad. Knowing that he is going to die, Paul hands over the work of
spreading the gospel to Timothy. But even more touching is Paul's
confession of deep loneliness. While in a prison waiting for his day
in court, he has only Luke, his doctor, with him. All the others
have left him; even some of his friends have deserted him.

Paul now begs Timothy to take along his winter coat, his
books and his parchments. It is cold in the jail; the hours are long
and monotonous. His active mind wants to occupy itself with
reading and maybe some writing.

These words are not complaints, but they do express tragedy.
However, if I would offer sympathy to Paul he would not accept it.
He speaks about the continuation of the gospel work by Timothy
and others; the ministry goes on. Paul himself is looking forward to
the crown of righteousness that will be given to him. Paul not only
has brought the gospel to thousands; he also lives in that gospel and
finds his victory in Jesus Christ.

My sense of tragedy dissipates when I see how Christ takes
Paul and every child of God and fills our hearts with the gifts of
comfort, hope, and trust.

Paul's request to bring his cloak and books gives me a deeper
insight into his attitude. Paul believes that his departure is at hand.
But he also admits that he might have to stay in prison during the
coming winter. Faith is to follow God and to leave the course of my
life to Him.

Someone once said that if he knew Jesus would come back
tomorrow, he would plant a tree today. It is important to look
ahead to glory, but also to realize that glory shines across the immediate future. Jesus leads me on the path of life today.

*As for a man who is factious, after admonishing him once or twice,
have nothing more to do with him (Titus 3:10).*

Is this pastoral care? Certainly it is unchristian to form fac-
tions in the church that fight each other, to destroy the unity of
Christian believers and to undermine the peace and well-being of
the congregation.

But it sounds equally unchristian to leave factious people
alone. In Christ's church we never give up hope of healing wounds
and restoring unity. We devote much time to bringing straying
sheep back into the flock. Such people should be warned of the
results of their sinful life. Church discipline may be invoked very
carefully to prevent the breach becoming even bigger. Hours and
days and weeks of consulting, admonishing, and praying seem to
be in order.

But Paul tells Titus to give a warning once or twice and then let
go. Why? Because the kingdom of Jesus Christ has no time to lose
itself in endless discussions. The preaching of the gospel, the
building up of the church, is urgent business. Satan tries to delay
the work of Christ with misunderstood demands for pastoral care.
Hours are wasted in consistories and homes when this apostolic
warning is not heeded.

Of course, we must decide when a person is truly factious. Not
every person who disagrees with the church leaders is trying to
destroy the unity and the well-being of the church. We need
wisdom to determine whether or not we are faced with genuine concerns.

But the glorious progress of the gospel must not be stopped by
anyone who cares only for himself. To follow this advice is not
loveless, for it shows love for Christ. And I can still pray for those
who are left behind.

So if you consider me your partner, receive him as you would receive me (Philemon :17).

After the slave Onesimus ran away from his master Philemon, he found refuge with Paul, who had occasionally stayed at Philemon's house. During his stay with Paul, the slave turned to Christ and became his dedicated helper, especially while Paul was in prison. Paul regards Onesimus as his child received in Christ, but he decides that the slave should return to his master.

Onesimus is understandably frightened to return. Run-away slaves were very harshly punished to set an example for all the other slaves. Knowing this, Paul gives him this letter appealing for mercy.

It would have been easier to leave matters as they were. Paul would have enjoyed having this friend around; Onesimus would have been very happy to serve God by serving Paul. And Philemon would not have been faced with the problem of what to do with a slave who has turned Christian and has Paul's support. Their relationship must have been so bad that Onesimus wanted to run away. Will it become better now?

This letter is far more than a personal appeal. It questions the impact of Christ upon relationships in this world. It would have been hypocritical to shout "Praise the Lord" for Onesimus's conversion without working towards restoration in his daily life. In the relations of management and labor, in education, in science, and in politics, the consequences of accepting Jesus as the Savior of the world are far-reaching.

In Christ, we all become partners. The struggle between the classes and the nations should be replaced by the sense of being co-workers in this world of God. Paul does not say that slavery should be abolished, for even that is not the final solution. Hardship still existed after abolition. Without a sense of becoming partners, nothing is solved.

The personal sacrifices to be brought by Paul, Onesimus, Philemon, by me and all Christians, are nothing compared to what Christ did for this world. I must bear the fruits of His labor.

But we see Jesus (Hebrews 2:9).

The people to whom this epistle is directed have given up hope.
When they first turned to Christ, everything was exciting. But now
they have lived in the gospel for many years and so little has happened. The Christian church is disappointing. Their lives are called
Christian, but little has really changed. Is it true that Christ is King
and rules the world? The Hebrews question the reliability of the Bible and the impact of Christ's victory on satan, and that hinders
their work and dedication. Apparently they are not attending
church services anymore and do not do the will of God as faithfully
as they should.

This letter often exhorts the Hebrews to persevere and keep up
the struggle. But that exhortation has little effect unless the hearts
of the readers change. That change can only be achieved when the
people look upon Christ. Then their actions will become reactions
to what He is doing.

But even looking upon Jesus is not the whole answer. He
seems to stall His return; apparently He rules even His church and
kingdom ineffectively.

Such a picture of Jesus may be disheartening. But if I review
what He did throughout His ministry, that motion picture gives me
a totally different image than a photo does. I see Jesus relinquish a
glory greater than that of the angels to accept a position of humiliation. But He overcomes the powers of sin and death; now I may
see Him crowned with glory and honor. In fact I may run to look
ahead and see the total victory of the last days. It would be foolish
to give up now while I run with Him down the home stretch.

We should exhort and admonish each other. But my greatest
comfort comes from looking at Jesus. I do not yet see everything in
subjection to Him, but it is. And one day I *will* see that it is true.

Let us leave the elementary doctrines of Christ and go on to maturity (Hebrews 6:1).

The epistle to the Hebrews is not easy reading. In places, it becomes very complicated and it does not present the simple gospel presented by some of the other epistles. And the author of this letter says that he means to express the gospel this way. The Holy Spirit disdains my efforts to reduce the Bible to the bare essentials.

Though I am a child of God, I do not have to retain a childish attitude. Even a child grows, maturing is essential to life. The author of this epistle wants to tell me to start growing up a bit. When you are able to chew some meat, you should not be still on the bottle. Believers must mature in Christ.

The author then makes the daring statement, "Let us leave the elementary doctrines of Christ." Can I ever do that? Sure. At the foot of the tree is the root, enormously important and perfectly essential. But without a trunk and branches and leaves and fruits, the root would not be a root; in fact, it would die.

So-called simple Christianity, charged with superficial joy, repetitive testimonies and emotional re-dedications, may be detrimental to the fruitfulness of Christ's work. The call to simplicity may be an escape from the urgent and difficult question of how to move on.

I have heard legitimate criticism of complicated doctrine and theologies and of stale systems of thinking. But just as legitimate is impatience with people who refuse solid food and incapacitate themselves for any substantial work in the kingdom of God. Refusing to think about how we should proceed is also perilous.

I should strive to develop a mind trained by practice to distinguish between good and bad. Going on to maturity means staying alive in Christ.

Not neglecting to meet together, as is the habit of some (Hebrews 10:25).

I know very little about the way the church services were organized in the early Christian church. But I do know that the services were less formal and more spontaneous than services in later centuries. Whoever wanted to contribute could do so, as long as a certain order was maintained. The meetings were held in the relaxed and unofficial atmosphere of a home.

Some say that the church should return to this unconstrained, joyful way of meeting together, sacrificing elaborate church buildings, expensive organs and the rigidly formal celebration of the sacraments and proclamation of the Word. I believe it is worth looking into this matter. But when people claim that to return to spontaneity would insure that the services would be better attended, that the services would have more meaning and draw more believers, I wonder. Even the Hebrew congregation had a problem with people who did not attend the communal meetings. It is not the form in which I worship that is all important, but rather the dedication of my heart.

There are many excuses for staying home: I can serve God just as well in my own home. The services are not what I think they should be and it is better not to make myself upset about them. I am so busy during the week that the day of rest should not be ruined by formalities. Sunday is a family day and we have to see each other at least one day a week. Each excuse has some truth to it.

But we in the Christian community need each other. We have to stir up one another to love and good works. Our confession should be known and held fast. The sacraments can only be celebrated in communion with God's children. Our task in the world can only be fulfilled by the whole community, not by each individual. Above all, when I go to church, I demonstrate my willingness to serve my God; I give myself to Him who gave Himself completely to me.

You have come to Mount Zion (Hebrews 12:22).

The letter to the Hebrews uses forceful language to admonish the congregation to be more faithful and active. It speaks of the Lord's vengeance, of a God who is a consuming fire.

However, the author of Hebrews does not mean to flog anybody into heaven with the whip of eternal damnation. The Old Testament and old covenant involved fear and trembling. Mount Sinai was a frightening place when God made His covenant with His people. Even Moses trembled with fear. A blazing fire, darkness, gloom, a tempest and the sound of a trumpet indicated the presence of God, and His people found that terrifying.

But that is all over. I do not have to come to Mount Sinai but to Mount Zion, the city of the living God. There the blood of Jesus speaks more graciously than the blood of Abel. I belong to the glory of God's grace and to the festal gathering in the new Jerusalem. I am delivered from fear and trembling.

The fact that the gloom of Mount Sinai is past does not mean that I can take life easy. When I know that my sins are forgiven, my goal becomes following and glorifying my Savior. To come to Mount Zion means that I am living in the sunshine of God's grace. Who would step out of that and back into the dark shadow of sin and death? The greatest motivation for faithfully serving God is not crippling fear but respect, awe, and praise for God's goodness in Jesus Christ. Throughout history, the church has often overlooked this point. Authority and discipline in the church must point to the cross.

Finally, if I have received so much, where is my gratitude? I should go to Mount Zion and see where the Lord's mercy has put me. Then I may ask God to help me respond better to His goodness.

You see that a man is justified by works and not by faith alone
(James 2:24).

Paul made it clear that grace is freely given and that I must accept it as a gift. By grace, I have been saved through faith; it is the
gift of God. This is not my own doing; it does not depend on
works, lest any man should boast. When the Galatians try to contribute even slightly to their salvation, Paul opposes them
vehemently.

Now brother James seems to say the opposite. How can the
Holy Spirit inspire both of these seemingly contradictory
statements? Or should I assume this is just a conflict of personal
opinions between Paul and James? Did the Reformers rightly emphasize faith alone? Or did the Roman Catholic Church just as
rightfully emphasize the importance of good works?

Only a very superficial reading of this epistle could create such
problems. James completely agrees with the doctrine of free salvation through faith alone. But he goes on to proclaim that when I
believe, I have only begun my journey through the kingdom of
God. Living faith must be working and doing things. A tree with no
fruit and no leaves is likely dead. Faith is not an object that I can
have lying around somewhere, that I show to other people
sometimes, and then put back in its place. A living faith has to
breathe and act and speak and love and sing and hope.

If I profess belief in God, I must bear fruit in a dedicated life.
If I do not, I may be in a worse position than the demons. They
believe that God is one, and they shudder (verse 19); at least they
react.

I must reassess my understanding of the word "faith." Then I
understand Paul and James agree completely about the place and
function of faith, living faith.

The prayer of faith will save the sick man, and the Lord will raise him up (James 5:15).

These words of James have drawn a lot of attention. Does prayer-healing still have a place in the Christian church? Reading this verse, I am afraid we have slipped terribly. I cannot explain the gap between this Biblical promise and the almost complete disappearance of this practise as centuries pass.

Paul and the other apostles hardly ever speak of prayer-healing. Certainly it existed, but it is not emphasized. James writes this letter to the churches of the Dispersion spread across Asia and Africa after severe persecution. These small groups are trying desperately to keep things going. But they experience considerable resistance and little growth. Their very survival seems threatened.

Now James, in the name of the Lord, gives them a mighty weapon—the special gift of healing. This gift will make a deep impression on their neighbors, and it will safeguard their existence by putting the fear of God in their attackers. It might even lead to the conversion of those who see the Lord at work. It seems that the Lord gives special powers to His people when He deems it necessary to defend His church and ensure the progress of His kingdom.

I may not lift this text out of its context to make it an absolute. Jesus did not heal all the sick in Israel. Neither is the Lord praised only through miraculous healings. But in His own time and in His own way, He uses His tools to promote the gospel.

This text is not a magic wand to wave over all situations, but evidence that when the Lord so desires, there will be healing by prayer and in faith. When God does not respond to my prayers as I would like, He obviously has other and better ways to achieve His ends.

James teaches that every healing has a purpose. I may not receive healing from my Father's hands. But I may open my hands to receive His gifts when they glorify Him.

He went and preached to the spirits in prison (I Peter 3:19).

Peter's confusing style of writing often leads to a misunderstanding of this text. Some say that between His crucifixion and death Jesus went to hell to preach the gospel and to release the believers of the Old Testament who could not go to heaven before Jesus' sacrifice. This widely accepted explanation has obscured a proper interpretation of the verse.

Jesus died, arose, and ascended into heaven. This verse refers to His ascension. Verse 22 states, "He has gone into heaven and is at the right hand of God." Peter writes that the ascension is a central event of the gospel.

In Noah's days, people did not accept the fact that salvation comes only through trusting the Word of God. Therefore they died in the flood. Noah himself needed to be saved from the floodwaters. But Jesus' death is followed by resurrection. When He ascends to the throne of God, He announces His complete victory. Thus, His ascension becomes the central proclamation of the gospel.

This is an important message to hear. The fruits of faith and dedication are not always visible in the world; I do not always see the victory of the church and of God's kingdom. When people doubt the gospel, I cannot prove its truth to them.

But today I can look upon Jesus and proclaim His ascension. The only way to the Father's throne is through Jesus. Christ's ascension into heaven means that He went ahead of me; there is nothing to separate me from God and the glorious hope of life in Him. There is no excuse for unbelief.

Noah's countrymen drowned because they rejected God's Word. How much more severe will be my judgment if I reject the message of an ascended Lord! He still calls me!

Humble yourselves under the mighty hand of God that in due time he may exalt you (I Peter 5:6).

This admonition is not particularly striking until I realize that it is spoken by the active, aggressive, and outspoken Peter. He took the lead among his fellow disciples, and even occasionally told Jesus what to do or not to do. Even after his denial of the Lord, Peter spoke the loudest on Pentecost. Now I listen to him speaking of humility, of waiting for the Lord, of hoping that in due time the Lord will take care of him. Peter also acknowledges the power of the devil, prowling around like a roaring lion. This does not sound like the forceful and impatient Peter.

This shows what the Lord can do. I pray for the Holy Spirit to change my life, but sometimes I give up hope that anything will really change. But here I see that what seems impossible can be achieved in time.

So there are two lessons. First, the Spirit's power *can* change a personality, a life. I can never claim that this is just the way I am and always will be. Even Peter can become a man who admonishes other believers to be patient.

But a second, equally important lesson is this: I should not expect change to happen at once. Peter's humility becomes evident in the epistles which he writes late in his life. Change takes time.

My sanctification is hindered by more than my resistance to God. Peter discovers satan behind my failures. The struggle is actually between God and the powers of darkness. Any change in me is a victory of the Lord over the powers of darkness. I should not underestimate the struggle. When I realize that I am a person in whom Jesus wants to be victorious, then it is no longer as hard to tell other people to humble themselves under the mighty hand of God.

We have the prophetic word made more sure (II Peter 1:19).

When Peter talks about Jesus and His salvation, he speaks from personal experience. He has spent years in Jesus' company. No doubt he remembers well the evening on the mountain top when the glory of God enveloped them and Moses and Elijah talked with Jesus. I expect him to tell people to listen to him because of this very special witnessing of Jesus' glory.

Peter does. But immediately he also tells his followers that this is not the main reason they should believe him. The Word of God is more solid ground to build their faith on.

The only Scriptures to which he could be referring are the writings of the Old Testament. They have been clearly fulfilled in the New Testament. Peter admonishes me to depend more on these books than on a lively description of his own life with Jesus. Jesus is not just a Savior who appeared all of a sudden. The promises of the old covenant have been fulfilled in His suffering and death and resurrection.

Personal witness of our experiences with Jesus can be very important. Peter does not shy away from them. But Peter does realize that faith must be based not on human experience, but rather, on the truth of the gospel. I must start with the promises given to me in God's Word; they are reliable and require me to give myself in faith and love. Then I may look around to see the results of God's power in other people's lives.

The Bible uses the word *witness* to mean *to attest to the truth*. Prophecy did not come by the impulse of man but by the Holy Spirit. The prophetic Word is more sure than any of my experiences and feelings.

No one who abides in him sins (I John 3:6).

How can anyone make this statement? Day by day my life convinces me that even though I believe in Jesus Christ and seek to follow my Master, still the old nature in me keeps on sinning. This is so clearly the Biblical message that I wonder how John can come to this apparently false conclusion. Even his own words witness against him. In the first chapter of this letter, he says that if I say I have no sin, I deceive myself and the truth is not in me. How can I square John's earlier confession with the statement, "No one who abides in Him sins"?

Perhaps my sin is evidence of my lack of abiding in Him. Is John saying that if I can strengthen my relationship with Jesus, I will become holy, sinning no more? Surely I have to rely on God's forgiving grace. Doesn't Paul say that he has not achieved what he hoped for, that he still sins, even though he does not want to? What does John mean then?

John uses strong language because he knows that people have to be shocked. This verse hits home and hits hard. John wants to tell me that when I abide in Jesus, I cannot live a life of sin anymore. "Sin" here means a way of life, to continue to let things go on in a sinful way, to find excuses for what is clearly against God's will. The Christian cannot live in sin; it is not the air that he breathes anymore.

When I see how Christ agonized in Gethsemane under the load of my transgressions, I can no longer indulge in them. Something must change. I must go back to a personal relationship with my Savior. I must not change or bend the Biblical rules and commandments for my life in order to please myself. John claims that I must go back to the source—my love for Jesus. I must admit that anyone who commits sin is of the devil but that in Jesus I do not sin anymore, no matter how strange that sounds.

If anyone comes to you and does not bring this doctrine, do not receive him into the house or give him any greeting (II John :10).

This seems a harsh and unchristian attitude. When people who do not bring the Christian message and doctrine call on me, John orders me to keep them standing on the doormat, to shut the door on them without even a greeting.

Today many people confront me with other faiths. Should I send them away without even greeting them? Isn't it my duty to convince them that they are wrong and to try to correct their false beliefs?

If they are open to accept my correction, if there is a glimmer of hope that I could win them back to the full gospel of Christ, the Bible urges me to try, by all means. But if they are trying to convert me, what is the use of talking? Is it my pride that I might be able to outmaneuvre them; is it curiosity about the outcome of the debate that keeps me talking to them?

John tells me to be extremely careful. First, if I start talking with these people, something they say may raise doubts in my mind about the validity of my own faith and trust in my Savior. I may think that I am strong enough to withstand any attack, but John tells me to be more humble. My pride may soon become a stumbling block if I underestimate the seductive power of satan. I must continue to ask God not to lead me into temptation.

Second, John tells me to be careful because when the person who does not bring the doctrine of Christ quotes Scripture and explains it incorrectly, I may not always have an immediate answer. Then they may go to other Christians and weaken their faith by declaring that I could not refute them.

John knows that spiritual strife is the attempt of satan and his antichrist to destroy God's work. The deceivers speak in the name of the arch-liar. But the Lord shelters me in His protective arms.

I pray that all may go well with you (III John :2).

John knows that Gaius is following the truth and acting as a child of God. Now John tells his friend that he wishes him health. His business and financial affairs are not second-rate affairs; they really count in God's kingdom. When visiting, I should not assume that I should only talk about the soul, and that anything else is merely small talk. "Spiritual" does not refer to a special area of life. Everything in my life should be spiritual—ruled and led by the Holy Spirit.

The Lord grants me health, success, and prosperity in addition to and sometimes even as a fruit of my relationship to Him. My body is not just a dirty container for my soul. It is a gift of God, and health and prosperity and power are of real interest to my Savior.

I must remember that health and prosperity are not given only for my own enjoyment. Gaius is reminded that he should give special care to the brethren who go around preaching the gospel and serving the congregations. They have no salary, and travel is expensive. As long as Gaius is healthy and can earn money, he can promote the kingdom of God by assisting these servants of God on their way.

This letter also addresses the problem of Diotrephes, the leader of the congregation. Apparently, he is so conceited that he will not recognize the authority of the men sent by John and hinders those who want to welcome them. Now Gaius has to stand up to this dictator and that takes courage. John prays that Gaius will be strong enough to do it. If the whole man stands firm in the service of the Lord, then the Lord will provide.

But you, beloved, build yourselves up on your most holy faith; pray in the Holy Spirit; keep yourselves in the love of God (Jude :20-21).

The similarity between the letters of Peter and Jude is striking. Most likely both men were concerned about the spiritual well-being of the church, they talked about it, and they used each other's writings to compose their respective epistles.

Jude reserves his strongest language for urging Christians to stay in Christ and to live a godly life. Does he forget that the Lord is the One who keeps His children safe from the attacks of the enemy? The Bible teaches that the Lord is my Keeper; I cannot keep myself. But Jude tells me I have to build up myself.

Jude, who speaks by the inspiration of the Holy Spirit, assures me I can keep myself in God's love. The covenant which the Lord made with me has two parties—God keeps me through my efforts to keep myself. I would be shirking my responsibility if I left out my side of the agreement. In order to stay in the love of God, in order to keep my body and my affairs in good shape, I have to walk in His way, open up His Word, and share in His work in this world. I must participate.

Jude wants to point out that trying to defend myself against the onslaught of the enemy is not enough. When I defensively lock the doors of my heart, I also lock out the light of God's grace. He wants me to be busy in His service.

Further, I must love those who are about to fall in the spiritual battle. I have to convince those who doubt, snatching them out of the fire. Mercy should be shown and prayers of intercession should be offered for them.

God is going on to the final victory. I have to stay in His love.

I know your works, your toil and your patient endurance (Revelation 2:2).

It must be frustrating for John in exile to be unable to do anything for the well-being of the churches but to write them a letter. So much heresy and so many antichristian forces are attacking the congregations; their love is growing cold and even dying in the face of persecution. If only he could go and see what is going on and do something about it.

Then Jesus tells John that nothing has gone wrong. He is still in command. While John is bound, He is free and He lives among the churches in all His power and love. John hears Christ say, "I know!" This message must be communicated to all the churches so that they may realize that though John is not present, Christ is.

These letters are not general remarks that can be applied to anyone in any circumstance. It is simplistic to say that every letter in Revelation applies directly to me, though I can learn a lot from them. Christ tells me in seven ways that He knows the special strengths and the special weaknesses of every church and every believer.

What a comfort! Jesus did not leave His church to the care of men like John. He walks among us and is deeply interested in the goings-on, for it is His own business.

Though this is comforting, it is also frightening. I cannot live my own life and avoid His searching eyes. Jesus says that He knows. When I posit excuses for my failures, He reminds me that nothing should prevent me from doing what I am supposed to do. The victory is won in Christ and I should share in it.

God knows and appreciates all my efforts even when they fall far short of His ultimate desires. But I may not use this as an excuse for inactivity.

I saw a Lamb standing (Revelation 5:6).

John sees the history of the universe written down in a book that is sealed. What happens in the world is not mere chance; we are not floating purposelessly through time and space. Rather, God has a master plan and His blueprint is in the sealed book. He is leading the world to its final destination. Satan has tried to ruin this, but in Jesus, God claims this world as His own. But I am not able to read the blueprint. Someone who has the power and the right to build the future must break the seals.

John sees somebody worthy to take the book and open the seals. He is the One who is able to instill meaning into world history and to lead it to its goal. He is the Lion of Judah.

Yet when John looks at this Lion, he sees a Lamb, a Lamb fresh from the slaughter. What a pathetic sight! Instead of the roaring power of a lion, John discovers the meekness of a lamb.

Princes, kings and rulers have tried to give leadership in this world, but all have failed. Why? Because nobody was willing to take away the cause of the problem—sin.

Man's sin gave satan the right to demolish God's plans. Nobody can build upon ruins of sin. But Jesus took away sin and a new start can be made. He is the Lion because He is the Lamb slain for the sins of the world. The Lamb is so mighty that He has become the Lion.

Through His Spirit, Christ is working on. I may take my place joyfully in His great work.

There were peals of thunder, voices, flashes of lightning, and an earthquake (Revelation 8:5).

What started the roaring thunderstorm, the lightning and loud noises? What made the earth tremble in an earthquake? Prayers. An angel came and took the incense, the prayers of the believers, (from the altar) and scattered it over the earth.

What relationship is there between my prayers and the loud noises? Well, I ask God to usher in His kingdom. I want His glory to be exalted and this world to be brought to its final end. But I should realize that this can never be accomplished without sacrifice and without the ordeals by which this world will be cleansed and purified. Deep down, I desire things to remain quiet. But out of love for God, I ask Him to take the hard way. Major surgery has to be performed, no matter how much blood will flow and how many tears will be shed.

God is willing to listen to all my small concerns and needs because He knows and loves me so well. But I may never lose sight of the great goal and glory of His kingdom. "Your will be done" is not a prayer of quiet submission; it is reaching out for the highest and greatest victory. When the armies of God advance, there will be loud noises and flashes of lightning.

If my prayers seem to go unanswered, perhaps God has mixed their incense with the fire of His desire to reach ultimate victory. Maybe my prayers evidence my lack of yearning for God's victory. Graciously, the Lord corrects or amends my prayers to make them what they should be. Then they are answered indeed.

Sometimes I am reluctant to pray, for I have found that an answer may require work and sacrifice. I must be ready for my world to be shaken when God answers my prayers.

The woman was given the two wings of the great eagle that she might fly from the serpent into the wilderness (Revelation 12:14).

The whole history of God's church is condensed into a few lines. They hinge on the birth of Jesus Christ. In the days of the Old Testament, satan tried to prevent the woman, the church, from bearing her child. When Christ walks the earth, the onslaught of the devil is so intense that the child is caught up to God, to His throne. Now the church is being pursued by an enemy maddened by defeat, out to do as much damage as he can before his final surrender.

If I don't recognize satan's assault on my life and on the church, it may be that I am blinded or half conquered by the evil one. But if I meet the demonic powers head on, I will experience God's comfort and protection.

Just as the woman is hated solely because she is the mother of the child, so I am persecuted only because of my relationship to Christ. If I no longer struggle with satan, it is because I no longer have a close relationship to my Savior.

Even as God supplies constant protection to His Son, so too He cares for me and the church. Whenever there is danger, the Lord guards and defends me. It may be a while before the woman is free from attack, but even now she is kept from the claws of the beast. I may not experience much comfort in my Christian life; I may only experience the safety of desert seclusion. But who cares? I would rather give up some so-called luxuries and live simply with my God.

When satan floods the desert, hoping that the woman will drown,the Lord saves her from this tribulation. The earth opens its mouth and swallows the flood. It is all God's work.

What is my responsibility? I must use the eagle's wings to fly to the shelter God offers me. No matter what hardships I encounter, I know the Lord provides an escape.

No one can buy or sell unless he has the mark (Revelation 13:17).

If somebody were to hold a pistol to my head and ask if I were a Christian, I don't think that I would deny my Lord. But when the antichrist will deny me because I will not acknowledge him, it will be far harder.

A moment's temptation is easier to endure than a long period in which I pay dearly for belonging to Christ and resisting satan. Doing without electricity, gas, and water, being unable to shop, losing my job or my business are extremely difficult to accept. Not only my life will be threatened, but also the lives of my spouse and my children. I may be strong enough to say no, but will they be able to bear the consequences of my actions? This page of the Bible presents a grim future. If I cannot show the sign of membership, I will not be accepted and will slowly starve.

Such a future would be unbearably bleak if I could not do anything about it now. But I can. I can remember God's promise to be near me during this terrible persecution. I can check my attitudes and priorities to see if I am ready and willing to let the non-essentials go if I am required to do so. Right now, I should examine my lifestyle and ask: Can I do without these, or am I so enslaved to them that they are a trap from which I cannot escape? Can I and my dependents go through these tribulations together? When everything is slowly taken away from me, will I still hang on to my Savior and resist the evil powers? How many times have I given up Jesus for something of less worth?

This passage does not present a threatening prospect. It asks, "What does Jesus mean to me?" I know I mean everything to Him. That should help me make my decision.

Blessed are those who are invited to the marriage supper of the Lamb (Revelation 19:9).

Various chapters of Revelation are in sharp contrast. I read about the powers of satan and his antichrist, and about a world full of hostility to God and His church. Then follows an even more gruesome description of what the Lord plans to do against these hostile forces in order to conquer them. What a contrast we have in chapter 19, an invitation to the glory of love and the fullness of mirth! The harlot who sought to lure God's people into unfaithfulness has been condemned, and the Bride is ready to attend the great wedding, dressed in fine linen, bright and clean.

The first part of Revelation has been a concise description of the conflicts that have occurred throughout time. Humanity called in the hostile forces; our sins caused this terrible conflict. It is hard for me to find joy in the judgments of God and in the eternal destruction of His enemies.

But His ultimate goal has always been to lead His people through painful suffering and darkness into His bright and everlasting victory. And in Jesus Christ, that goal has become a fact. The future is certain. I now have the invitation in my hands.

The only question that can remain is, "Am I invited to that great wedding feast?" Yes, the Word of God is one great invitation! God does not want to sit at the supper alone. He does whatever He can to get people there. The invitation has been sent; will I go?

There shall be no night there (Revelation 21:25).

The glory of life eternal is so magnificent that human words cannot describe it. It can only be expressed as the opposite of all that has ruined this present life. There will be no more death, no mourning, no crying, no pain. The Lord is going to wipe the tears from our faces. Above all, there will be no more sin to separate us from God and His joyful presence. Satan will no longer accuse us before God's face; he will be sent to his proper place.

Surprisingly, there will be no temple anymore. God's presence will be everywhere and constant; the communion between us will be perfect. Even the sun and moon are ridiculously insignificant compared to the light of the Lamb.

Finally, there will be no night: no more difficulties in finding the way, no more fears of lurking danger, no more twilight gloom. Jesus described a future without Him as utter darkness and called satan's actions the works of darkness. Now the gospel preaches, "There will be no night there." I don't know exactly what that means, but it is enough to know that this will be a day that never ends.

For the present I must walk on through the night, but the bright stars of God's promises beckon me to march on. The horizon already glows with the dawn of eternity. Jesus Christ is the Sun of Righteousness through whom God calls me out of darkness into His glorious light.

In the radiancy of His Glory I shall see His face, and night shall be no more!